EASY BIKING
IN NORTHERN CALIFORNIA

FOGHORN OUTDOORS®

EASY BIKING
IN NORTHERN CALIFORNIA

Third Edition

Ann Marie Brown

AVALON
TRAVEL

FOGHORN OUTDOORS EASY BIKING IN NORTHERN CALIFORNIA

Third Edition

Ann Marie Brown

Printing History
1st edition—1999
3rd edition—November 2004
5 4 3 2 1

Avalon Travel Publishing
An Imprint of
Avalon Publishing Group, Inc.

AVALON
publishing group incorporated

Some photos and illustrations are used by permission
and are the property of the original copyright owners.

ISBN: 1-56691-673-9
ISSN: 1086-7848

Editors: Mia Lipman, Christopher Jones
Series Manager: Marisa Solís
Acquisitions Editor: Rebecca K. Browning
Copy Editor: Deana Shields
Production Coordinators: Jacob Goolkasian, Justin Marler, Darren Alessi
Graphics Coordinator: Justin Marler
Cover and Interior Designer: Darren Alessi
Map Editor: Olivia Solís
Cartographers: Mike Morgenfeld, Kat Kalamaras, Suzanne Service, Ben Pease
Indexer: Laura Welcome

Front cover photo: © John Elk III

Printed in the United States of America by Malloy

About the Author

The author of 12 outdoor guidebooks, Ann Marie Brown is a dedicated California outdoorswoman. She hikes, bikes, and camps more than 150 days each year in a committed effort to avoid routine, complacency, and getting a real job.

Ann Marie's work has appeared in *Sunset, VIA,* and *Backpacker* magazines. As a way of giving back a little of what she gets from her experiences in nature, she writes and edits for several environmental groups, including the Sierra Club and Natural Resources Defense Council. When not riding down a California trail, Ann Marie resides in her home near Yosemite National Park.

In addition to *Foghorn Outdoors Easy Biking in Northern California,* Ann Marie's other guidebooks include:

Foghorn Outdoors 101 Great Hikes of the San Francisco Bay Area
Foghorn Outdoors 250 Great Hikes in California's National Parks
Foghorn Outdoors Bay Area Biking
Foghorn Outdoors California Hiking (with Tom Stienstra)
Foghorn Outdoors California Waterfalls
Foghorn Outdoors Easy Camping in Southern California
Foghorn Outdoors Easy Hiking in Northern California
Foghorn Outdoors Easy Hiking in Southern California
Foghorn Outdoors Northern California Biking
Foghorn Outdoors Southern California Cabins & Cottages
Moon Handbooks Yosemite

For more information on these titles, visit Ann Marie's website at www.annmariebrown.com.

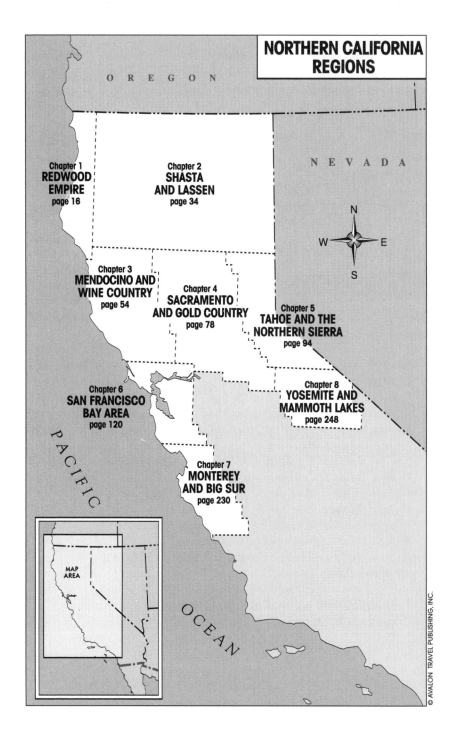

NORTHERN CALIFORNIA REGIONS

OREGON

NEVADA

Chapter 1
REDWOOD EMPIRE
page 16

Chapter 2
SHASTA AND LASSEN
page 34

Chapter 3
MENDOCINO AND WINE COUNTRY
page 54

Chapter 4
SACRAMENTO AND GOLD COUNTRY
page 78

Chapter 5
TAHOE AND THE NORTHERN SIERRA
page 94

Chapter 6
SAN FRANCISCO BAY AREA
page 120

Chapter 8
YOSEMITE AND MAMMOTH LAKES
page 248

Chapter 7
MONTEREY AND BIG SUR
page 230

PACIFIC

OCEAN

MAP AREA

© AVALON TRAVEL PUBLISHING, INC.

© ANN MARIE BROWN

Contents

Our Commitment

We are committed to making *Foghorn Outdoors Easy Biking in Northern California* the most accurate and enjoyable biking guide to the area. With this third edition you can rest assured that every ride in this book has been carefully reviewed and accompanied by the most up-to-date information. Be aware that with the passing of time some of the fees listed herein may have changed, road conditions may have upgraded (or downgraded), and trails may have closed unexpectedly. If you have a specific need or concern, it's best to call the location ahead of time.

If you would like to comment on the book, whether it's to suggest a ride we overlooked, or to let us know about any noteworthy experience—good or bad—that occurred while using *Foghorn Outdoors Easy Biking in Northern California* as your guide, we would appreciate hearing from you. Please address correspondences to:

Foghorn Outdoors Easy Biking in Northern California, 3rd edition
Avalon Travel Publishing
1400 65th Street, Suite 250
Emeryville, CA 94608
email: atpfeedback@avalonpub.com

If you send us an email, please put "Easy Biking in Northern California" in the subject line.

How to Use This Book

Foghorn Outdoors Easy Biking in Northern California is divided into eight chapters that encompass the following geographical regions: Redwood Empire, Shasta and Lassen, Mendocino and Wine Country, Sacramento and Gold Country, Tahoe and the Northern Sierra, San Francisco Bay Area, Monterey and Big Sur, and Yosemite and Mammoth Lakes. Navigating this guide can be done easily in two ways:

1. If you know the general area you want to visit within one of the regions, turn to the map at the beginning of that chapter. You can determine which bike routes are in or near your destination by finding their corresponding numbers on the map. Opposite the map is a table of contents listing each route in the chapter by map number and page number. Turn to the corresponding page for the route that interests you.

2. If you know the name of the route—or the name of the surrounding geographical area or nearby feature (town, national or state park or forest, lake, etc.)—look it up in the index and turn to the corresponding page.

About the Ride Number and Name

Each ride in this book has a number and name. The ride's number allows you to find it easily on the corresponding chapter map. The name is either the actual trail or street name (as listed on signposts and maps), or a name I've given to a series of trails or routes. In these cases, the ride's name is taken from the focal point of the route—usually a geographic landmark, such as a ridge it traverses or the destination it reaches.

About the Ride Descriptions

At the top of each ride description, you'll find six pieces of key information:

Total distance—This is the total round-trip mileage for the ride.

Biking time—This is the estimated time it will take to complete the ride. Remember that times may vary due to your level of riding experience, the weather, and the number and length of any breaks taken.

Type of trail—This notes the kind of trail surface or surfaces you'll encounter, such as a dirt road, a single-track trail, or a paved recreation path.

Type of bike—This recommends a road bike, mountain bike, or either, depending on the trail.

Steepness—This provides an estimate of the amount of hill-climbing the ride requires. Trails are rated as "mostly level," "rolling terrain," or "steep sections." A trail that is mostly level necessitates only an occasional change of gears, whereas a trail with steep sections may require you to pause and catch your breath occasionally.

Skill level—This provides an estimate of the riding skills required to complete the route. Trails are rated as "easiest," "moderate," or "challenging." Trails with the "easiest" rating have a completely smooth surface and are suitable for families with young children and for riders getting on a bike for the first time after a long absence. Trails with a "moderate" rating are suitable for families with older children and for strong beginners who enjoy small challenges. On moderate trails, surfaces may not be completely smooth, but they do not require any special skills for riding. Finally, trails with a "challenging" rating are best for those who feel comfortable handling occasional technical obstacles, such as rocks or tree roots, and who can comfortably maneuver through tight turns and follow a narrow line with good balance.

About the Maps

Each chapter in this book begins with a map of the region it covers. Every ride's starting point is noted by a number on the map. These points are placed as precisely as possible, but the scale of these maps often makes it difficult to pinpoint a ride's exact starting point. I advise you to purchase a detailed map of the area, especially if it is new to you.

Some of the rides also feature a trail map. However, if the area is new to you, or if you would like to see topographic lines, I recommend obtaining a more detailed map. If you are riding in a national, state, county, or regional park, pick up a park trail map from the visitors center or entrance station. Bike and outdoors shops also carry detailed maps.

MAP SYMBOLS

———	Road Route	○	City
- - - -	Unpaved Road Route	○	Town
— — —	Trail Route	**ℙ**	Trailhead Parking
— — —	Other Trail	**Start**	Start of Ride
········	Other Trail (Bikes Prohibited)	■	Point of Interest
═══	Divided Highway	★	Natural Feature
═══	Primary Road	▲	Mountain
———	Secondary Road	⚑	State Park
- - - - -	Unpaved Road	⛺	Campground
		⩘	Waterfall

© ANN MARIE BROWN

Biking Tips

Safety

Like the Boy Scout motto says, you must be prepared. It's easy to set off on a bike ride, especially near your home, carrying nothing except maybe your wallet and keys. We've all done it from time to time. But even on the shortest spin through the neighborhood or local park, it's wise to have a few items with you. Some riders carry all of the following items on every ride, and some carry only some of the items some of the time. But each of the following could prove a real lifesaver:

1. A helmet for your head. They don't call them "brain buckets" for nothing. Don't get on your bike without one; many parks require them, and the ones that don't, should. Just as you wear your seat belt when you drive, wear your helmet when you ride. Make sure yours fits properly, and strap it on securely.

2. Food and water. Being hungry or thirsty spoils a good time, and it can also turn into a potentially dangerous situation. Even if you aren't the least bit hungry or thirsty when you start, you will feel completely different after 30 minutes of riding. Always carry at least two water bottles on your bike, and make sure they are full of fresh, clean water when you head out. Add ice on hot days, if you wish. For a two- to three-hour ride, carrying 100 ounces of water is not overkill, especially in summer. Many riders prefer to wear a bladder-style backpack hydration system, which has the extra advantage of providing room to carry a few snacks or car keys. Always bring some form of calories with you, even if it's just a couple of energy bars. If you carry extras, you'll be the hero or heroine who gives them to a rider in need.

3. Cycling gloves and cycling shorts. These make your trip a lot more comfortable. Cycling gloves have padded palms, so the nerves in your hands are protected from extensive pressure when you lean your upper body weight on the handlebars. Cycling shorts have chamois or other padding in the saddle area, and it's obvious what that does.

4. A map of the park or roads you are riding. Sometimes trails and roads are signed, sometimes they're not. Signs get knocked down or disappear with alarming frequency, due to rain, wind, or souvenir hunters. Get a map from the managing agency of the park you're visiting; all their names and phone numbers are in this book.

5. A bike repair kit. How many and which tools to carry are a great subject of debate. At the very least, if you're going to be farther than easy walking distance from your car, carry what you need to fix a flat tire. Great distances are covered quickly on a bike. This is never more apparent than when a tire goes flat 30 minutes into a ride and it takes two hours to walk back. So, why walk? Carry a spare tube, a patch kit, tire levers, and a bike pump attached to your bike frame. Make sure you how to use them.

Many riders also carry a small set of metric wrenches, Allen wrenches, and a couple of screwdrivers, or some type of all-in-one bike tool. These are good for adjusting derailleurs and the angle on your bike seat, making minor repairs, and fidgeting with brake and gear cables. If you're riding on dirt trails, carry extra chain lubricant with you, or at least keep some in your car. Some riders carry a few additional tools, such as a spoke wrench for tightening loose spokes or a chain tool to fix a broken chain.

6. Extra clothing. On the trail, weather and temperature conditions can change at any time. It may get windy or start to rain, or you can get too warm as you ride uphill in the sun, and then too cold as you ride downhill in the shade. Wear layers. Bring a lightweight jacket and a rain poncho with you. Tie your extra clothes around your waist or put them in a small daypack.

7. Sunglasses and sunscreen. Wear them both. Put on your sunscreen 30 minutes before you go outdoors so it has time to take effect.

8. A bike lock. It comes in handy if you want to stop for anything. Many of the trails in this book combine a bike ride with a short hike or a visit to a winery, museum, or historic site. If you are planning to stop anywhere, even to use a restroom, a bike lock is valuable. Never leave your bike unlocked and unattended.

9. A first-aid kit and emergency money for phone calls. See below for more details.

First Aid and Emergencies

Like most of life, bicycling is a generally safe activity that in the mere bat of an eye can suddenly become unsafe. The unexpected occurs—a rock in the trail, a sudden change in road surface, a misjudgment or momentary lack of attention—and suddenly, you and your bike are sprawled on the ground. Sooner or later, it happens to everyone who rides. Usually, you look around nervously to see if anybody saw you, dust yourself off, and get back on your bike. But it's wise to carry a few emergency items just in case your accident is more serious: A few large and small adhesive bandages, antibiotic cream, and an ace bandage can be valuable tools. I also carry a Swiss army knife with several blades, a can opener, and scissors. If I don't need it for first aid, I'll use it for bike repair or picnics. Finally, it's a good idea to carry a candle and matches in a waterproof container, just in case you ever need to build a fire in a serious emergency.

Some riders carry a cell phone everywhere they go, but be forewarned that this is not a foolproof emergency device. You won't get cell reception in many areas, particularly in non-urban places. Carry a cell phone if it makes you feel better, but don't rely on it.

Always bring along a few bucks so you can make a call from a pay phone or buy food and drinks for yourself or someone else who needs them.

Bike Maintenance

Most bike-related problems won't occur if you do a little upkeep on your machine. Remember to check your tire pressure, seat height, brakes, and shifters before you begin each ride. Lubricate your chain and wipe off the excess lubricant. Make sure all is well before you set out on the trail.

If you ride often, also clean your bike and chain frequently, lubricate cables and derailleurs, tighten bolts, and check your wheels for alignment. Don't wait to have your bike worked on when you bring it into the shop occasionally; learn to perform your own regular maintenance, and do it frequently.

Fat Tires vs. Skinny Tires

Thinking about buying a new bike? Wondering what type of wheels would suit you best? This book includes rides for skinny tires (road bikes) and rides for fat tires (mountain bikes). Many rides in this book are suitable for either type of bike. Generally speaking, a mountain bike is more versatile and well-suited to all types of trail surfaces—dirt, paved, or mixed. Many adults who return to bicycling after years away from the sport find that a mountain bike, with its upright handlebar positioning and wider tires, is more comfortable to ride. Also, the huge range of gears now available on mountain bikes (usually somewhere around 21 speeds) makes climbing hills a lot easier.

Another type of bike, called a "crossover," has become popular in the last decade. This bike is a mix between a road bike and a mountain bike, with tires that are somewhere in between fat and skinny, and a frame that is similar to that of a mountain bike, but without all the bells and whistles. If you plan to ride mostly on pavement but want to make occasional forays on dirt trails, a crossover bike may be right for you.

Take a trip to your local bike store and test ride a few bikes. Make sure a friendly, knowledgeable salesperson helps you get the right "fit" in a bike, no matter which type of bike you select. If you test ride a few different models, you'll see a wide variation in the way a bike can fit your torso, arms, and legs. A good fit is far more important than what brand of bike you buy or how many speeds your bike has.

If you're riding with children who are too young to be on their own bikes, you can choose between child seats, which are positioned directly behind your saddle, or child trailers, which are separate units with wheels. The trailer hooks on to your bike, and the child rides behind you in his or her own little vehicle. Trailers are great, but they are only useful on paved trails. A child seat is usually more versatile and can be used on varied terrain.

Mountain Biking Tips for Beginners

If you've never mountain biked before, you may be surprised at how much time you spend walking instead of riding. You'll walk your bike up steep grades, down steep grades, and in level places where the terrain is too rugged. Mountain bikers frequently have to deal with rocks, boulders, tree roots, sand traps, holes in the ground, stream crossings, eroded trails, and so on. Often the best way to deal with these obstacles is to walk and push your bike. Use this technique to your advantage. If something looks scary, dismount and walk. If you are unsure of your ability to stay in control while heading downhill, or of your capacity to keep your balance on a rough surface, dismount and walk. It will save you plenty of bandages.

Learn to shift gears before you need to. This takes some practice, but it's easier to shift before you're halfway up the hill and the pedals and chain are under pressure. When you see a hill coming up ahead, downshift.

Play around with the height of your seat. When the seat is properly adjusted, you will have a slight bend in your knee while your leg is fully extended on the lower of the two pedals.

Take it easy on the handlebar grips. Many beginners squeeze the daylights out of their handlebars, which leads to hand, arm, shoulder, and upper back discomfort. Grip the handlebars loosely, and keep a little bend in your elbows.

Learn to read the trail ahead of you, especially when riding downhill. Keep your eyes open for rocks or ruts, which can take you by surprise and upset your balance.

Go slow. As long as you never exceed the speed at which you feel comfortable and in control, you'll be fine. This doesn't mean that you shouldn't take a few chances, but it's unwise to take chances until you are ready.

Mountain Biking Etiquette

Mountain bikes are great. They give you an alternative to pavement, a way out of the concrete jungle. They guarantee your freedom from auto traffic. They take you into the woods and the wild, to places of natural beauty.

On the other hand, mountain bikes are the cause of a lot of controversy. In the past 15 years, mountain bikers have shown up on trails that were once the exclusive domain of hikers and horseback riders. Some say the peace and quiet has been shattered. Some say that trail surfaces are being ruined by the weight and force of mountain bikes. Some say that bikes are too fast and clumsy to share the trail with other types of users.

Much of the debate can be resolved if bikers follow a few simple rules, and if non-bikers practice a little tolerance. The following is a list of rules for low-impact, "soft cycling." If you obey them, you'll help to give mountain biking the good name it deserves:

1. Ride only on trails where bikes are permitted. Obey all signs and trail closures.

2. Yield to equestrians. Horses can be badly spooked by bicyclists, so give them plenty of room. If horses are approaching you, stop alongside the trail until they pass. If horses are traveling in your direction and you need to pass them, call out politely to the rider and ask permission. If the horse and rider moves off the trail and the rider tells you it's okay, then pass.

3. Yield to hikers. Bikers travel much faster than hikers. Understand that you have the potential to scare the daylights out of hikers as you speed downhill around a curve, overtake them from behind, or race at them head-on. Make sure you give other trail users plenty of room, and keep your speed down when you are near them. If you see a hiker, slow down to a crawl, or even stop.

4. Be as friendly and polite as possible. Potential ill will can be eliminated by friendly greetings as you pass: "Hello, beautiful day today . . . ." Always say thank-you to other trail users for allowing you to pass.

5. Avoid riding on wet trails. Bike tires leave ruts in wet soil that accelerate erosion.

6. Riders going downhill should always yield to riders going uphill on narrow trails. Get out of the way so they can keep their momentum as they climb.

Protecting the Outdoors

Take good care of this beautiful land you're riding on. The primary rules are to leave no trace of your visit, pack out all your trash, and try not to disturb any animal or plant life. But you can go the extra mile and pick up any litter you see on the trail or road. Carry an extra bag to hold litter until you get to a trash receptacle, or just keep an empty pocket for that purpose.

If you have the extra time or energy, you could also join a trail organization in your area or spend some time volunteering in your local park. Biking and hiking trails need constant maintenance, and most of the work gets done by volunteers. Anything you do to help this lovely planet will be repaid to you many times over.

Best Bike Rides

Of the 110 rides in this book, here are my favorites in nine categories:

Best Combination Bike-and-Hike Rides

Fern Canyon & Falls Loop Trails, Mendocino and Wine Country, p. 57. It's a short and easy pedal and hike to Russian Gulch Falls, a 36-foot waterfall that drops into a rocky fern grotto in Russian Gulch State Park.

Bear Valley Trail Bike & Hike, San Francisco Bay Area, p. 131. This easy, level biking trail in Point Reyes National Seashore accesses a short hike to a coastal overlook at Arch Rock.

Skyline-to-the-Sea Trail, San Francisco Bay Area, p. 224. An 11.6-mile round-trip bike ride in Big Basin Redwoods State Park brings you to a short trail to one of the Bay Area's most spectacular waterfalls.

General Creek Loop, Tahoe and Northern Sierra, p. 104. At the far end of this easy loop ride through Sugar Pine Point State Park, you can lock up your bike and take a one-mile hike through the forest to diminutive Lily Lake.

Best Mountain Bike Rides for Families

Bizz Johnson National Recreation Trail, Shasta and Lassen, p. 49. The first 6.7 miles of this 25-mile-long railroad grade are easy pedaling along the scenic Susan River canyon, perfect for all levels of riders.

Sugar Pine Railway, Sacramento and Gold County, p. 89. Two stretches of this old railroad grade, one from Lyons Reservoir and one from Fraser Flat near Strawberry, make excellent easy riding for families.

General Creek Loop, Tahoe and Northern Sierra, p. 104. A pretty loop through pine and fir forest starts and ends at General Creek Campground in Sugar Pine Point State Park.

Bear Valley Trail Bike & Hike, San Francisco Bay Area, p. 131. This excursion in Point Reyes National Seashore is easy enough for bikers of any ability, and it leads to a spectacular coastal overlook.

Perimeter Trail, San Francisco Bay Area, p. 152. This 5.5-mile, nearly level trail circumnavigates Angel Island in the middle of San Francisco Bay, providing outstanding views and some interesting history lessons.

Tennessee Valley Trail, San Francisco Bay Area, p. 161. Biking families will enjoy this easy, wide dirt road that rolls gently out to Tennessee Beach, a black gravel pocket beach framed by jagged bluffs on both sides.

Best Paved, Car-Free Recreation Trails

Monterey Peninsula Recreation Trail, Monterey and Big Sur, p. 240. This 29-mile round-trip trail runs from Marina to Pacific Grove, passing famous

Monterey attractions such as Cannery Row and the Monterey Bay Aquarium.

Truckee River Recreation Trail, Tahoe and Northern Sierra, p. 99. Lake Tahoe has several excellent paved recreation trails, but this pathway along the scenic Truckee River is the best of the lot.

Nimitz Way Bike Trail, San Francisco Bay Area, p. 170. Perched on the tip of San Pablo Ridge in Tilden Regional Park, Nimitz Way offers the best views of any paved trail in East San Francisco Bay.

Sawyer Camp Recreation Trail, San Francisco Bay Area, p. 199. This trail in the pristine San Francisco watershed lands near Hillsborough travels the length of Lower Crystal Springs Reservoir and leads through marshlands to southern San Andreas Lake.

Hammond Trail, Redwood Empire, p. 27. A 13-mile out-and-back from Mad River in McKinleyville leads to windswept Clam Beach County Park.

Sacramento River Trail, Shasta and Lassen, p. 43. This 9.8-mile paved path in Redding is the hub of a well-developed trail system in and around town, connecting to sights such as the Turtle Bay Museum and Redding Arboretum.

Eagle Lake Trail, Shasta and Lassen, p. 47. Ride your bike on the south shore of Eagle Lake, the second largest natural lake in California and one of the best spots in Northern California for bird-watching.

Yosemite Valley Bike Path, Yosemite and Mammoth Lakes, p. 251. The best way to visit car-choked Yosemite Valley is to park your car and ride your bike past its spectacular granite walls and waterfalls.

American River Parkway: Beals Point to Negro Bar, Sacramento and Gold County, p. 87. Ride the most scenic stretch of this 32.8-mile-long paved trail, one of the oldest and longest recreation trails in the United States.

Best Rides for Tricycles/Training Wheels

Howarth Park & Spring Lake Park Trails, Mendocino and Wine Country, p. 65. If you need more than just a bike ride to entertain the kids, these two Santa Rosa–area parks offer two small lakes, rowboat rentals, and an amusement park with a carousel, miniature train, animal barn, and pony rides.

Lafayette-Moraga Regional Trail, San Francisco Bay Area, p. 173. If you start your ride at Moraga Commons, you can take the little ones out-and-back as far as they are comfortable, then return for some play time on the park's playground.

Half Moon Bay Bike Path, San Francisco Bay Area, p. 205. This small-town bike trail paralleling the coast is a safe, level place to teach kids to ride. When they tire of their bike lessons, take them to the neighboring beach.

Los Gatos Creek Trail, San Francisco Bay Area, p. 215. Vasona Lake

County Park is ideally suited for family fun, with a section of the nine-mile-long Los Gatos Creek Trail running through it, plus a miniature train, carousel, and children's play area.

Bidwell Park, Sacramento and Gold Country, p. 79. This shady city park in downtown Chico has a wide, safe road for riding on, plus water fountains, picnic tables, benches, and children's play areas situated along the route.

Best Rides Through History

Old Railroad Grade: East Peak to West Point Inn, San Francisco Bay Area, p. 159. Take a ride through Mount Tamalpais history on this out-and-back ride on the old Mount Tamalpais Scenic Railway route, home of the "Crookedest Railroad in the World."

Bizz Johnson National Recreation Trail, Shasta and Lassen, p. 49. Where cyclists ride on the Bizz Johnson Trail today, in the early 1900s thundering locomotives rumbled through the Susan River canyon, carrying heavy loads of logs and lumber.

Perimeter Trail, San Francisco Bay Area, p. 152. Visit the many remaining buildings on Angel Island, which has had a long and varied history as a military outpost, Russian sea otter hunters' site, and immigrant detention center.

Hardrock Trail, Sacramento and Gold Country, p. 82. From 1850 to 1957, the land at what is now Empire Mine State Historic Park was one of the biggest and richest gold mines in the state, with more than 300 miles of underground tunnels and shafts.

Bodie Ghost Town Ride, Yosemite and Mammoth Lakes, p. 254. Pedal your wheels through the well-preserved 1870s ghost town at Bodie State Historic Park.

Best Oceanfront Rides

Old Haul Road/Ten Mile Coastal Trail, Mendocino and Wine Country, p. 55. The Old Haul Road in MacKerricher State Park travels right next to wide open beaches, coastal dunes, and rocky coves north of Fort Bragg.

Gerstle Cove to Stump Beach Cove Trail, Mendocino and Wine Country, p. 62. Watch for sea otters and seals as you cruise this level trail on grassy bluffs above the Gerstle Cove Marine Reserve.

Wilder Ranch Bluffs Ride, Monterey and Big Sur, p. 233. Cruise along the marine terrace at Wilder Ranch State Park and view sea arches and cliffs, a seal rookery, sandy beaches, and a hidden fern cave.

17-Mile Drive, Monterey and Big Sur, p. 242. The seven-mile coastal stretch of 17-Mile Drive is full of jaw-dropping coastal scenery, plus grand mansions and golf courses.

Coastal Trail & Great Highway Bike Path, San Francisco Bay Area, p. 192. The wild side of San Francisco can be seen on Coastal Trail at Land's

End, with its million-dollar views of crashing surf, offshore outcrops, Golden Gate Bridge, and the Marin Headlands.

Best Rides for Wildlife-Viewing
Coastal Trail, Redwood Empire, p. 21. Here in Prairie Creek Redwoods State Park is your best chance of sharing the trail with a 1,000-pound Roosevelt elk (or a whole herd of them).

Eagle Lake Trail, Shasta and Lassen, p. 47. Eagle Lake, the second largest natural lake in California, is a prime spot for bird-watching, particularly for eagles and osprey.

Lake Almanor Recreation Trail, Shasta and Lassen, p. 45. Lake Almanor near Chester boasts the largest summer population of ospreys in California.

Arcata Marsh & Wildlife Sanctuary Trail, Redwood Empire, p. 29. A short ramble around Arcata Marsh gives you the chance to catch a glimpse of an osprey, peregrine falcon, kingfisher, or heron. The marsh is a home or rest stop for more than 200 bird species.

Tidelands Loop & Newark Slough Trail, San Francisco Bay Area, p. 190. Two of the largest egret colonies in California are found in the Don Edwards San Francisco Bay National Wildlife Refuge, as well as plentiful small mammals such as foxes and rabbits.

Best Single-Track Rides
Clikapudi Trail to Jones Valley Camp, Shasta and Lassen, p. 39. Ride this three-mile out-and-back or the entire 9.7-mile loop at Shasta Lake, then take a dip in the lake's cool turquoise waters.

Waters Gulch & Fish Loop Trails, Shasta and Lassen, p. 36. Parts of this Shasta Lake ride may be extremely challenging for beginners, but this is a great place to shore up your single-track skills.

Oak Bottom Channel/Great Water Ditch, Shasta and Lassen, p. 41. This scenic single-track skirts the edge of Whiskeytown Lake and serves up water views at almost every twist and turn.

Shoreline Trail, San Francisco Bay Area, p. 148. China Camp State Park offers a mellow single-track trail and a scenic location on San Pablo Bay, with blue-water vistas from more than 1,500 shoreline acres.

Horseshoe Lake Loop, Yosemite and Mammoth Lakes, p. 265. This short but sweet single-track loop around Horseshoe Lake in the Mammoth Lakes Basin is so fun, you'll probably ride it twice around.

Best Rides to Waterfalls
Fern Canyon & Falls Loop Trails, Mendocino and Wine Country, p. 57. On this easy trip for families, ride a paved path and then hike to Russian Gulch Falls, a 36-foot waterfall in Russian Gulch State Park near Mendocino.

Skyline-to-the-Sea Trail, San Francisco Bay Area, p. 224. This bike-and-hike trip takes you to a 70-foot waterfall in a beautiful redwood forest at Big Basin Redwoods State Park.

Yosemite Valley Bike Path, Yosemite and Mammoth Lakes, p. 251. You can ride practically to the base of Lower Yosemite Falls on this bike path in Yosemite Valley.

Coastal Trail, Redwood Empire, p. 21. This loop ride in Prairie Creek Redwoods State Park travels past three tall, narrow waterfalls, including 80-foot-high Gold Dust Falls.

Redwood Empire

Redwood Empire

L and of the tallest trees, dwelling place of the giants, the Redwood Empire is home to some of the largest remaining stands of old-growth sequoia sempervirens, or coast redwoods. These magnificent trees grow to more than 350 feet tall and live as long as 2,000 years, contributing to one of the most remarkable habitat areas in California—and, in fact, the world.

These behemoth trees are the reason visitors flock to the Redwood Empire. Although the area boasts a rugged and beautiful coastline, quaint towns like Arcata and Trinidad, and wide, free-flowing rivers, the redwoods are the main draw. Nowhere else in California can you gaze up at such an abundance of the world's tallest living things.

Although a redwood forest is considered a monosystem, many other plants live alongside the big trees, including ferns of all kinds, vine maples, huckleberry, salmonberry, and redwood sorrel. The Redwood Empire also features a wealth of wildlife, most notably its herds of giant Roosevelt elk. Adult male elk can weigh more than 1,000 pounds; their larger-than-life stature and huge antlers seem strangely appropriate among the giant redwoods. It's not uncommon to spot elk grazing while riding your bike on road or trail. Although they seem gentle, give them plenty of room.

Black bears also roam the redwood forests, searching for acorns and berries. Mountain lions and bobcats prefer the high grassland prairies, which are also good birding spots. The rivers and streams of the Redwood Empire, particularly the Smith and Klamath Rivers, are renowned for steelhead and salmon fishing.

No wonder these precious resources are preserved under the umbrella of Redwood National and State Parks, a co-managed park system that extends for 50 miles up the California coast and includes Redwood National Park, Jedediah Smith Redwoods State Park, Prairie Creek Redwoods State Park, and Del Norte Coast Redwoods State Park. Clearly, this is land worth protecting.

Although the area is infamous for rain, the summer months in the Redwood Empire are actually quite dry. The region receives an average of 69 inches of rain per year—almost six feet—but 90 percent of it occurs November–March. Summer can be foggy, but this dense marine layer brings life-giving moisture to the giant redwoods. Bicyclists would be well advised to always carry extra layers when riding in the Redwood Empire, because fog, wind, rain, and sunshine can be encountered all in one day, or in one bike ride.

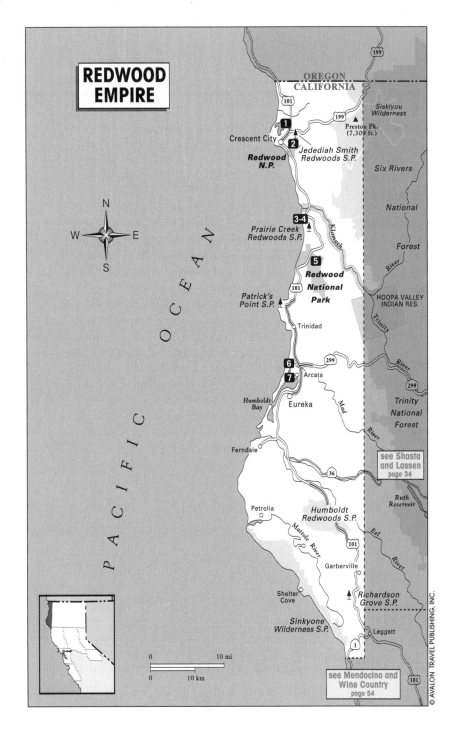

REDWOOD EMPIRE

OREGON
CALIFORNIA

Siskiyou
Wilderness

Preston Pk.
(7,309 ft.)

1

Crescent City

2

Jedediah Smith
Redwoods S.P.

Redwood
N.P.

Six Rivers

National

3-4

Prairie Creek
Redwoods S.P.

Forest

5

Redwood
National
Park

HOOPA VALLEY
INDIAN RES.

Patrick's
Point S.P.

Trinidad

6

7

Arcata

Humboldt
Bay

Eureka

Trinity

National

Forest

Ferndale

see Shasta
and Lassen
page 34

Petrolia

Humboldt
Redwoods S.P.

Ruth
Reservoir

Garberville

Richardson
Grove S.P.

Shelter
Cove

Leggett

Sinkyone
Wilderness S.P.

see Mendocino and
Wine Country
page 54

P A C I F I C   O C E A N

N
W   E
S

0   10 mi
0   10 km

© AVALON TRAVEL PUBLISHING, INC.

1 LAKE EARL & YONTOCKET INDIAN VILLAGE TRAIL

Tolowa Dunes State Park, off U.S. 101 near Crescent City

Total distance: 7.0 miles   **Biking time:** 1.5 hours

Type of trail: Dirt and gravel double-track

Type of bike: Mountain bike

Steepness: Mostly level   **Skill level:** Easiest

Tolowa Dunes State Park is so far north that it is almost out of California. Located just a few miles and a few turns off U.S. 101 north of Crescent City, the park doesn't see much recreation traffic except for occasional locals-in-the-know. Set smack on the coast and surrounded by miles of lowlands that roll gently to the sea, this place is perfect for an easy bicycling trip.

Tolowa Dunes State Park encompasses 5,000 acres of land and water, including Lakes Earl and Tolowa, oceanfront beaches and sand dunes, and a huge coastal wetland. This diverse landscape attracts an array of birds and wildlife, including the rare Canada Aleutian goose and peregrine falcon. Although much of the park is undeveloped, the area north of the lakes and

Lake Earl & Yontocket Indian Village Trail

© ANN MARIE BROWN

south of the Smith River is crossed by a seldom-used biker/hiker/equestrian trail. The path leads through coastal meadows to a Yontocket Indian cemetery and a view of the Smith River.

One year, I rode my mountain bike on this trail on the day before Thanksgiving. Under a gray wintry sky, the marshy landscape was resplendent with harvest colors. Every possible shade of green, gold, red, and orange showed in the trailside foliage. In contrast to the steel blue of the ponds and wetlands, the brilliantly colored ferns and meadow grasses seemed to glow with vibrancy in their final days before going dormant for the winter.

The trailhead is a little tricky to spot (follow the directions below exactly), but once you find it, the rest of the trip is a breeze. The trail is a gravel roadbed, composed of very fine stones that are as smooth as glass under your wheels. You glide up and down a series of small hills, passing some environmental campsites at the start of the trail, then cruise all the way to the park's northeastern boundary near where the Smith River reaches the ocean. Stay on the wide main path, ignoring the single-track spur trails, which quickly dissipate into sand.

At the first junction, which is signed for the marsh to your left and the ponds to your right, go right. At the next trail split, take the left fork (still the main trail) and you'll wind up at the Yontocket Indian Memorial Cemetery, which was once the site of a thriving Native American village. Climb the small hill to the cemetery for a good view of the Smith River and surrounding marshes.

At this point, you are almost three miles from the trailhead. From here, you can ride only .5 mile farther, veering to the right past the cemetery to the gated park boundary. There's no way to loop back; just turn around at the boundary sign. The ride back is mostly downhill and pure fun.

One possible minus at Tolowa Dunes State Park is that the place is popular with hunters, so you may hear the sound of shooting in the distance, particularly in the autumn months. Waterfowl hunting is permitted in the park on Saturdays, Sundays, and Wednesdays only. If hunting offends your sensibilities, plan your trip for the other days of the week. Or visit in spring or early summer, when the grasslands are alive with colorful displays of wildflowers.

Information and Contact
There is no fee. For more information and a map, contact Tolowa Dunes State Park, 1375 Elk Valley Road, Crescent City, CA 95531, 707/445-6547 or 707/464-6101, ext. 5151, website: www.parks.ca.gov.

Directions
From U.S. 101 in northern Crescent City, drive northwest on Northcrest Drive, which later becomes Lake Earl Drive, for 5.8 miles. Turn left on Lower Lake Road and drive 2.4 miles. Turn left on Kellogg Road and drive .6 mile (follow the signs for Kellogg Beach/Coastal Access) to the trailhead. The trail sign is set back from the road and can be difficult to spot. Watch for a dirt and gravel trail on the right, where there is a small pullout.

2 HOWLAND HILL ROAD

Jedediah Smith Redwoods State Park, off U.S. 101 near
Crescent City

Total distance: 4.0 miles

Type of trail: Paved road

Type of bike: Mountain bike or road bike

Steepness: Steep sections

Biking time: 1.0 hour

Skill level: Moderate

Howland Hill Road is bordered by one of the most incredible fern displays
in the Redwood Empire, and for that reason alone you should take this
bike ride. If that isn't enough to motivate you, consider that the ferns grow
in the understory of one of the finest old-growth redwood groves in northwestern California. To ride here is to be wowed by the trees.

You will have to deal with some car traffic on Howland Hill Road,
which is a dirt road open to passenger vehicles but closed to trailers and
motor homes. The road sees the heaviest traffic in summer, so visit October–May for the fewest cars and the greatest chance of seeing the majestic
redwoods in peace.

You can avoid most of the cars, and a big hill, by riding only the portion of Howland Hill Road that is described here. The quietest section is
the stretch farthest from Stout Grove, where most park visitors head to see

an enormous stump on Howland Hill Road

Stout Tree, the largest redwood in the park. You may miss out on Stout Tree on this trip, but you'll see plenty of other big, magnificent redwoods. Plus, you leave your car at the hikers' trailhead for Boy Scout Tree Trail, so when you're finished riding, you have the option of hiking a mile or more among the big trees.

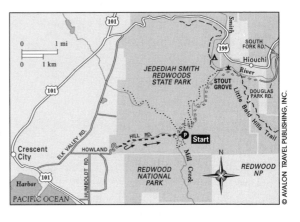

From Boy Scout Tree Trailhead, head west on your bike, following Howland Hill Road toward Crescent City. After almost two level miles, the road starts to ascend toward Howland Summit; turn around when you don't want to climb anymore. This gives you about a four-mile round-trip. The trail directions are simple, so you can focus on your surroundings, which consist almost entirely of redwoods, ferns, and as much greenery per square foot as the earth can deliver. Ride and be humbled by this magnificent forest.

Options

If you want more time and mileage in the big trees, you can also ride east from Boy Scout Tree Trailhead for a mile or two. The entire length of the road in both directions makes a 10.4-mile round-trip.

Information and Contact

There is no fee. For more information and a map, contact Jedediah Smith Redwoods State Park, 1375 Elk Valley Road, Crescent City, CA 95531, 707/445-6547 or 707/464-6101, ext. 5112, website: www.parks.ca.gov.

Directions

In Crescent City, head south on U.S. 101 and turn east on Elk Valley Road. Drive 1.1 miles and turn right on Howland Hill Road. Drive 1.5 miles to where the pavement turns to dirt at Howland Summit. Continue 2.5 miles farther to Boy Scout Tree Trailhead on the left.

3 COASTAL TRAIL

Prairie Creek Redwoods State Park, off U.S. 101 near Orick

Total distance: 6.0 miles   **Biking time:** 1.5 hours

Type of trail: Dirt single-track

Type of bike: Mountain bike

Steepness: Mostly level   **Skill level:** Moderate

Imagine a single-track trail that runs parallel to the ocean, framed by coastal bluffs and a mossy spruce forest. Imagine an abundance of wildlife along the trail, fearless enough to stand still and let you take pictures. Imagine three waterfalls tucked into the forest, like secret treasures waiting to be discovered.

Okay, now imagine that this trail is open to bikes. Sound impossible? Yes, but it is possible. Coastal Trail in Prairie Creek Redwoods State Park is one of the best easy mountain bike trails in all of California. Don't miss a chance to ride here.

Depending on the season, getting to the trailhead may require some effort. The driving route is a seven-mile stint on unpaved Davison Road, which may or may not be graded, depending on the season. In wet weather the road may be partially flooded and full of potholes; in dry weather it can be as smooth as asphalt. Where the road ends at Fern Canyon Trailhead, head due north (straight) from the parking area, following the Coastal Trail. The trickiest part of the whole trip is in the first 100 yards,

Roosevelt elk along the Coastal Trail

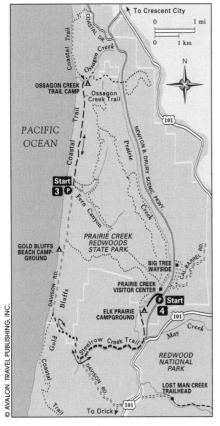

where you have to cross a few streams and plow through an often wet and muddy forested stretch. Walk your bike through here if need be. Once you're out of the trees and on to the open coastal bluff, the trail is drier and more hard-packed, making the riding easy.

Although you can't always see the ocean, its nonstop roar accompanies you. You ride along the inland perimeter of flat grassland bluffs, just before they intersect with steep cliffs on your right. In between the cliffs and the grasslands lies a narrow strip of forest—mostly alders and mossy Sitka spruce—where the waterfalls are hidden.

At one mile in, you come to the first waterfall, but you can barely hear or see it through the trees. Listen carefully for the faint sound of water falling, then peek into the forest canopy to see it. If you are riding too fast, you'll miss it, but even if you do, two more waterfalls await. Each one is a tall, narrow plume of water cascading down the hillside.

What you can't miss are the huge Roosevelt elk that roam this coastal prairie, munching on grasses all day long to feed their 700- to 1,000-pound bulk. Often you will see them as you drive in to the trailhead, but you will most likely see more as you ride along the Coastal Trail. Although they appear to be gentle animals, give them plenty of room. They are much bigger than you are, and you are in their territory.

The second waterfall is more easily spotted; it has a little clearing in front of it and a wooden viewing bench. The third waterfall is only about 100 yards beyond the second and is the easiest of all to find. A little spur trail leads right to it. Walk your bike into the forest and take a minute to appreciate these watery wonders.

In the final mile of the bikes-allowed section of the Coastal Trail, you move inland, away from the oceanside bluffs, and enter into a narrow strip of forest. Your turnaround point is at the junction with Ossagon Trail. Although Ossagon Trail is also open to bikes, it ascends immediately and returns to the highway in 1.8 miles. Better to turn around and head back on the Coastal Trail, experiencing the magic all over again.

Options

You can also begin your ride at Elk Prairie Campground at Prairie Creek Redwoods State Park by following Steelrow Creek Trail (see the following trail description) to its end at Davison Road, then turning right and following Davison Road to its end at Fern Canyon Trailhead and the start of the Coastal Trail.

Information and Contact

A $6 day-use fee is charged per vehicle. A park map is available at the entrance kiosk. For more information, contact Prairie Creek Redwoods State Park, Orick, CA 95555, 707/464-6101, ext. 5301, or 707/445-6547, website: www.parks.ca.gov.

Directions

From Eureka, drive north on U.S. 101 for 41 miles to Orick. Continue north for 2.5 more miles to Davison Road, then turn left (west) and drive eight miles to the Fern Canyon Trailhead. You pass the entrance kiosk where you pay your day-use fee about halfway in. No trailers or motor homes are permitted on unpaved Davison Road.

4 STEELROW CREEK TRAIL
Prairie Creek Redwoods State Park, off U.S. 101 near Orick

Total distance: 8.0 miles   **Biking time:** 2.0 hours

Type of trail: Paved, gravel double-track and dirt single-track

Type of bike: Mountain bike

Steepness: Mostly level   **Skill level:** Moderate

In my best daydreams, mountain biking is like this: I am riding through a fern-filled canyon with towering redwood trees on one side and a deep, lush ravine on the other. The foliage is so thick it makes a tunnel just high and wide enough for me to ride through. Nobody is around except for the animals and birds of the forest, who welcome me with their calls. The trail is smooth and hard, and I glide along in perfect rhythm. . . .

It's time to wake up from my daydreams, because it's all for real at

Prairie Creek Redwoods State Park. Steelrow Creek Trail is a slice of bicycling heaven. It's easy enough for beginners to ride, but so much fun that even experienced mountain bikers will delight in it.

You won't need a map—the trail is well-marked the whole way. The first few hundred yards border a huge meadow, aptly named Elk Prairie, where a herd of Roosevelt elk often hang out and entertain the tourists. Beyond the meadow, the trail moves away from the campground and park roads, and all vestiges of civilization are left behind. The trail narrows from double-track to single-track and disintegrates from an old paved road to a gravel roadbed to plain old dirt and mud.

As you ride, the canyon drops off steeply on your left. It's filled with big redwood trees—they're second growth, but big nonetheless. You're surrounded by a lush treasury of ferns, azaleas, salmonberry, red alders and other shade- and water-loving plants and trees. Water-loving? That's right, it rains a lot here, but don't let that stop you from riding. Just make sure you have some dry clothes to change into back in your car.

At nearly three miles, you reach a gate across the trail, which is only 50 yards from the edge of Davison Road, a graded dirt road with some car traffic. This is your turnaround point, which means you get to experience the magic all over again, heading in the opposite direction.

Steelrow Creek Trail

Options

If you don't mind sharing the road with cars, you can continue riding along Davison Road (a dirt road). Turn right on Davison Road to ride to Fern Canyon Trailhead. Lock up your bike and take a short hike through this magnificent fern-lined canyon.

Information and Contact

A $6 day-use fee is charged per vehicle. A park map is available at the entrance kiosk. For more information, contact Prairie Creek Redwoods State Park,

Orick, CA 95555, 707/464-6101, ext. 5301 or 707/445-6547, website: www.parks.ca.gov.

Directions
From Eureka, drive north on U.S. 101 for 41 miles to Orick. Continue north for approximately five more miles and take the Newton B. Drury Scenic Parkway exit. Turn left, following the signs for one mile toward the visitors center. Turn left at the sign for Elk Prairie Campground/Visitors Center, drive through the entrance kiosk, then continue straight to the day-use parking areas. Begin riding on Steelrow Creek Trail.

5 LOST MAN CREEK TRAIL
Redwood National Park, off U.S. 101 near Orick

Total distance: 3.0 miles   **Biking time:** 1.0 hour

Type of trail: Dirt road

Type of bike: Mountain bike

Steepness: Mostly level   **Skill level:** Easiest

Is it possible to visit the Redwood Empire and not fall in love with the giant redwood trees and the deep green of the forests? You'd have to be pretty jaded not to. Take Lost Man Creek Trail, for example. No matter what the weather is like, the scenery is a treat for the senses. Trees that are hundreds of years old are everywhere you look, moss hangs from the alders, ferns grow to huge sizes. These sights and more are the reason that bikers and hikers flock here every year to be awed and humbled by the Redwood Empire's majestic forests.

A little surveying on a map will tell you that Lost Man Creek Trail is much longer than the mileage suggested above. After the first four miles, the trail reaches Holter Ridge and follows it for six more miles. However, the operative word in Holter Ridge is "ridge," meaning you have to gain about 1,400 feet in elevation to ascend it. But why bother? The first 1.5 miles of Lost Man Creek Trail are almost perfectly level as the path follows alongside gurgling Lost Man Creek. Those who want a gorgeous, easy ride through first- and second-growth redwoods can go out and back almost effortlessly, turn around when the trail starts to climb, then have a picnic at the trailhead and sit around gawking at the trees. This is a perfect trip for families with small kids. Stronger riders can tackle the hill, continuing as far as they darn well please.

© ANN MARIE BROWN

Lost Man Creek Trail

The trail itself is an old gravel roadbed, smooth as silk and covered with a soft bed of fallen leaves and conifer needles. The only obstacles to overcome are the abundant bright yellow and green banana slugs. Try to avoid squashing them as they slowly slug across the road.

For the first mile, you ride along the creek, where a couple of wide bridge crossings offer eye-opening peeks into the beautiful stream canyon. The bridges can be slippery when wet, which they often are, since it rains frequently on this stretch of coast. One bridge is curiously signed "Weight Limit 19 Tons," a little odd for a road that is no longer open to vehicles.

The big attraction is the trees, of course, and luckily they provide some cover if it rains. In addition to the huge redwoods, thick stands of alders grow on the streambanks. When they lose their leaves in winter, a dense lichen completely covers every inch of their trunks and branches like a thick fur coat.

Options

Want to add some mileage to your ride without having to go up? The paved portion of Lost Man Road, which you drove in on to get to the trailhead, is another riding option. You may encounter a few cars, but not many since the road dead-ends at the trailhead. Riding out and back from the trailhead to Lost Man Road's intersection with U.S. 101 adds 1.8 miles to your trip.

Information and Contact

There is no fee. For more information and a free map, contact Redwood National Park Headquarters at 1111 Second Street, Crescent City, CA 95531, 707/464-6101, website: www.nps.gov/redw.

Directions

From Eureka, drive north on U.S. 101 for 41 miles to Orick, then continue north for three more miles to the well-signed turnoff for Lost Man Road (on the right). Drive .9 mile to the end of the pavement, where the trailhead is located.

6 HAMMOND TRAIL
Humboldt County Parks, off U.S. 101 in McKinleyville

Total distance: 13.0 miles

Biking time: 2.0 hours

Type of trail: Paved bike trail

Type of bike: Road bike or mountain bike

Steepness: Rolling terrain

Skill level: Easiest

The movement to convert abandoned railroad lines to multiuse trails for bicyclists, equestrians, and anyone else under non-motorized power has gained a lot of momentum in California, a state that is home to thousands of miles of unused railroad track. Hammond Trail is a proud example of this movement's success: It presents a safe and easy route from Arcata to McKinleyville, grand views of the coast and rural farmlands, beach access, and a ride through a historic railroad bridge that is closed to all motorized traffic. Two short sections of the trail follow quiet neighborhood streets, but the remainder is paved, car-free recreation trail.

The trail begins at an old railroad bridge across the Mad River, a key piece of McKinleyville's history. The original bridge on this site was of the wooden covered variety, built in 1905. When it deteriorated, it was replaced by the existing steel truss bridge in 1941. It was used by Hammond Lumber Company for its railroad until 1961.

Hammond Trail passes through the farmlands of Arcata Bottoms—a Northern California version of the English countryside with green fields and grazing cows and horses—then continues north through Hiller Park, a small community park. A stretch through dense coastal forest leads to Murray Road and a neighborhood of large, odd-looking houses built to resemble castles (some developer's imaginative idea). Beyond Murray Road, bikers and horses split off from hikers and follow the trail on the west side of U.S. 101 (hikers cross an environmentally sensitive area over Widow White Creek). A quarter-mile stretch on Letz Avenue connects to a vista point overlooking Trinidad Head to the north and the entire Mad River estuary. The trail's final stretch provides access to the brayed tan sands of Clam Beach.

Options
All of the country roads in the Arcata Bottoms area and around Mad

River County Park are suitable for easy biking, as they are flat and have very little auto traffic.

Information and Contact
There is no fee. For more information, contact Humboldt County Parks, 1106 Second Street, Eureka, CA 95501, 707/445-7651, website: www.co.humboldt.ca.us.

Directions
From U.S. 101 in Eureka, drive north 10 miles to the north end of Arcata, then take the Giuntoli Lane exit and head west (left). Cross over the freeway, then turn right on Heindon Road and drive .3 mile. Turn left on Miller Lane and drive .8 mile. Turn right on Mad River Road and drive 1.6 miles to an old steel railroad bridge. Park in the dirt pullouts by the bridge.

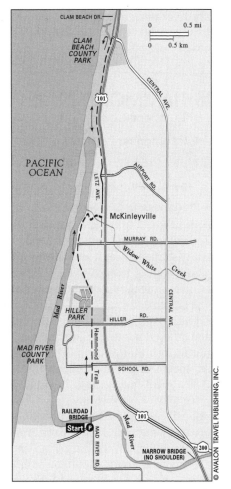

7 ARCATA MARSH & WILDLIFE SANCTUARY TRAIL

City of Arcata, off U.S. 101 in Arcata

Total distance: 2.0 miles

Biking time: 1.0 hour

Type of trail: Dirt and gravel single-track

Type of bike: Mountain bike

Steepness: Mostly level

Skill level: Easiest

Few wildlife refuges have policies friendly toward bicyclists; most of them forbid riders for fear of scaring off the wildlife they are trying to protect. Arcata Marsh is an exception to the rule, a small sanctuary built near a wastewater treatment facility that allows bike riders, as well as walkers and anglers, to tread on its gravel levees. This allows those of us on two wheels the opportunity to see birds—tons of them—as well as bucolic views of marsh and shoreline.

There are only a couple of miles of trails at Arcata Marsh, so don't come here expecting a major workout. You're better off showing up with your binoculars, camera, or fishing pole, or maybe just a good book in your bike bag. This is a bike ride for nature lovers, not speed demons on wheels. Come with the hope of catching a glimpse of an osprey, peregrine falcon, kingfisher, egret, heron, or at least some gulls and mud hens.

© ANN MARIE BROWN

Arcata Marsh

The history of Arcata Marsh is a good recycling story: The land here was formerly a sanitary landfill, but thanks to some forward thinking on the part of city officials it was converted to 150 acres of fish and wildlife habitat in four freshwater and saltwater marshes and one small lake, set right along Humboldt Bay. The variety of saltwater and freshwater habitat attracts a huge diversity of birds; Arcata Marsh is a home or rest stop for more than 200 species.

Besides bird-watching, fishing is probably the most popular activity here. Anglers spread out on the bay side of the marsh, casting from the levee that separates Franklin R. Klopp Recreation Lake from Arcata Bay. You can ride on a trail that tops the levee and goes all the way around the lake, plus a connecting trail that runs parallel to the access road (I Street) and is routed inland, toward the wind sock at the waste treatment center.

On our trip, we probably did more stopping than riding. Allow plenty of time to enjoy the views, watch the fishermen, identify the birds, and take photographs. This is not a place where you'll want to hurry.

Information and Contact
There is no fee. For more information and a free map, contact the City of Arcata, 736 F Street, Arcata, CA 95521, 707/822-5953, website: www.arcatacityhall.org.

Directions
From U.S. 101 in Eureka, drive north about 10 miles to Arcata, then take the Samoa Boulevard exit west and drive .6 mile to I Street. Turn left (south) and drive one mile to I Street's end at the parking area for Arcata Marsh. Start riding on the trail between the parking lot and the lake.

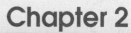

© ANN MARIE BROWN

Shasta and Lassen

Shasta and Lassen

I n the northeastern corner of California lies a part of the state where most people have never set foot. Ranging from the Oregon border south to Redding and from the Nevada border west through the Klamath Mountains, this northern interior is both the least populated and least visited region of the Golden State. Yet it is bestowed with some of California's most spectacular scenery: a landscape of rugged mountains, raging rivers in steep canyons, and vast expanses of sagebrush flats and pine- and fir-covered ridges. This is the land where ospreys and eagles soar, and remnants of volcanoes sputter and fume.

Two national parks are found here, both celebrating the region's volcanic past: Lava Beds National Monument, with its 300 lava-tube caves, vast volcanic cinder landscape, and western juniper forests; and Lassen Volcanic National Park, California's best example of recent geothermal activity. Then there is 2.1-million-acre Shasta-Trinity National-al Forest, dominated by mighty Mount Shasta, a dormant volcano whose summit attains the lofty height of 14,162 feet. At its base is Shasta Lake, the largest reservoir in California, which is part of another federally managed parkland: Whiskeytown-Shasta-Trinity National

Recreation Area. Both Shasta and Whiskeytown Lakes offer mountain bikers some of the best single-track riding in the state.

Wildlife is plentiful in the northeast corner of the state. Black bears roam the mountainsides; herds of mule deer and pronghorn antelope migrate through the plains. Eagle Lake, the second largest natural lake in California, is one of the best spots in Northern California for bird-watching. Lake Almanor, near Chester, has the largest summer population of ospreys in California. Paved recreation trails at these two lakes make them accessible to families and novice riders who are camping or visiting for the day.

A sense of history is also prevalent. Old mine sites, water ditches, and structures from the Gold Rush era can be explored on Whiskeytown Lake's trails. The Bizz Johnson Trail in Susanville is built on a circa-1900s railroad grade. Where cyclists ride today, thundering locomotives once rumbled through the canyon carrying heavy loads of logs and lumber.

The only thing you won't find in northeast California is a crowd. And that may be the best reason of all to come here and ride your bike.

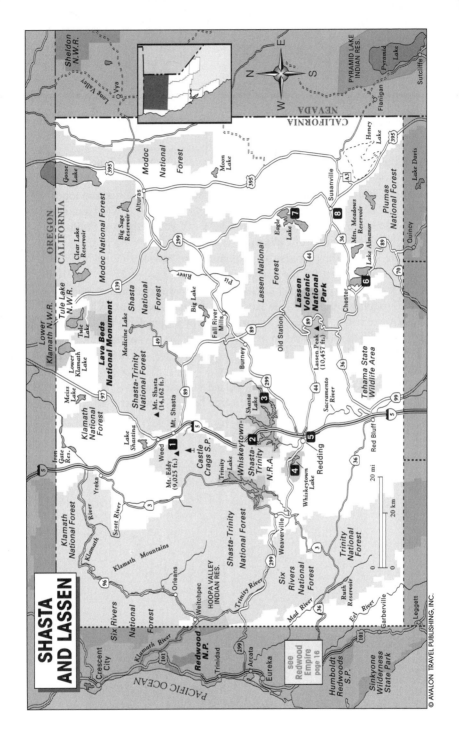

1 SISKIYOU LAKE NORTH SHORE

Shasta-Trinity National Forest, off I-5 near Mount Shasta

Total distance: 4.0 miles   **Biking time:** 1.0 hour

Type of trail: Dirt roads

Type of bike: Mountain bike

Steepness: Mostly level   **Skill level:** Easiest

If you're vacationing at Shasta Lake and all the water-skiers and loud party boats are starting to wear you down, a trip to Siskiyou Lake could be the antidote. Siskiyou Lake is one of the few reservoirs in California that was built specifically for quiet kinds of recreation; the lake speed limit is 10 miles per hour. As a bonus, the water managers leave the lake level alone even when other lakes in the area are drawn down. Deep blue and full to the brim, Siskiyou Lake is for scenery-lovers, surrounded by a dense conifer forest with Mount Shasta holding court in the background. Now, doesn't that sound like a great setting for a bike ride?

The key to your trip is riding on the north shore of the lake, not the busier south shore where the marina and campground are located. Your route is on Forest Service dirt roads that only rarely see car traffic, because the main attractions are on the other side of the lake, reachable by pavement.

Start riding from where you parked your car, near the start of North Shore Road. The first two-thirds of a mile give no indication that you are about to come to beautiful Siskiyou Lake, so when you get your first view through the trees, it's a great surprise.

You pass several turnoffs on your left leading to dirt parking areas and shoreline access. Take any of them if you'd like to drop in a fishing line or just sit by the water's edge. You may notice a single-track trail leading along the shoreline of the lake; it looks tempting to ride, but leave it for the anglers who built it. (Trout fishing is popular here in spring, bass fishing in summer.)

The dirt road becomes rougher as you ride to the west end of Siskiyou Lake, where the reservoir gradually narrows until it becomes not a lake at all, but the Sacramento River. The road condition varies greatly according to what time of year you ride—it is smoothest and most tightly compacted in late summer and fall. Fall is probably the best season to ride here anyway, as the surrounding pine and fir forest gets lit up by occasional splashes of color from deciduous oaks.

On your way out or upon your return, make a stop at the first dirt parking lot on the northeast edge of the lake (the first left turnoff you'll see on your ride out) for a terrific view of Mount Shasta on clear days.

Options

If you can manage to cross the Sacramento River (it's fairly easy to carry your bike across in late summer and fall, but nearly impossible earlier in the year, when the water level is high), you can make a 10-mile loop out of this trip by riding back on Siskiyou Lake's south shore. Food and supplies are available at Siskiyou Lake Camp Resort.

Information and Contact

There is no fee. For more information, contact Siskiyou Lake Camp Resort, P.O. Box 276, Mt. Shasta, CA 96067, 530/926-2618, website: www.lakesis.com.

Directions

From Redding, drive north on I-5 for 60 miles to the town of Mt. Shasta, then take the central Mt. Shasta exit and turn left. Go west over the overpass and drive .5 mile to South Old Stage Road. Turn left on South Old Stage Road and drive .2 mile until you come to a Y in the road. Veer right on to W.A. Barr Road and drive .7 mile to North Shore Road, where you turn right. Park your car in the pullout where the pavement turns to dirt. Begin riding west on the dirt road.

2 WATERS GULCH & FISH LOOP TRAILS

Shasta-Trinity National Forest, off I-5 on Shasta Lake

Total distance: 6.8 miles   **Biking time:** 1.5 hours

Type of trail: Dirt single-track

Type of bike: Mountain bike

Steepness: Steep sections   **Skill level:** Challenging

When you're ready for a single-track challenge, but not ready for long mileage or steep uphills that climb halfway to the stars, you're ready to ride on Waters Gulch and Fish Loop Trails at Shasta Lake. The trails roll along with only short ups and downs but offer multiple lessons in technical riding, with plenty of bridges to cross, rocks strewn along your path, exposed tree roots, tight turns, and steep drop-offs into Shasta Lake. Better keep your eyes on the road.

For beginning mountain bike riders, the best advice is to slow down and not attempt anything that looks too tricky. If you find yourself wondering if you can negotiate a tight curve or make it across a narrow bridge, don't try it. Stop and walk your bike. Also, keep your speed down at all times, staying prepared for surprise tight turns and the trail's steep drop-offs.

All disclaimers aside, this ride is pure fun, plus the surrounding forest of pines and oaks and the views of the Sacramento River Arm of Shasta Lake are lovely. If you stop to stare at the bright blue lake surface, you might get lucky and see a golden eagle or an osprey go fishing. As you ride, oak leaves frequently get caught in your spokes, making a great shuffling sound as your wheels spin.

Waters Gulch and Fish Loop are separate but connecting loops. What ties them together is a .6-mile stretch on Packers Bay Road, which you drive on in your car on your way to the trailhead. You can ride out and back on the single-track in both directions for a 6.8-mile round-trip, or, if you decide after the first leg that you've had enough of this path's technical challenges, you can return downhill on pavement for a 4.0-mile round-trip.

Either way, start riding on Fish Loop, a short path around a small peninsula on Packers Bay. The trail gets narrower as manzanita bushes crowd in and brush your ankles. Fish Loop offers the best riding of the day and wonderful lake views, but it's over in only .7 mile. Too soon.

Go left where Fish Loop connects to Waters Gulch Trail and undulate up and down through more manzanita and dense oak forest. The trail moves away from the lake as it crosses the strip of land separating Packers

overlooking Lake Shasta from Waters Gulch Trail

Bay from Waters Gulch. As it nears the water again, the path becomes more technical in nature and ascends more steeply. This is a good place to consider whether or not you will be comfortable returning downhill on this trail, or if you should loop back on pavement. Much of the upper part of Waters Gulch Trail has been heavily eroded and is quite rocky and narrow; the drop-off into a neighboring creek is nearly vertical. A couple

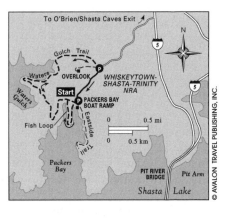

of stairstep-style drops and an extremely tight double switchback may give you pause. (I walked my bike here both up- and downhill.) But shortly beyond the switchbacks, you're at the upper terminus of the trail, and probably feel disappointed (or perhaps lucky?) that it's over. Simply turn around and ride back or take the pavement downhill.

Remember that this is Shasta Lake, not Mount Shasta, so daytime temperatures in the summer months can be extreme. Plan your ride around the thermometer.

Options
Beginners should ride just Fish Loop Trail and return to the parking lot, instead of connecting to Waters Gulch, the more technical of the two trails.

Information and Contact
There is a $6 fee per vehicle for parking at the boat ramp. For more information and a map, contact Shasta-Trinity National Forest, Shasta Lake Ranger District, 14225 Holiday Road, Redding, CA 96003, 530/275-1587, website: www.fs.fed.us/r5/shastatrinity.

Directions
From I-5 at Redding, drive north for 15 miles and take the O'Brien/Shasta Caverns exit. Cross the freeway and get back on I-5 heading south. Drive one mile and take the Packers Bay exit. Drive 1.6 miles to the end of the road at the boat ramp. The trailhead for Fish Loop Trail is on the right side of the parking lot, 20 yards below a separate trailhead for Waters Gulch Trail.

3 CLIKAPUDI CREEK TRAIL TO JONES VALLEY CAMP

Shasta-Trinity National Forest, off I-5 on Shasta Lake

Total distance: 3.0 miles

Type of trail: Dirt single-track

Type of bike: Mountain bike

Steepness: Rolling terrain

Biking time: 1.0 hour

Skill level: Moderate

The name Clikapudi comes from the Wintu Native American word *klukupuda,* meaning "to kill." Fortunately, it's a reference to a battle between the Wintu and local traders in the 1800s, and does not reflect the difficulty of this trail's single track.

In fact, this single-track is downright manageable, even for people who don't have a lot of technical riding experience. The surface is more smooth than rocky, the curves are graceful and not tight, and the main obstacles are hikers and horses, not rocks and tree roots. With only two short but challenging hills and a fair amount of shade from black oaks and conifers, this is a good trail for building your confidence on single-track. At the few difficult spots, simply dismount and walk.

rolling single-track on the Clikapudi Creek Trail

The critical element with riding at Shasta Lake is timing. Show up in the late summer or fall, and you'll hit hard-packed trails. Show up in the spring, and you'll slide all over the place. I recommend riding here in the fall, when the forest is most colorful. The black and white oaks turn yellow and orange, contrasting with the crimson bark of madrones and manzanita. If you like conifers in your forest, plenty of Douglas firs and pines

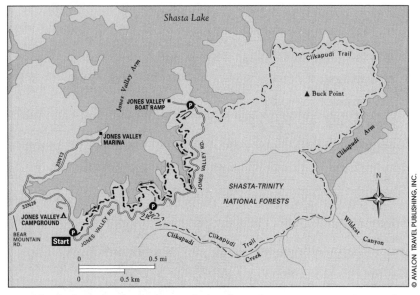

Shasta Lake

Clikapudi Trail

Jones Valley Arm

JONES VALLEY
BOAT RAMP

▲ Buck Point

JONES VALLEY
MARINA

Clikapudi Arm

33N13

JONES VALLEY RD.

SHASTA-TRINITY

NATIONAL FORESTS

N

33N26

JONES VALLEY ▲
CAMPGROUND

JONES VALLEY RD.

BEAR
MOUNTAIN
RD.

Start

Clikapudi

Clikapudi Trail

Wildcat Canyon

Clikapudi Creek

0   0.5 mi

0   0.5 km

© AVALON TRAVEL PUBLISHING, INC.

provide shade and color year-round. Another advantage to an autumn trip is that the place is usually deserted; even nearby Jones Valley Campground is often empty.

The entire Clikapudi Creek Trail is a 9.7-mile loop, with a more difficult, steeper section on the north side of Jones Valley Road, but you don't need to ride all of it to have a great trip. The mileage listed above assumes that you ride only on the south (lake) side of Jones Valley Road, making an out-and-back trip rather than a loop. That keeps you near the water's edge the entire time.

Start at the boat ramp's western Clikapudi trailhead (there's another one on the east side), then ride south and west to Lower Jones Valley Campground. You pass a junction with a sharp left turn about one mile in; this is the route for those who are crossing to the north side of Jones Valley Road to ride the entire Clikapudi loop. Continue straight for another .5 mile to the campground, then where the trail ends near the picnic area, turn around and ride back.

Options

Those who wish to ride farther can pick up the trail at the other Clikapudi trailhead on the east side of the boat ramp parking lot and follow it for another three miles, heading up the Clikapudi cove of Shasta Lake. The trail stays relatively level all along the lake; it is only when it leaves the water that it begins to climb and get more technical. The truly ambitious can ride the entire 9.7-mile loop.

Information and Contact

There is a $6 fee per vehicle for parking at the boat ramp. For more information and a map, contact Shasta-Trinity National Forest, Shasta Lake Ranger District, 14225 Holiday Road, Redding, CA 96003, 530/275-1587, website: www.fs.fed.us/r5/shastatrinity.

Directions

From I-5 in Redding, take Highway 299 east for 5.5 miles to Bella Vista. Just past the small town, turn left on Dry Creek Road and drive six miles to a fork in the road. Go right on Bear Mountain Road. Drive one mile and turn right on Jones Valley Road. Continue past the turnoff for Jones Valley Marina, following the signs for the Jones Valley campgrounds. Drive past the campgrounds to the end of the road at the Forest Service boat-launching facility and parking area. Start riding at Clikapudi Creek Trailhead on the left (west) side of the parking lot (there is another trailhead on the east side of the lot).

4 OAK BOTTOM CHANNEL/ GREAT WATER DITCH

Whiskeytown National Recreation Area, off Highway 299 west of Redding

Total distance: 6.6 miles

Biking time: 1.5 hours

Type of trail: Dirt single-track

Type of bike: Mountain bike

Steepness: Rolling terrain

Skill level: Moderate

If you like riding on single-track and you enjoy lakeside trails, Oak Bottom Channel Trail is a perfect fit. It skirts the edge of Whiskeytown Lake, providing stunning blue-water views at almost every turn.

The trail is also known as Great Water Ditch (including on some park maps), but it is signed on both ends as Oak Bottom Channel Trail. It is built on one of the area's many water ditches, which were part of the original irrigation system that developer Levi Tower built in the Gold Rush days to supply his hotel, farm, and mining operations.

The trail starts at Oak Bottom campground's access road and runs to Carr Powerhouse, which is part of a huge water regulation system somewhat more complicated than Levi Tower's: The powerhouse diverts water from the Trinity River, stores it in Trinity Lake, sends it by tunnel to Whiskeytown Lake, then sends it to Keswick Reservoir and into the Sacramento River. All in an

riding the Great Water Ditch at Whiskeytown Lake

effort to keep the Central Valley from looking like a desert.

From the dirt pullout and trailhead along the Oak Bottom Camp access road, head downhill immediately for about 30 yards, then follow the single-track as it curves in and around the lakeshore. The trail runs between Whiskeytown Lake and Highway 299, so you are wowed by lake views the whole way. One section snakes through what may be the biggest manzanita bushes in all of Shasta-Trinity. The only minus is the road noise.

Where the trail ends at a paved road, follow the pavement to Carr Powerhouse Road, then cross Clear Creek and ride to the left to Carr Powerhouse and a picnic area. Picnic tables sit underneath the massive power lines coming from the Carr Powerhouse. It's a good place for a rest stop, as long as all that electricity being generated doesn't make you too nervous.

Options

To add four more miles to your ride, turn right after crossing Clear Creek (the road is pavement but soon turns to dirt, then single-track). After several steep uphill switchbacks, turn right, go straight at the next junction, then watch for a steep trail heading sharply downhill to the right. Now you're on Mill Creek Trail and will shortly reach the El Dorado Mine site. After examining the old mine buildings, continue on Mill Creek Trail past the ranger's house to the Tower Historic District and Tower Gravesite. Then return the way you came.

Information and Contact

There is no fee. For more information and a free trail map, contact Whiskeytown National Recreation Area, P.O. Box 188, Whiskeytown, CA 96095-0188, 530/246-1225, website: www.nps.gov/whis.

Directions

From I-5 at Redding, take Highway 299 west for 13 miles (five miles west of the Whiskeytown Lake Visitor Information Center). Turn left at the sign for Oak Bottom Campground and Marina. Drive .2 mile on the Oak Bottom access road and park in the pullout on the right.

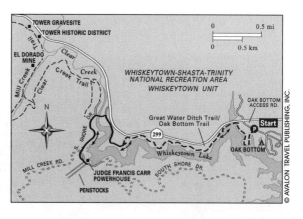

5 SACRAMENTO RIVER TRAIL
City of Redding, off Highway 299 in Redding

Total distance: 9.8 miles

Biking time: 1.25 hours

Type of trail: Paved bike trail

Type of bike: Road bike or mountain bike

Steepness: Rolling terrain

Skill level: Easiest

If ever there was a perfect, easy trail for teaching someone how to ride a bike, or for taking a casual Sunday afternoon ride with a friend, Sacramento River Trail is it. It takes you away from the hustle and bustle of downtown and offers plenty of good places to sit on a bench and watch the water roll by.

Not surprisingly, the multiuse trail is popular with Redding locals, and you'll see plenty of dog-walkers, anglers, baby strollers, and joggers in addition to dozens of squirrels and small flocks of quail. If you visit in midsummer, you can pick a few handfuls of blackberries along the trail (careful, they stain your cycling gloves). If you time your trip for fall, you'll witness one of Redding's finest displays of autumn color.

The first mile of trail west from Riverside Drive is so tame and suburban-feeling, you'll be a little surprised when you suddenly enter wide-open foothill country. Here, the paved trail seems out of place against the rugged landscape. At 2.5 miles, you reach a 418-foot-long hiker-and-biker footbridge across the Sacramento River, just before Keswick Dam. A technological wonder, the bridge is considered to be environmentally safe

© JOHN KLEINFELTER

Sacramento River Trail

because it is a "concrete stress-ribbon," meaning it is supported by 200-plus steel cables in its concrete deck instead of pilings or piers dug into the riverbed.

Across the bridge, the trail loops back on the river's north side. This side is steeper and has more tight curves, making it less popular with walkers and joggers. At a junction with the Diestlehorst Bridge that would lead back to the starting point, continue straight on a trail extension that runs into downtown Redding. The trail continues through Caldwell Park, across Market Street, and to the new Turtle Bay Museum. The trail bridge by the museum, built in 2003, is as architecturally stunning as the museum itself. Called Sundial Bridge, it looks like a boomerang with harp strings, and it functions as a sundial. The floor of the span, built of frosted glass panels, is lit up at night.

Options

In the near future, Sacramento River Trail will connect to nine-mile Sacramento River Rail Trail, an abandoned rail bed that leads to Shasta Lake. The Bureau of Land Management and Shasta County are working together to make that happen.

Information and Contact

There is no fee. For more information and a free map, contact City of Redding Community Services, 530/225-4512, website: www.ci.redding.ca.us. Or contact the Redding Convention and Visitors Bureau, 530/225-4100, website: www.visitredding.org.

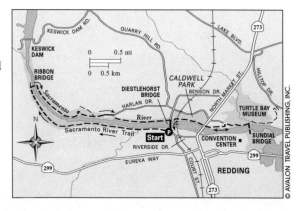

Directions

From I-5 at Redding, take Highway 299 west for two miles to its junction with Highway 273 heading north (North Market Street). Veer right on Highway 273, then turn left (west) on Riverside Drive. Don't cross over the river; go straight into the parking area at Riverside Park. Ride west on the bike trail from the parking area.

6 LAKE ALMANOR RECREATION TRAIL
Lassen National Forest, off Highway 36/89 near Chester

Total distance: 19.0 miles **Biking time:** 2.0 hours

Type of trail: Paved bike trail

Type of bike: Road bike or mountain bike

Steepness: Rolling terrain **Skill level:** Easiest

Lake Almanor Recreation Trail is a popular paved path for campers staying at Lake Almanor's five campgrounds, but you don't have to be camping here to take advantage of it. Lake Almanor, at 4,500 feet in elevation near the south side of Lassen Volcanic National Park, is one of the largest man-made lakes in California—13 miles long and six miles wide, with 28,000 surface acres. It's well known among anglers, who ply its waters for rainbow trout, brown trout, and chinook salmon. It's also popular with water-skiers in summer.

The recreation trail makes a perfect family bike trip, and its 19-mile round-trip length is long enough to make you feel like you got some exercise.

low water at Lake Almanor at summer's end

Unfortunately, the path follows the lakeshore for only a small portion of its length, but still it's quite pretty. Much of it runs through fragrant stands of pine, fir, and incense cedar, and it passes meadows covered in wildflowers in spring and early summer. Interpretive signs are posted at several points along the trail, explaining the local flora and fauna.

Start your ride at the trail's northern terminus; after 2.5 miles of pedaling through the forest, you pass by Lake Almanor's boat ramp and two campgrounds. Soon thereafter, you ride by Jake's Lake, an ephemeral wetland that dries up by midsummer. More pedaling through the pines and firs brings you to Dyer View day-use area at 6.5 miles, and then the end of the trail at 9.5 miles (at yet another campground). Nothing to do now but turn your wheels around and cruise back home.

As you ride, keep your eyes peeled for ospreys and bald eagles; they are frequently seen from the lake's west shore. Lake Almanor has the largest summer population of ospreys in California.

Information and Contact

There is no fee. For more information, contact Almanor Ranger District, Lassen National Forest, 900 East Highway 36, P.O. Box 767, Chester, CA 96020, 530/258-2141, website: www.fs.fed.us/r5/lassen.

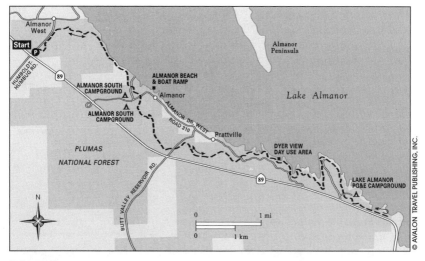

Directions

From Chester, drive three miles west on Highway 36/89, then turn left (south) on Highway 89 and drive 4.3 miles. Turn left across from Humbug-Humboldt Road and park at the signed trailhead.

⑦ EAGLE LAKE TRAIL

Lassen National Forest, off Highway 36 near Susanville

Total distance: 10.0 miles   **Biking time:** 1.0 hour

Type of trail: Paved bike trail

Type of bike: Road bike or mountain bike

Steepness: Mostly level   **Skill level:** Easiest

Was Eagle Lake named for our national bird? Yes, indeed. From the shores of Eagle Lake, bald eagles and ospreys are commonly seen. During one bike ride here, I spotted both of those remarkable birds, plus white pelicans, western grebes, Canada geese, a great blue heron, a beaver, mule deer, and golden-mantled ground squirrels by the dozens. Eagle Lake is one of the best places to see wildlife in Northern California.

It's not too surprising, considering a few facts: Eagle Lake is the second largest natural lake in California, after Lake Tahoe. Fed by natural, underwater springs, the lake is in an enclosed basin with no natural outlets. As a result, its water is extremely alkaline. Only one species of trout can survive in it—the Eagle Lake rainbow trout. This fish is coveted for its size, fighting ability, and taste. Humans, as well as ospreys and eagles, find them quite delicious.

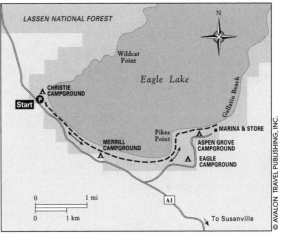

Eagle Lake's paved recreation trail starts at Christie Campground near site number 12. The path stays right along the lake's south shore for the entire ride, curving in and out of pine forest and meadows, passing sandy beaches, and offering nearly nonstop views of the water. Because the trail runs through several campgrounds, you have many chances for water breaks. Four miles out, the marina store is an option for snacks. Bike rentals are also available if you forgot to bring your own. A highlight along the trail is the wheelchair-accessible fishing area by the marina, which is also a prime bird-watching spot. Nearby Gallatin Beach is marked off for swimming.

The lake elevation is 5,100 feet, so it's often cool and comfortable up here, even when the nearby Susanville area is much warmer.

Information and Contact

There is no fee. For more information, contact Eagle Lake Ranger District, Lassen National Forest, 477-050 Eagle Lake Road, Susanville, CA 96130, 530/257-4188, website: www.fs.fed.us/r5/lassen.

Directions

From Susanville on Highway 36, drive west for three miles and then turn north on County Road A-1, Eagle Lake Road (next to the ranger station). Drive 14 miles to the lake, then follow the signs to Christie Campground.

8 BIZZ JOHNSON NATIONAL RECREATION TRAIL

BLM Lands and Lassen National Forest, off Highway 36 near Susanville

Total distance: 13.4 miles   **Biking time:** 2.0 hours

Type of trail: Dirt road

Type of bike: Mountain bike

Steepness: Mostly level   **Skill level:** Easiest

The Bizz Johnson National Recreation Trail is one of the great success stories of the rails-to-trails movement in the United States. The longest rail trail in California, it follows the path of the Southern Pacific Railroad's Fernley and Lassen branch line between Susanville and Mason Station, four miles north of Westwood. Southern Pacific operated logging, freight, and passenger trains over the line 1914–1955. Through the cooperative efforts of the Bureau of Land Management, U.S. Forest Service, and many community groups, the abandoned rail line is now a 25.4-mile-long trail for bikers, hikers, and horseback riders.

one of two railroad tunnels on the historic Bizz Johnson Trail

The wide dirt-and-gravel road is ideal for mountain biking. Those looking for an easy ride will want to keep to the first 6.7 miles of the trail for a mellow cruise along the scenic Susan River. Beyond those miles, the trail has a steeper grade and loses much of its scenic value.

The trail begins at the Susanville Railroad Depot and museum, which is open daily, including holidays. The first half mile runs through Susanville's neighborhoods, then reaches the Millerton Road trailhead and enters the scenic Susan River canyon. Both sides of the trail are lined with fascinating volcanic rocks; the pretty river flows mellifluously alongside. A highlight for many riders, especially kids, is the point where the trail passes through two old railroad tunnels (one 800 feet long and one 400 feet long, both extremely dark inside). If bridges are your thing, not tunnels, the trail crosses nine of them.

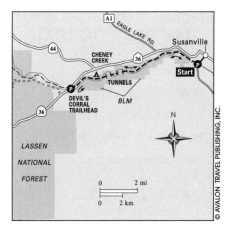

Your turnaround point is the Devil's Corral Trailhead at 6.7 miles. Here, you simply turn your wheels around and head back, enjoying the lovely river canyon all over again.

So, who was Bizz Johnson, anyway? He was a former California Congressman who worked on this project and many other public works.

Information and Contact

There is no fee. For more information and a free map, contact Bureau of Land Management, Eagle Lake Field Office, 530/257-0456, website: www.ca.blm.gov/eaglelake. Or contact Eagle Lake Ranger District, Lassen National Forest, 477-050 Eagle Lake Road, Susanville, CA 96130, 530/257-4188, website: www.fs.fed.us/r5/lassen.

Directions

From Highway 36 in Susanville, head east through town as the road becomes Main Street. At the first stoplight, turn right on South Weatherlow Street. Drive .4 mile to the railroad depot on the left.

© ANN MARIE BROWN

Mendocino and Wine Country

Chapter 3

Mendocino and Wine Country

The Mendocino and Wine Country region encompasses a vast and diverse landscape ranging from wave-swept beaches, rugged cliffs, and rolling sand dunes to vineyard-covered hills and valleys. Despite the technological advances of our modern 21st century, this area has retained its pastoral character more than perhaps anywhere else in California. Highway 1 winds up the rocky Pacific coast past seaside villages with population counts lower than their elevation—which is close to sea level. In much of the grassland hills east of the Sonoma and Mendocino coast, you're likely to see many more sheep or cows than people. The talk in the towns is about the crab harvest, or how many head of cattle are grazing in what plot of land, or whether or not grapes can grow in the coastal hills.

This peaceful, rural countryside is a marvelous setting for a bike ride, and the area is blessed with an abundance of parks. Within a few miles of the Mendocino town limits are three state parks where bicycling is permitted—Van Damme, Russian Gulch, and MacKerricher. And if you're clamoring for a fine meal or a bed-and-breakfast to ease you out of the saddle at the end of the day, visitors are always welcome at the charming shops and business establishments in downtown Mendocino.

Like the Mendocino coast, the neighboring Sonoma coast also offers unforgettable coastal scenery. Rugged headlands, rocky promontories, and sandy coves provide breathtaking panoramas. Trails at Salt Point State Park give mountain bikers the opportunity to take in the coastal drama.

Also unforgettable are the inland valleys, where U.S. 101 runs north from Santa Rosa to Wine Country. Most people think of Sonoma and Napa as Wine Country, but the wine-growing regions expand into several other valleys as well: Alexander Valley east of Geyserville, Dry Creek Valley west of Geyserville, and the Russian River Valley between Guerneville and Healdsburg. Fortunately, bicycling and wine-tasting go together like, well, a bold merlot and French bread smothered in Camembert. Several of the Wine Country's parklands offer great biking opportunities for casual riders seeking a little fresh air and exercise: Annadel State Park, Sugarloaf Ridge State Park, and Jack London State Historic Park, among others. For a perfect day-trip, plan a morning bike ride topped off by an afternoon of wine-tasting.

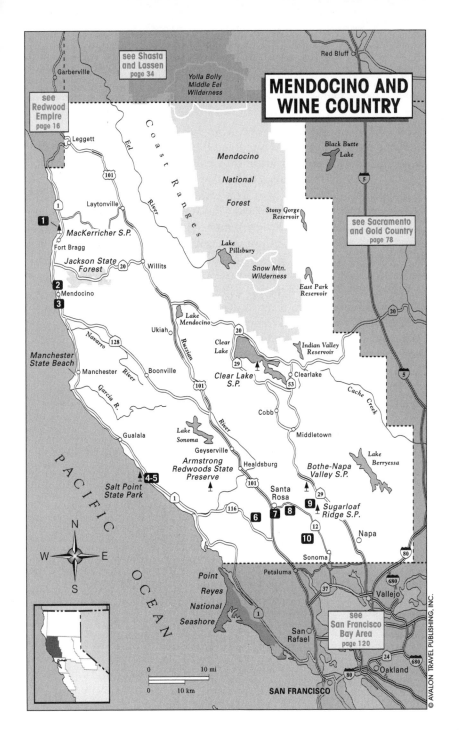

1 OLD HAUL ROAD/TEN MILE COASTAL TRAIL

MacKerricher State Park, off Highway 1 near Fort Bragg

Total distance: 6.4 miles   **Biking time:** 1.0 hour

Type of trail: Paved road

Type of bike: Road bike or mountain bike

Steepness: Mostly level   **Skill level:** Easiest

First, the good news: Old Haul Road in MacKerricher State Park is one of the few trails around Mendocino where you can ride right alongside the ocean waves, enjoying miles of coastal scenery. It's a car-free, paved recreation trail, suitable for all kinds of riders and beach lovers.

Now the bad news: Old Haul Road, also called Ten Mile Coastal Trail, has suffered serious storm damage over the years, and parts of it are completely washed away, replaced by millions of grains of blowing sand. State park managers have been hoping for funds to repair it (and an aged railroad trestle that connects Old Haul Road to Fort Bragg and beyond); but so far, they're still just hoping.

But that hasn't stopped bikers from using Old Haul Road, a historic railroad grade built in 1915 for transporting redwood logs to the mill in Fort Bragg. Bicyclists arrive in great numbers every sunny day and share the trail with hikers, baby strollers, dogs on leashes, and even some equestrians. Everybody has a good time.

A 3.2-mile oceanside section from Ward Avenue south to the closed-off railroad trestle over Pudding Creek in Fort Bragg allows uninterrupted

© ANN MARIE BROWN

ocean views from Old Haul Road

easy riding. The first stretch passes by wide-open beaches, dunes, and coastline, then enters the main camping and day-use area of MacKerricher State Park. Here, you might want to get off your bike and do some exploring around Laguna Point, where harbor seals and tidepools are plentiful along the rocky shore. South of the park the trail becomes somewhat less scenic; it passes behind the backs of seaside motels and provides occasional views of the Georgia-Pacific Lumber Company's smokestacks. Still, looking westward, you'll find that the open ocean is your constant companion—a symphony of white sand and wavy seas.

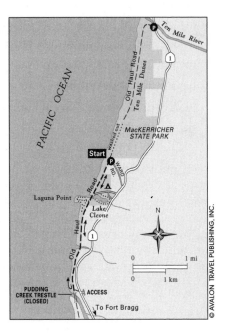

Options

To experience more of Old Haul Road, drive north on Highway 1 to just south of the Ten Mile River bridge, where the trail's northern terminus is located. From here, you'll get a couple of miles in the saddle (riding southward) before the pavement vanishes in the sand. This is the western edge of the 1,285-acre sand dune complex called Ten Mile Dunes, home to 12 threatened or endangered species, including the western snowy plover. If you wish to explore this area, head for the beach instead of walking on the fragile dunes.

Information and Contact

There is no fee. A map/park brochure is available at the entrance station. For more information, contact MacKerricher State Park, P.O. Box 440, Mendocino, CA 95460, 707/937-5804 or 707/937-4296, website: www.parks.ca.gov.

Directions

From Mendocino, drive 13 miles north on Highway 1 to Ward Avenue (four miles north of Fort Bragg and one mile north of MacKerricher State Park). Turn left and drive .7 mile to the road's end at a small parking area.

2 FERN CANYON & FALLS LOOP TRAILS

Russian Gulch State Park, off Highway 1 near Mendocino

Total distance: 3.2 miles

Biking time: 1.0 hour

Type of trail: Paved bike trail

Type of bike: Road bike or mountain bike

Steepness: Mostly level

Skill level: Easiest

The Fern Canyon Trail at Russian Gulch State Park is hardly long enough to be considered a bike trail, yet it is always popular with riders of all ages and abilities. Why? Because cycling on the forested, fern-lined Fern Canyon Trail is only one part of the adventure; part two comes when you lock up your bike at the paved trail's terminus and take a hike to Russian Gulch Falls, a gushing 36-foot waterfall that drops into a rocky fern grotto. The falls are framed by toppled tree trunks and hundreds of ferns in a lush, picturesque setting. After a good rain, Russian Gulch Falls really pours, but it is lovely to see even in the dry summer months.

Russian Gulch Falls

The trail directions are a breeze. Just get on your bike and ride from the trailhead at the edge of the campground, following the smooth paved path 1.6 miles to a junction, where you'll find a few picnic tables and a bike rack. Here, you must lock up your bike and continue on foot to the waterfall. Two trail choices will get you there: a short, .7-mile route accessing it from the north, or a longer, 2.3-mile route accessing it from the south. After viewing the falls, you can either return the way you came or hike the alternate trail back (for a three-mile round-trip hike). Then it's back in the saddle for a quick return ride to the trailhead.

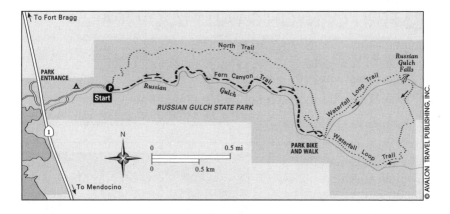

Note that the bike ride itself will probably take you less than an hour, but allow at least an extra hour to hike to (and hang out at) the waterfall. And don't forget to bring along a bike lock.

Options
You could easily combine this short bike-and-hike trip with a similar adventure on the nearby Fern Canyon Trail in Van Damme State Park (see the following trail description).

Information and Contact
A $6 day-use fee is charged per vehicle. A park map is available at the entrance kiosk. For more information, contact Russian Gulch State Park, P.O. Box 440, Mendocino, CA 95460, 707/937-5804 or 707/937-4296, website: www.parks.ca.gov.

Directions
From Mendocino, drive two miles north on Highway 1 to the entrance to Russian Gulch State Park on the left. Turn left, then left again immediately to reach the entrance kiosk. Continue past the kiosk and turn left again to cross under the highway. Drive through the campground to the Fern Canyon Trail parking area. (If the camp is closed for the winter, you must park near the recreation hall and ride through the campground.)

3 FERN CANYON TRAIL

Van Damme State Park, off Highway 1 near Mendocino

Total distance: 5.0 miles   **Biking time:** 2.0 hours

Type of trail: Paved trail

Type of bike: Road bike or mountain bike

Steepness: Rolling terrain   **Skill level:** Easiest

Fern Canyon Trail

It's a bit confusing: Within five miles of the Mendocino coast are two Fern Canyon Trails. Both are paved bike trails, both were built on old logging roads, both are in state parks, and both carve their way through flora-rich canyons, paralleling streams.

Here's the difference: The Fern Canyon Trail in Russian Gulch State Park has an optional add-on hike to a waterfall (see the previous trail description). The Fern Canyon Trail in Van Damme State Park, described here, crosses Little River dozens of times, revealing spawning salmon and steelhead in the winter months. The trail also has an option for an add-on mountain bike ride or hike to a pygmy forest of miniature cypress and pine trees.

Both trails are worth a visit. The Fern Canyon Trail in Van Damme State Park has one big catch, though. During the rainy season, its multiple bridges are removed, so you can't travel past the first mile. Generally, you can count on the entire trail being open April–October, but always phone the park before making a special trip. Storm damage in the 1990s closed the trail for extended periods, and if Mother Nature gets in the mood, it could happen again. One 50-yard-long, washed-out stretch in the first mile of trail serves as a reminder of these stormy days. Most riders carry their bikes over the break in the pavement.

The first 2.5 miles are nearly level, curving through Little River's lush canyon lined with redwoods, firs, alders, berry bushes, and, of course, the inevitable

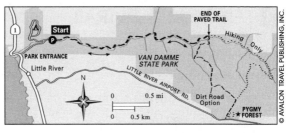

ferns—10 different kinds are found here. Where the pavement ends, two trails continue onward: a 2.5-mile, hikers-only trail (skinny-tire riders can lock up their bikes at the bike rack and hike this path) and a 1.2-mile dirt road that is open to mountain bikes. Both trails lead to the pygmy forest, where sandy, highly acidic soil has produced miniaturized flora. Mountain bikers, be prepared for a brief but substantial climb to get there. Those who have elected to hike instead of ride this stretch will probably want to turn it into a 3.7-mile loop by combining the hiking trail and the dirt road.

Options

You can turn this bike-and-hike trip into an overnight camping trip, if you wish. At 1.7 miles in, you pass a few environmental campsites (meaning campsites with minimal facilities), which are available by prior reservation from the park office (contact information below).

Information and Contact

A $6 day-use fee is charged per vehicle. A park map is available at the entrance kiosk. For more information, contact Van Damme State Park, P.O. Box 440, Mendocino, CA 95460, 707/937-5804 or 707/937-0851, website: www.parks.ca.gov.

Directions

From Mendocino, drive three miles south on Highway 1 to the entrance to Van Damme State Park on the left. Turn left and continue past the kiosk to the Fern Canyon Trail parking lot at the east end of the campground.

4 PYGMY FOREST TRAIL LOOP

Salt Point State Park, off Highway 1 near Jenner

Total distance: 4.5 miles **Biking time:** 1.5 hours

Type of trail: Dirt roads

Type of bike: Mountain bike

Steepness: Steep sections **Skill level:** Moderate

If you've been eating too much abalone with garlic and butter on your trip to Salt Point State Park, here's a ride where you'll work off some calories. Pygmy Forest Trail is a workout, but it's definitely worth the effort. When it's all over, you can have another serving of those tasty shellfish for which this stretch of coast is known.

Check your calendar before you go. The state park opens its trails to mountain bikers April–October only in order to protect the trails in the wet and muddy months. (Abalone season runs April–November, which coincides nicely.)

You may eye the uphill fire road leading from the parking lot with some suspicion. However, once you get through the first 200 yards of strenuous climbing, you turn left onto a nice level stretch. (Ignore the trail sign that points straight uphill for the pygmy forest—you're taking a slightly easier route.) Enjoy the smooth ride through pine and fir trees, catch your breath, and turn right at the next intersection. Climb. Climb some more. Walk your bike when you can't stand climbing any more. The trail is not terribly steep, but rather a slow, relentless uphill, gaining about 500 feet in elevation. Mild grumbling is okay, but extensive grumbling is not permitted, since you can make the entire 1.5-mile climb in less than 30 minutes, even if you walk half of it.

As you ascend, you may notice a change in the forest around you. The soil becomes drier and more sandy the higher you go. Rhododendrons spring up among the trees, which appear less dense than they were at the lower elevations. Finally, the trail tops the ridge at 900 feet and you're in the pygmy forest. Azaleas and rhododendrons flourish in the sandy, acidic soil. Cypress, pine, and redwood trees grow in dwarfed versions. It's a strange contrast to the "normal" conifer and hardwood forest you've been riding in.

The trail narrows to single-track, with a few sandy and rocky spots to keep things interesting. Keep your speed down and watch out for other trail users who may be coming the opposite way through the pygmy forest. If you've made it this far, you might as well ride the rest of the loop instead of turning around, because the remainder is pure fun—all flat or downhill. The trail descends through the pygmy forest, then meets up with a fire road where you can turn left or right. Right goes straight home, but if you have any energy remaining, turn left instead for a level .5 mile. The trail leads to a wide meadow, called a coastal prairie. Take a moment to watch for wildlife in these grasslands and then turn your bike around and begin the descent back to the campground at Highway 1. When you reach two water tanks halfway down, stay to the left to take a slightly different route than the one you rode up.

Information and Contact
A $6 day-use fee is charged per vehicle. A park map is available at the entrance station. For more information, contact Salt Point State Park, 25050 Coast Highway 1, Jenner, CA 95450, 707/847-3221, website: www.parks.ca.gov.

Directions
From Jenner at Highway 1, drive north on Highway 1 for 20 miles to Salt Point State Park. Turn right at the Woodside Campground entrance (if you reach Gerstle Cove, you've gone too far). Continue past the entrance kiosk to the parking lot for the hike/bike camp. Start riding on the dirt fire road that leads from the far side of the lot, signed as "Pygmy Forest, 2 miles."

5 GERSTLE COVE TO STUMP BEACH COVE TRAIL
Salt Point State Park, off Highway 1 near Jenner

Total distance: 2.4 miles   **Biking time:** 45 minutes

Type of trail: Dirt roads

Type of bike: Mountain bike

Steepness: Mostly level   **Skill level:** Easiest

If you're prepared for some coastal wind, the Salt Point State Park trail from Gerstle Cove to Stump Beach Cove is a spectacular, level bike trip across grassy bluffs, with classic ocean views every pedal-turn of the way. The ride is short and level enough so that kids can enjoy the ride equally with adults. And because the Gerstle Cove Marine Reserve is just below the blufftop trail, you'll have plenty of opportunities to glimpse some marine life.

While the coastal vistas here are unparalleled, to enjoy them you must time your trip right and dress properly. Make sure you arrive April–October, the only months when the park's trails are open to bikes. Then, ride

Stump Beach Cove, Salt Point State Park

this trail as early in the morning as possible, before the wind picks up speed. On this trail, it's just you, the wind, the bluffs, and the open ocean. If 2.4 miles doesn't sound like much of a bike workout, try it when the wind is howling at 50 miles per hour, which it sometimes does here. Bring a jacket with you, always.

Start riding from the parking area at Gerstle Cove. Ride your bike back up the park road about 100 yards and pick up the dirt fire road signed as "Authorized Vehicles Only." Prepare to be awed by the rocky coastline, vast kelp beds, harbor seals swimming in the surf, and seabirds swooping and diving overhead. Waves crash against the cliffs, sometimes causing a fine mist to dampen your face. You may even see a California gray whale passing by on its yearly migration.

Ignore any trail spurs and stay on the main fire road, leaving the single-track for hikers. Occasionally, the route turns inland, moving away from the sea. In springtime, the trailside grasslands bloom profusely with lupines, poppies, and coastal paintbrush.

When you reach Stump Beach Cove, the trail loops around to the right, skirting the edge of the cove and coming to an end at Highway 1. Ride all the way to the highway and then just turn around, enjoying all the views one more time on your return trip.

Information and Contact

A $6 day-use fee is charged per vehicle. A park map is available at the entrance station. For more information, contact Salt Point State Park,

25050 Coast Highway 1, Jenner, CA 95450, 707/847-3221, website: www.parks.ca.gov.

Directions
From U.S. 101 at Santa Rosa, drive west on Highway 116 for 33 miles, through Sebastopol and Guerneville, to Highway 116's intersection with Highway 1 near Jenner. Continue north on Highway 1 for 20 miles to Salt Point State Park. Look for the Gerstle Cove entrance on your left. Drive through the entrance kiosk, then head straight for .7 mile to the day-use area.

6 JOE RODOTA TRAIL
Sonoma County Regional Parks, off Highway 116 between Sebastopol and Santa Rosa

Total distance: 5.6 miles   **Biking time:** 1.0 hour

Type of trail: Paved bike trail

Type of bike: Road bike or mountain bike

Steepness: Mostly level   **Skill level:** Easiest

Sebastopol is the kind of unspoiled Sonoma town where you can still smell the apples in the fall. Sure, the city has grown up. Yes, things aren't the way they were in the old days. But Sebastopol still manages to retain its rural, small-town feel. The old rail trail that runs from Sebastopol to Santa Rosa is the perfect kind of bike path for this town—a level, easy route on which you can ride through farmland and inhale the apple-scented air.

Pull that old beach cruiser out of your dusty garage, because on Joe Rodota Trail, you won't even need to shift. The trail's history is obvious (it's an old railroad line). The route is completely straight and level; along the way, you cross three bridges, which are placed on top of old train trestles.

The trail starts near the Town Plaza in Sebastopol, which has both a bike shop and an ice-cream store, fulfilling all of a cyclist's basic needs. The first part of the route is more bucolic than its latter miles, which enter more suburban territory as the trail approaches Santa Rosa. Although the entire bike path parallels busy Highway 12, it is sheltered from the freeway by trees for the first 1.5 miles. Benches are situated along the trail, allowing you to take a break and enjoy the view to the south over farm country.

The trail intersects with roads at a few points, but most are just ranch roads with little traffic. There is one major intersection about two miles in where you must stop and look carefully before crossing, but otherwise you are mercifully separated from automobiles until the bike route comes to an end at Merced Avenue, .5 mile from the Santa Rosa city limit. Nothing to do here but turn around and ride back.

Options

This trail is a piece of the larger West County Trail system in Sebastopol. It is possible to connect to other stretches of the trail system by following Sebastopol streets to Analy High School at Moore Street.

Information and Contact

There is no fee. For more information, contact Sonoma County Regional Parks Department, 2300 County Center, Suite 120A, Santa Rosa, CA 95403, 707/565-2041 or 707/823-7262, website: www.sonoma-county.org/parks.

Directions

From U.S. 101 at Santa Rosa, drive northwest on Highway 116 (Petaluma Boulevard) to downtown Sebastopol, just before its junction with Highway 12. Turn left on Burnett Street in Sebastopol and park in the city lot, which allows three hours of free parking. Ride your bike out the east side of the lot and cross Petaluma Boulevard to the start of the trail.

7 HOWARTH PARK & SPRING LAKE PARK TRAILS

Sonoma County Regional Parks, off Highway 12 in Santa Rosa

Total distance: 5.0 miles   **Biking time:** 1.0 hour

Type of trail: Paved bike trail

Type of bike: Road bike or mountain bike

Steepness: Rolling terrain   **Skill level:** Easiest

Howarth Park and Spring Lake Park are adjacent parks, run by the city of Santa Rosa and county of Sonoma, respectively. They are well-loved by locals, but virtually unknown outside the Santa Rosa area. Thousands of people drive within five miles of them on their daily commute without ever knowing of their existence or their myriad charms. In addition to sharing a paved bike trail, the parks have two lakes with fishing opportunities and rowboat rentals, a campground, boat ramp, hiking and horseback-riding trails, and enough game courts and children's play sets to keep an entire family happy for a year. There is even an amusement park called K Land at Howarth Park, with a carousel, miniature train, animal barn, and pony rides during summers and school vacations.

The bike trail that runs through both parks is perfect for a one-hour workout. It forms a loop that you can circle once or twice and has a few small hills to get your leg muscles working. One family I know comes here regularly on weekends; one parent plays with the kids while the other rides the bike trail, then they switch roles.

If you start your ride at Howarth Park by Lake Ralphine, you can avoid paying the entrance fee at Spring Lake Park. Lake Ralphine is much smaller than Spring Lake, but it's still popular with young anglers, who fish from shore for bass, trout, and bluegill. The bike trail

Lake Ralphine, Howarth Park

passes Lake Ralphine's southeast edge, heading through oak-studded hills to Spring Lake. The trail loops around Spring Lake; I'd suggest riding to the left first, since the trail is routed up a hill and over the dam, offering great views of the 75-acre lake.

Constructed as a flood-control reservoir in 1962, Spring Lake offers decent fishing prospects for trout and bass and plenty of picnic spots with views of ducks, reeds, and water. Although swimming is not allowed in the lake, a separate swimming lagoon is on its east side. The bike trail passes it on the way to the campground and boat ramp.

As you ride through the boat ramp parking area, the trail gets a little tricky to follow. You go up a short hill, then turn right at Jackrabbit Parcourse/Picnic Area and ride through it to pick up the bike path again (on your right). In less than a quarter mile, you descend to the fork where you first entered the loop; turn right to ride the loop again or left to head back to Howarth Park, Lake Ralphine, and your car.

Options

Mountain bikers have the option of heading off on various dirt trails that intersect with the paved trail. Be sure to get updated information about which trails are open to mountain bikes. Maps with trail designations are posted throughout the park.

Information and Contact
There is no fee. For more information, contact Sonoma County Regional Parks Department, 2300 County Center, Suite 120A, Santa Rosa, CA 95403, 707/565-2041 or 707/823-7262, website: www.sonoma-county.org/parks.

Directions
From U.S. 101 in Santa Rosa, take the Fairgrounds/Highway 12 exit. Highway 12 becomes Farmers Lane as it heads through downtown Santa Rosa. Turn right on Montgomery Drive and continue for one mile. Turn right on Summerfield Road and drive .3 mile, then turn left into Howarth Park. Drive straight up the hill to the upper parking lot, next to Lake Ralphine. The bike path begins on the right side of the lake.

8 LAKE ILSANJO TRAIL LOOP
Annadel State Park, off Highway 12 in Santa Rosa

Total distance: 6.3 miles   **Biking time:** 1.5 hours

Type of trail: Dirt roads

Type of bike: Mountain bike

Steepness: Steep sections   **Skill level:** Moderate

Annadel State Park is a horsey kind of place. When you count the horse trailers in the parking lot, hoofprints all over the place, and horse "evidence" along the trail, you might think more horses visit here than people. Luckily, horses are generous by nature, and they don't mind sharing the trail to Lake Ilsanjo with easy bikers, as long as we mind our trail manners.

So, let's review: When you see a horse and rider coming toward you on the trail, what do you do? Stop riding, pull over to the side, smile a lot, and let them pass. If you're heading in the same direction as they are and need to pass, call out gently and cheerfully, without shouting, and ask the rider's permission. Give the horse plenty of time to move off the trail. That way, you won't scare the daylights out of a 1,500-pound animal.

In addition to being a horsey place, Annadel is also a mountain biker's place. Not just the ranch roads but also most of the single-track at Annadel is open to bikes. That's convenient, because you need to cover a lot of ground to see Annadel's 5,000 acres, filled with woodlands, meadows, creeks, wildflowers, and even a 26-acre lake.

grasslands and oaks near Lake Ilsanjo in Annadel State Park

Pick up a park map at the ranger kiosk on your way in. Since 1997, Annadel's multiple trails have been undergoing reconstruction and repair in an effort to protect the park's delicate meadows, marshes, and archaeological sites. The work is ongoing, so carry a recently updated map with you as you ride. Start your trip at the trailhead at the end of Channel Drive, heading uphill over 1.5 miles on Warren Richardson Trail. The wide ranch road steadily ascends through a dense and shady Douglas fir forest, with a few redwoods and bay laurels for variety. In a few stretches, the trail goes level just long enough for you to catch your breath.

You know you are nearing the lake when you start to descend into open meadows dotted with oak trees. The trail takes you to the east side of the lake, providing great views of blue water and plenty of waterfowl. Veer left on Canyon Trail to circle around the lake and over its dam. Fishing is fair in Lake Ilsanjo, with anglers lining up along the shore to cast for black bass and bluegill. If you're curious about the origin of the lake's moniker, "Ilsanjo" is a combination of Ilsa and Joe, the names of the land's former owners.

To loop back, bear left on Rough Go Trail and head away from the lake to connect to Live Oak Trail, then North Burma Trail. Turn right on North Burma Trail. Most of this return stretch is nearly level, but an abundance of rocks in the trail may slow you down. Annadel is famous for its rocks; in the early 1900s, the area was extensively quarried to provide cobblestone for the city of San Francisco.

When you rejoin Warren Richardson Trail, go left and enjoy an easy coast back down to the parking lot. Be sure to turn left at the hairpin turn that you rode through on the way up; when coasting downhill, it's easy to continue straight instead of making that turn, in which case you'll head off on Two Quarry Trail and probably won't be home in time for supper.

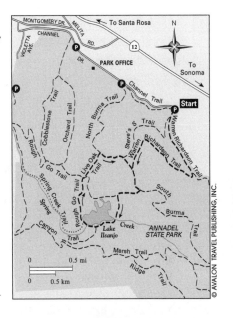

Options

Beginning riders can skip the loop and just ride up the hill to the lake's eastern edge and back, for a four-mile round-trip with no technically challenging stretches. More advanced riders can make a slightly longer loop by continuing straight on North Burma Trail after visiting the lake, then following Channel Trail back to the parking lot. Make sure you have a park map with you.

Information and Contact

A $4 day-use fee is charged per vehicle. Park maps are available at the ranger station. For more information, contact Annadel State Park, 6201 Channel Drive, Santa Rosa, CA 95409, 707/539-3911 or 707/938-1519, website: www.parks.ca.gov.

Directions

From U.S. 101 in Santa Rosa, take the Fairgrounds/Highway 12 exit. Highway 12 becomes Farmers Lane. Turn right on Montgomery Drive and follow it for 2.7 miles (veering to the right), then turn right on Channel Drive. Follow Channel Drive into the park, stop at the ranger station, then drive to the end of the road and park in the lot (a total of 2.2 miles on Channel Drive).

9 MEADOW & HILLSIDE TRAIL LOOP

Sugarloaf Ridge State Park, off Highway 12 near Kenwood

Total distance: 2.5 miles   **Biking time:** 1.0 hour

Type of trail: Dirt roads

Type of bike: Mountain bike

Steepness: Steep sections   **Skill level:** Moderate

With its entrance set farther off the main road, Sugarloaf Ridge is often overlooked in a cluster of close-together Sonoma state parks, including Annadel, Sugarloaf, and Jack London. Getting there requires a four-mile drive off Highway 12 to the park entrance, set 1,000 feet below the top of Sugarloaf Ridge, elevation 2,200 feet. Much of the ascent is accomplished on the drive up, so you're rewarded with spectacular views of Sonoma Valley without having to do a lot of climbing on your bike ride.

You will get a workout, however, especially on the return leg of this loop. Whereas Meadow Trail is mostly flat, Hillside Trail ascends about 300 feet in .5 mile and then drops back down, reminding your heart and lungs of their respective functions.

From the day-use parking area, ride up the paved park road for .25 mile, toward the horse corral area, then ride through the horse camp gate. At the far end of the horse camp, the pavement ends. On the right is a gate and gravel trail, signed as "Meadow Trail." Follow it for .8 mile, passing by the junctions with Gray Pine and Brushy Peaks Trails on your left, and then loop to your right on Hillside Trail.

Here comes the workout. Although Meadow Trail was sunny and open, Hillside Trail is shaded by oaks, laurel, and madrone, and if it's at all warm outside, you'll be grateful for the canopy. After climbing for .6 mile (pant, pant), you start to descend and pass a water storage tank. Don't rush downhill, or you'll miss the best part of this ride, which is an overlook with a picnic table about 100 yards beyond the tank. A short spur trail leads to the overlook (ride too fast and you'll miss it), where, lo and behold, there's a spring and a water spigot. Hopefully, your biking partner remembered to pack along some good food, since you're here at this picnic table with a fine view of the valley. Have lunch and celebrate having made the ascent to such a great spot.

On the way downhill, the gravel service road turns to dirt and eventually single-track, so try to keep your eyes on the trail as you descend. You will be continually distracted by the views. When you reach an intersection where Hillside Trail heads to the right and a nature trail leads straight ahead, stay on Hillside Trail. Pass another hiking trail, then cross Sonoma Creek and take a short jaunt through a meadow. The trail leads back to a gate at the horse corral area, just a few dozen yards from where you started. Ride back on the pavement to your left to the parking area and your car.

Options
Bikers seeking an aerobic workout can try their lungs on Stern Trail and Bald Mountain Trail, which lead from the parking lot by the entrance kiosk to the summit of 2,729-foot Bald Mountain. Much of the route is paved, but the climb is relentless (a 1,500-foot ascent in less than three miles).

Information and Contact
A $6 day-use fee is charged per vehicle. A park map is available from the entrance kiosk. For more information, contact Sugarloaf Ridge State Park, 2605 Adobe Canyon Road, Kenwood, CA 95452-9004, 707/833-5712 or 707/938-1519, website: www.parks.ca.gov.

Directions
From U.S. 101 in Santa Rosa, take the Fairgrounds/Highway 12 exit. Highway 12 becomes Farmers Lane. Continue on Highway 12 for 11 miles to Adobe Canyon Road. Turn left and drive 3.5 miles to the park entrance kiosk. Pay the entrance fee, then continue straight and park in the day-use parking area on the left. Ride your bike farther up the park road, following the pavement to the far end of the horse camp. Where the pavement ends, take the gravel trail signed as "Meadow Trail."

10 LAKE TRAIL LOOP
Jack London State Historic Park, off Highway 12 in Glen Ellen

Total distance: 2.7 miles   **Biking time:** 1.0 hour

Type of trail: Dirt roads

Type of bike: Mountain bike

Steepness: Steep sections   **Skill level:** Moderate

Author Jack London wanted beauty, and so he "bought beauty, and was content with beauty for awhile." Those were his words describing his love affair with his Sonoma ranch and its surrounding hills, which are now part of Jack London State Historic Park.

London, famous for his novels *Call of the Wild* and *The Sea Wolf,* which made him one of the most popular and highest paid fiction writers of the

the extravagant Pig Palace enjoyed by Jack London's beloved pigs

early 1900s, wanted to build his home in Glen Ellen to escape city life. After two years of construction, his ranch dream house caught fire and burned to the ground just days before he and his wife were to move in. It was a devastating loss, both personally and financially, for the Londons. The couple lived on the ranch in a small wood-frame house until Jack London's death in 1916.

In the 1950s, several parcels of this land became state park property, and today, the park has grown to 800 acres with several miles of fire roads that are open to bikes. Many of the trails are quite steep as they rise toward the summit of Sonoma Mountain. For easy bikers, the best ride is the 2.7-mile round-trip to London's ranch lake and an overlook beyond. You can begin or end your trip with a visit to Jack London Museum at the park's visitors center, which has interesting exhibits and photographs from the author's life.

Even without the historical slant, this ride is a winner. Take the paved trail from the parking lot to the picnic area (walk your bike on this 100-yard section), then pick up the dirt fire road signed as "Lake Trail." Head right, past the barns and winery buildings. Turn right at the sign for Pig Palace—the extravagant pigsty enjoyed by London's beloved pigs. Check out this elaborate stone structure, then return to the main path. Skirting past carefully tended vineyards, the road forks at a gate; bike riders must stay on the wide road to the left. Climb for .5 mile through mixed hardwoods and Douglas firs all the way to the lake.

London's prized lake is more of a pond nowadays. With sediment continually encroaching upon it, it has shrunk to half its original size. A redwood log cabin that was used as a bathhouse still stands. The Londons swam, fished, and entertained guests at the lake. Ride around the lake's left side, following the trail signed "Mountain Trail to Mountain Summit." It's a hard, switchbacked climb over .3 mile, but worth the effort. When you reach a junction with Fallen Bridge Trail, you're at May's Clearing vista point, and the view of the valley to the south is breathtaking.

Retrace your route when you're ready, but control your speed on the way downhill. The park has a strict 15-mile-per-hour speed limit, and with the number of horses and hikers on the trail and around the ranch grounds, it makes sense to obey it.

Options
From the vista point at May's Clearing, you can continue uphill on Mountain Trail for another 1.5 miles to the next vista point.

Information and Contact
A $6 day-use fee is charged per vehicle. A park map is available at the entrance station. For more information, contact Jack London State Historic Park, 2400 London Ranch Road, Glen Ellen, CA 95442, 707/938-5216 or 707/938-1519, website: www.parks.ca.gov.

Directions
From Sonoma on Highway 12, drive north for 4.5 miles to Madrone Road and turn left. At the end of Madrone Road, turn right on Arnold Drive and follow it for three miles into Glen Ellen, then turn left on London Ranch Road. Follow London Ranch Road for one mile to the park entrance kiosk. Park in the day-use area on the right (not in the visitors center lot on the left). The trail leads from the parking area.

Chapter 4

© ANN MARIE BROWN

Sacramento and Gold Country

Sacramento and Gold Country

The Sierra Nevada foothills region surrounding the north–south corridor of Highway 49 is a history-rich area known as the Gold Country, or the Mother Lode. This is the place where James Marshall discovered gold in January 1848, sparking a huge and frenzied migration westward. When it became known that a rich vein of gold ran from Mariposa to Downieville, the history of California and the West was forever changed. Although other areas of California experienced their own Gold Rush, it was the Mother Lode that ultimately produced the richest deposits of ore.

Evidence of the area's mining past is obvious, from historic brick and wooden buildings to old bridges, mines, water ditches, and an abundance of antique shops. Many of the region's towns have barely changed since their heyday: Streets are just wide enough for two stagecoaches to pass, buildings are constructed of stones from local rivers and streams, and storefronts look like they are right out of a movie set. You can travel for many miles in the Gold Country without ever seeing a traffic light. There's a whole lot of California here just waiting to be rediscovered, preferably on two wheels that roll along wild-flower-covered hills in springtime.

The landscape of the Gold Country is made up of low-elevation foothills studded with oaks and pines and deeply carved, roaring river canyons. Hot weather is to be expected in summer, which means the trails in this region are best for bicycling in autumn, winter, and spring.

Also included in this region is the Central Valley, with its endless acres of cotton, orchards, and grazing lands and its famous rivers: the Sacramento, American, and Feather, among others. Extending for hundreds of miles from these rivers are marshy wetlands that attract ducks and waterfowl. The Central Valley, which may seem like an empty wasteland to hurried drivers on I-5 or Highway 99, is a place of critical refuge for millions of birds on the Pacific Flyway. From the seat of a bike, and at the mellower speed of your own leg power, it is possible to develop a new appreciation for this vast landscape of grasslands and waterways. All that wildlife just can't be wrong.

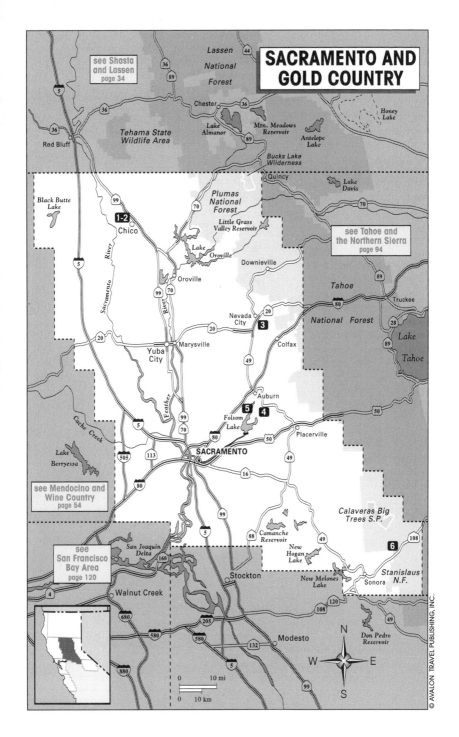

SACRAMENTO AND GOLD COUNTRY

see Shasta
and Lassen
page 34

Lassen
National
Forest

Honey
Lake

Chester

Red Bluff

Tehama State
Wildlife Area

Lake
Almanor

Mtn. Meadows
Reservoir

Antelope
Lake

Bucks Lake
Wilderness

Black Butte
Lake

Quincy

Lake
Davis

Plumas
National
Forest

Chico **1-2**

Little Grass
Valley Reservoir

see Tahoe and
the Northern Sierra
page 94

Lake
Oroville

Downieville

Oroville

Tahoe

Truckee

National Forest

Nevada
City **3**

Marysville

Yuba
City

Colfax

Lake
Tahoe

Auburn **4**

Folsom
Lake **5**

Cache Creek

Lake
Berryessa

Placerville

SACRAMENTO

see Mendocino and
Wine Country
page 54

Calaveras Big
Trees S.P.

6

see
San Francisco
Bay Area
page 120

San Joaquin
Delta

Camanche
Reservoir

New
Hogan
Lake

Stanislaus
N.F.

Walnut Creek

Stockton

New Melones
Lake

Sonora

Don Pedro
Reservoir

Modesto

N
W   E
S

© AVALON TRAVEL PUBLISHING, INC.

0   10 mi

0   10 km

1 BIDWELL PARK RIDE

City of Chico, off Highway 32 in Chico

Total distance: 6.6 miles

Biking time: 1.0 hour

Type of trail: Paved bike trail

Type of bike: Road bike or mountain bike

Steepness: Mostly level

Skill level: Easiest

Chico is a bike-riding kind of town. Its downtown stretch on Main Street has bike racks on almost every corner, three bike stores in the space of two blocks, and municipal buses rolling by with bike carriers mounted on their backs. Like many other college towns, Chico has made way for its bike-riding students at California State University by adding bike lanes to major streets and printing up a local map with suggested routes for bicyclists. But the town has gone beyond mere bike accommodation with its conversion of rail trails to bicycle trails, and with Bidwell Park, a 3,600-acre park that is largely closed to vehicle traffic so that bicyclists can have a field day.

Visitors and locals alike enjoy Bidwell, considered the third largest city park in the United States. Access is easy: Starting from 4th and Main Streets in downtown Chico, ride down 4th Street straight into the park. (You can also drive into the park from 4th Street and park in one

Lower Bidwell Park offers easy riding through plentiful shade trees.

of several small lots, but parking is limited.) In .5 mile, the park road is blocked off to cars, so the route becomes blissfully free of auto traffic. Since this is a two-lane road (called South Park Drive) and not a bike trail, there is plenty of room for bikers traveling in both directions, as well as for multitudes of walkers, joggers, baby-stroller pushers, and the like. Situated along the route are water fountains, picnic tables, benches, and children's play areas. The first main grouping of facilities is at One Mile Recreation Area, one mile in on your right.

Although Bidwell Park can get quite hot in summer, it is well-protected by shade trees. Oaks, maples, sumacs, and other deciduous trees line the route—enough of them to make you sometimes forget you are in the middle of a big town. Their leaves put on quite a color show in autumn. Because of the density of the trees, you may be surprised when the route suddenly intersects with a well-traveled city street, Manzanita Avenue. With that dose of reality, you must make a decision: cross the road and continue into Upper Bidwell Park, or turn around and ride the north side of the loop back to your starting place. Road bikers can ride only .5 mile farther into Upper Bidwell; the pavement ends at Five Mile Recreation Area. Mountain bike trails continue up into the hills from there (see Options, below).

To turn around at Manzanita Avenue and complete a 6.6-mile loop ride on pavement, walk your bike to the left across the Manzanita bridge over Chico Creek (watch for cars). Pick up the bike trail again on your left; it turns into a park road called Peterson Memorial Way. Now you're on the north side of the creek, heading west. You'll finish the trip at Mangrove Avenue, near the park's west end; turn left here and ride two blocks, winding up back on 4th Street, near the park entrance.

Options

Mountain bikers can use the paved loop as a warm-up for the trails in Upper Bidwell Park. From the east end of the paved trail in the lower park, cross Manzanita Avenue, follow the bike path to Five Mile Recreation Area, then continue beyond it and turn right on Wildwood Avenue to pick up the bike path for .8 mile to the end of the pavement and a gate. Ride the dirt road beyond the gate for up to four more miles to Devil's Kitchen Parking Area.

Information and Contact

There is no fee. For more information, contact the City of Chico Parks and Recreation, 411 Main Street, Chico, CA 95928, 530/895-4972, website: www.chico.ca.us.

Directions

From Highway 32 heading east into Chico, stay on Highway 32 as it becomes Nord Avenue, Walnut Street, and finally West 9th Street, and turns left. Drive about 10 blocks on West 9th Street until you reach Main Street, then turn left. Turn right on East 4th Street and park.

2 CHICO TO DURHAM BIKE PATH
Butte County, off Highway 32 near Chico

Total distance: 5.0 miles   **Biking time:** 1.0 hour

Type of trail: Paved bike trail

Type of bike: Road bike or mountain bike

Steepness: Mostly level   **Skill level:** Easiest

A converted rail trail in Chico leads out of town, through ranch lands rich with fragrant almond groves, and heads south to the small town of Durham. The route is pleasant enough, but the reward at the end of the trail is the reason that many Chico natives ride here again and again: a French bakery that serves unforgettable croissants and pastries. Pack along your Sunday paper and make a leisurely morning out of this trek.

The trail's beginning does not look promising. It starts in a less-than-scenic industrial area, but things look better as you ride. The paved Chico to Durham Bike Path parallels Midway Road for its entire length, leaving urban Chico behind. The nearby road noise somewhat disturbs the bucolic ambience, but at least you are completely separate from the cars.

An abandoned Sacramento Railroad line, the bikeway is level and straight, a typical converted rail trail. But unlike many rail trails, this one sees little traffic except from bicyclists since it isn't located in the center of town with easy pedestrian access. It's unlikely you'll have to dodge novice in-line skaters, wayward dogs on long leashes, or walkers strolling three and four abreast. Instead, you can relax and enjoy the pastoral views of rural farms. If you are fortunate enough to ride here in February or March, you will inhale the intoxicating fragrance of almond trees in bloom. Some farmers plant their trees in alternating rows of male and female trees, which produces alternating rows of pink and white flowers. It's quite a show in early spring.

The bike path ends at Jones Avenue, just shy of Durham. If you don't mind riding on a quiet road with occasional car traffic, continue south on

Jones Avenue (don't ride on busy Midway Road) for two more miles until you reach Durham-Dayton Highway. Turn right, cross the railroad tracks, and ride about 300 yards into Durham. Turn right on Midway and ride less than 50 yards to the aforementioned French bakery/café, on the right side of the road.

If you add on the two-mile road ride to the Durham bakery, your round-trip mileage will increase from five miles to nine. But there are cinnamon pastries, chocolate croissants, and gourmet coffee waiting for those who put in the extra effort. For many, the payoff is adequate.

Information and Contact
There is no fee. For more information, contact Butte County Department of Public Works, 7 County Center Drive, Oroville, CA 95965, 530/538-7681, website: www.buttecounty.net.

Directions
From Highway 32 heading east into Chico, stay on Highway 32 as it becomes Nord Avenue and Walnut Street. Turn left on West 2nd Street, drive about 10 blocks, then turn right on Broadway. In .5 mile, Broadway becomes Park Avenue (Highway 99), and in one mile, Park Avenue veers left and Midway Road continues straight. Stay on Midway Road and park along the road. The bike trail is on the left, starting at the junction of Midway and Hegan Lane.

3 HARDROCK TRAIL
Empire Mine State Historic Park, off Highway 20 in Grass Valley

Total distance: 3.0 miles
Biking time: 1.0 hour

Type of trail: Dirt double-track

Type of bike: Mountain bike

Steepness: Rolling terrain
Skill level: Easiest

It's a toss-up whether the best reason to come to Empire Mine State Historic Park is to immerse yourself in its fascinating hardrock mining history or to ride your bike on its smooth and scenic trails. When you visit, you should certainly do both. Check out the mine museum, take the mine tour, and learn all about the history of this gold-rich land, then hop on your bike and start cruising the park's trails. As you ride through this lovely Sierra foothills forest, you may wonder why the mine owners didn't give up hardrock mining and invent mountain biking instead.

Hardrock Trail

The land you are riding on made up one of the biggest and richest hardrock gold mines in the state 1850–1957, with more than 300 miles of underground tunnels and shafts. Unfortunately, the mine owners completely destroyed the land—like mountain biking, environmentalism had not yet been invented—but Mother Nature has largely healed herself. What stands today is a profusion of pines, white and black oak trees, big manzanita bushes, and the scattered remains of mine structures.

Hardrock Trail, which begins .75 mile down the road from the park visitors center, is your starting point. This trail allows you the option of adding on a challenging one-mile loop trip to Osborn Hill. The route is well signed and passes by several mines, starting with the W.Y.O.D. mine, which stood for "Work Your Own Diggins." Here, the wealthy mine owner allowed the peon miners to lease sections of the mine, then try to dig up their own fortune. Not surprisingly, no one got rich in this fashion except the mine owner.

Past the W.Y.O.D. mine, turn left at the fork (.5 mile in), which is Short Loop Trail on the park map. After a brief climb, this trail brings you to an overlook above the mine-yard buildings. Head right, past the Orleans mine and stamp mill, and cross Little Wolf Creek on a wooden bridge. Here, you have the option of continuing uphill to Osborn Loop Trail (look for the turnoff on the left after the creek crossing) or turning right and heading back along the ridge on Long Loop Trail. Long Loop Trail cuts through a lovely grove of trees, which is particularly spectacular in fall, when the oaks turn yellow.

If you decide to ride Osborn Loop, take the left turnoff after the creek and head uphill, passing by several abandoned mine sites on your way to a great lookout over the entire 700-acre park and the Sacramento Valley. Osborn Loop reconnects with Long Loop Trail. Ride west on Long Loop Trail across the ridge and then downhill, past the cutoff for Short Loop Trail and the W.Y.O.D. mine, back to your starting point.

Information and Contact
There is no fee for bike riding in Empire Mine State Historic Park, but there is a $1.50 fee per person for the mine tour. Trail maps are available at the visitors center. For more information, contact Empire Mine State Historic Park, 10791 East Empire Street, Grass Valley, CA 95945, 530/273-8522, website: www.parks.ca.gov.

Directions
From the junction of Highway 49 and I-80 near Auburn, take Highway 49 north to Grass Valley and Highway 20. Exit on Highway 20 east (toward Grass Valley), which becomes Empire Street. Follow it for three miles to the Empire Mine State Historic Park visitors center. Buy a park map at the visitors center, then drive back down the road .75 mile (the way you came in) and park in the dirt lot on the left (south) side of the road. The trailhead for Hardrock Trail is clearly marked.

4 QUARRY ROAD TRAIL
Auburn State Recreation Area, off Highway 49 near Auburn

Total distance: 10.8 miles **Biking time:** 2.5 hours

Type of trail: Dirt double-track and single-track

Type of bike: Mountain bike

Steepness: Rolling terrain **Skill level:** Moderate

Beginning mountain bikers can easily become discouraged in Auburn State Recreation Area. From the novice's standpoint, the local trails climb with the average grade of a skyscraper. Their surfaces are rutted and rocky. The sun beats down upon them year-round. But still, the region is wildly popular with mountain bikers. Every trailhead is filled with cars, and every car sports a bike rack. What's a wannabe to do?

Head for Quarry Road Trail, which follows the south side of the canyon

Quarry Road Trail

of the Middle Fork of the American River. The trail, really a wide road, starts near the confluence of the North and Middle Forks and runs for 5.4 miles to Main Bar (spelled "Maine Bar" on some maps). It's mostly level and smooth, with only three steep but short climbs over its entire distance. Quarry Road presents few technical challenges, except for the discipline it requires to keep your eyes on the trail instead of watching the beautiful American River flow by. It is very important to pay close attention, however: Some sections of trail have washed out in winter storms, and the drop-offs are severe.

One of Quarry Road's great charms is that it is a breeze to follow. It sticks to the river's edge for its entire distance and is frequently marked with small "WST" signs, which stand for Western States Trail (although technically, this is the "alternate" Western States Trail, a lengthy equestrian trail). The few spur trails that intersect it are all clearly signed "No Bikes."

If it is a warm day, you'll have plenty of company in the first half mile, as sunbathers wander with their inner tubes in search of a good swimming hole. The level of solitude increases as you progress into the canyon. An old quarry, the trail's namesake, is the first notable landmark. The path gets slightly more technical (read: rocky) beyond the quarry.

Quarry Road continues, rolling up and down tiny hills, for several miles of uninterrupted riding and great vistas of the steep river canyon. The canyon's slopes are punctuated by a few foothill pines—scraggly-looking conifers with gray-green needles—and some interesting rock outcrops. A

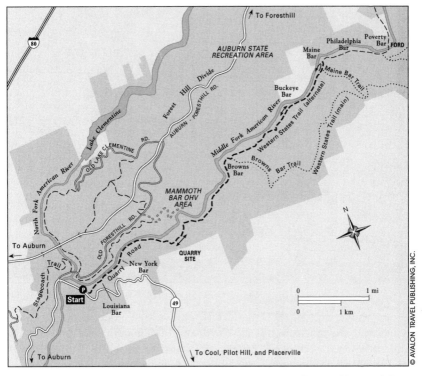

few offshoot trails lead down to the river. Follow any of them if you wish to cool off.

After about four miles, you leave the sunshine and the river views and head into dense oak and pine forest, where the trail narrows. You reach Main Bar at 5.4 miles, where Main Bar Trail takes off on the right and bikes are prohibited. Relax at the picnic table for a few minutes, then turn around and ride westward, enjoying the river canyon all over again.

Options

A good turnaround point for families with young children is at the quarry. Beyond this point, the trail gets rougher.

Information and Contact

There is no fee. For more information and a free park map/brochure, contact Auburn State Recreation Area, 501 Eldorado Street, Auburn, CA 95602, 530/885-4527, website: www.parks.ca.gov.

Directions

From Sacramento, take I-80 east to Auburn and exit at Highway 49 south.

Head southeast through Auburn on Highway 49 for three miles. At the bottom of the canyon, where Highway 49 turns right and crosses a bridge over the river, set your odometer. In .4 mile, turn left on a dirt road (it's easy to miss). Quarry Road Trail is the gated dirt road by the parking area.

5 AMERICAN RIVER PARKWAY: BEALS POINT TO NEGRO BAR

Folsom Lake State Recreation Area, off I-80 at Folsom Lake

Total distance: 7.0 miles **Biking time:** 1.0 hour

Type of trail: Paved bike trail

Type of bike: Road bike or mountain bike

Steepness: Rolling terrain **Skill level:** Easiest

American River Parkway is one of the oldest and longest paved bike paths in the United States, a 32.8-mile trail leading all the way from Discovery Park in Sacramento to Folsom Lake. More than 500,000 people ride the trail each year. Some hardy riders pedal the whole thing out and back for 65.6 miles of paved recreation trail riding, but since some sections are far more scenic than others, easy riders might as well stick to the best part—riding westward from Beals Point at Folsom Lake.

The American River Parkway is one of the oldest and longest paved bike trails in the United States.

© ANN MARIE BROWN

Start at the trail's eastern terminus. After leaving the Beals Point parking area (which can be an absolute zoo on summer weekends because of the lake's sandy beach and swimming areas), pick up the bike trail and ride to your left (west). Numbers painted on the trail's surface mark your mileage. You are starting at

32.8; the numbers drop as you ride west—31, 30, 29, etc.

Your first vistas are of Folsom Lake as you ride around its northwest edge on a wing of huge, 340-foot Folsom Dam. The 18,000-acre reservoir was created in 1955 by building a main concrete dam on the American River, as well as several wing dams and dikes. Here's a fact you can't live without knowing: Folsom Dam contains enough concrete to build a sidewalk three feet wide from San Francisco to New York City.

Next you ride by a place you've heard about, but never thought you'd visit: Folsom State Prison. Fortunately, your surroundings quickly become less foreboding as you pedal through acres of grasslands with the American River at your side. Bird-watching is popular in this stretch.

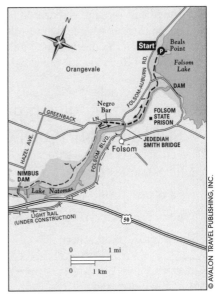

At three miles out, the river is dammed once again, this time by Nimbus Dam. You ride past Lake Natoma, which is smaller and quieter than Lake Folsom. Just beyond the highway bridge before Negro Bar is a high overlook above the lake, where little boats float by and people wade near the shore. A turnaround here, near mileage marker 29, makes a seven-mile round-trip.

Options

From the overlook near Negro Bar, continue onward another 6.5 miles to Nimbus Fish Hatchery. A turnaround here makes a 20-mile round-trip. You have a slight uphill on the way back to Folsom Lake, but it doesn't amount to much.

Information and Contact

A $7 day-use fee is charged per vehicle at Beals Point. For more information, contact Folsom Lake State Recreation Area, 7806 Folsom-Auburn Road, Folsom, CA 95630, 916/988-0205. Or for information on and a map of the entire American River Parkway, contact the American River Parkway Foundation, P.O. Box 188437, Sacramento, CA 95818, 916/456-7423, website: www.arpf.org.

Directions

From I-80 in Sacramento, drive east for 15 miles and take the Douglas Road exit near Roseville. Drive east 5.3 miles on Douglas Road, then turn right on Auburn-Folsom Road and drive 1.7 miles. Turn left at the sign for Beals Point; you'll cross the bike path as you drive to the parking area.

6 SUGAR PINE RAILWAY

Stanislaus National Forest, off Highway 108 near Strawberry

Total distance: 5.6 miles

Biking time: 1.0 hour

Type of trail: Dirt road

Type of bike: Mountain bike

Steepness: Rolling terrain

Skill level: Moderate

The old Sugar Pine Railway tunnels through dense forest alongside the Stanislaus River.

Sugar Pine Railway was named for the very large sugar pines that were harvested in this area and shipped along the railroad line 1906–1965. A portion of that rail route, called the Strawberry Branch, is the basis for this trail along the sun-dappled Stanislaus River.

The trail starts at the river bridge near Fraser Flat Campground. Heading to your right (east), the dirt path starts out wide but eventually narrows to single-track. It's simple to follow; the path hugs the river and there are no turnoffs. Watch for an old wooden flume on the river's far side, known as the Philadelphia Ditch. Built in 1899 to supply gold miners with water to work their diggings, the flume is currently used by Pacific Gas and Electric Company to carry water and generate power from the Stanislaus River.

At 2.2 miles, the trail narrows considerably, turns away from the river, and heads uphill through meadows and forest. At 2.8 miles, the single-track ends at a paved road, Old Strawberry Road. You can turn around here for a 5.6-mile round-trip or ride into the town of Strawberry for lunch, adding a couple more miles to your day. To do so, turn left on the pavement. Ride one mile on Old Strawberry Road, then turn right on Strawberry Drive and come out to the Strawberry Inn. If you're not in the mood for a sit-down lunch, there's a grocery store across the street.

Options

Head over to Lyons Reservoir to pedal another piece of the old railroad grade. Drive seven miles west on Highway 108 to Lyons Reservoir Road, two miles east of Mi-Wuk Village. Turn right on Lyons Reservoir Road (open May–October only) and drive 2.1 miles to the day-use area. Park and ride to your left on the gated dirt road. This trail is even easier, wider, and smoother than the Fraser Flat section of the rail trail. The path runs for five level miles to its end at a neighborhood on Middle Camp Road. A turnaround here adds 10 miles to your day.

Information and Contact

There is no fee. For more information, contact Stanislaus National Forest, Summit Ranger District, 1 Pinecrest Lake Road, Pinecrest, CA 95364, 209/965-3434, website: www.fs.fed.us/r5/stanislaus.

Directions

From Sonora, drive east on Highway 108 for 30 miles to the Fraser Flat turnoff, nine miles east of Mi-Wuk Village and two miles west of Strawberry. (If you reach Cold Springs Store, you've gone too far east.) Turn left on Forest Service 4N01, signed for Fraser Flat and Spring Gap. Drive 2.5 miles to Fraser Flat Bridge.

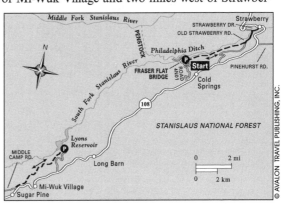

Chapter 5

© ANN MARIE BROWN

Tahoe and the Northern Sierra

Tahoe and the Northern Sierra

or most visitors, the Tahoe region is clearly defined by its 22-mile-long, azure blue lake—"a noble sheet of blue water lifted six thousand three hundred feet above the level of the sea, and walled in by a rim of snow-clad mountain peaks," in the eloquent words of Mark Twain. The 10th deepest lake in the world (1,645 feet at its deepest point), with remarkable water clarity, it is among the most notable features in the landscape of North America.

Bicycling visitors to the Tahoe region will note two other outstanding features besides the mammoth lake: rocks and hills. Mountain bikers frequently encounter both elements when riding through Tahoe's spectacular High Sierra scenery. In conjunction with the heart-pumping, high-elevation air, these obstacles can make even casual rides around Lake Tahoe a bit challenging.

But that's not to say there aren't opportunities for riders who want to take it strictly easy. Tahoe is laced with paved bike paths, from the scenic Truckee River Recreation Trail, which closely follows the rushing waters of the Truckee, to the more pedestrian West Shore Trail, which parallels busy Highway 89 from Tahoe City to Sugar Pine

Point. Novice to intermediate mountain bike riders will find dirt trails to suit their abilities in the canyons of the lake's west shore. And for those who just want to coast downhill, not crank uphill, several Tahoe ski resorts operate their lifts in the summer so mountain bikers can be whisked to high summits, then cruise downhill on two wheels (see the list of Northern California Mountain Bike Parks in the Appendix).

The only disappointing fact about biking around Tahoe is that the season is so short. Snow can fall as early as mid-October, and the spring melt can hold off until June. Mountain bikers may find that even though trails may be snow-free as early as Memorial Day, they may be too wet to ride until mid- or late July.

Because of the brief season, thousands of riders take to the roads and trails of Tahoe each year during a few months' period. To avoid the crowds, the best time to visit is usually September and October, when most of the summer visitors have gone home. And how fortunate, because that's when Tahoe's famous fall color show occurs. It's worth the wait.

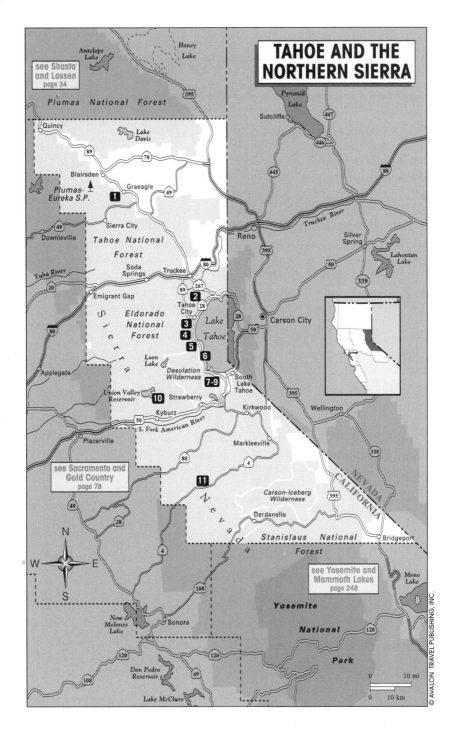

1 MILLS PEAK LOOKOUT

Plumas National Forest, off Gold Lake Highway near Graeagle

Total distance: 6.6 miles   **Biking time:** 2.0 hours

Type of trail: Dirt road

Type of bike: Mountain bike

Steepness: Steep sections   **Skill level:** Moderate

The reward of a bike ride to a fire lookout is always the same: an impressive
vista from a summit with a
wide scope on the surrounding terrain. Although fire
lookouts are a favorite destination of mountain bikers,
by their nature they are
rarely attained without a
steep climb.

Mills Peak Lookout in
the Gold Lakes Basin is the
exception. Perched on a
rocky escarpment at 7,310
feet in elevation, the lookout offers an all-encompass-
ing view of the Mohawk
Valley and the Sierra Buttes
to the south, but with a
total climb of only 900 feet
from the trailhead.

The well-graded dirt lookout road is open to cars and
gets some traffic on summer

Mills Peak Lookout, elevation 7,310 feet

weekends, so a weekday ride
is preferable. It's virtually impossible to get lost, because the road is marked
with black arrows on orange signs nailed to trees (snowmobile markers).
The surface is only a little rocky and not technical at all, and although it's
uphill all the way, the grade is quite moderate. This is a great ride for strong
beginners looking for an aerobic workout.

And what a feeling of accomplishment when you reach the summit and
are wowed by the expansive view of the Gold Lakes Basin. The lookout
tower itself is a square white cabin built in 1932. It is staffed somewhat
inconsistently July 4–October 1 each year. Even if the tower is closed, you

can check out the marvelous view from its base, which is almost as good as from the top.

On the ride back downhill, be sure to stop at Red Fir Nature Trail 1.1 miles from the lookout (or 2.2 miles from Gold Lake Highway). Lock up your bike and take a short walk through the marvelous red fir forest, where the staghorn moss on the trees' large trunks gives an indication of the previous winter's snow level.

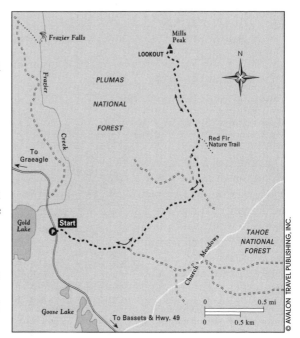

Options

If you return to your car still bounding with energy, ride north .5 mile on Gold Lake Highway and turn right at the sign for Frazier Falls. Ride 1.8 miles to the signed trailhead, then lock up your bike and take the .5-mile walk to the plunging 250-foot cataract. The round-trip ride to the Frazier Falls trailhead will add 4.6 nearly level miles to your ride, making an 11.2-mile day.

Information and Contact

There is no fee. For more information, contact Beckwourth Ranger District, Plumas National Forest, P.O. Box 7, Mohawk Road, Blairsden, CA 96103, 530/836-2575, website: www.fs.fed.us/r5/plumas.

Directions

From Graeagle, head south on Highway 89 for 1.5 miles, then turn right (west) on Gold Lake Highway, also signed as "Lakes Basin Recreation Area." Drive seven miles to the sign for Mills Peak Lookout (.5 mile south of Gold Lake Campground). The lookout road is on the left; park in the gravel pullout on the right side of Gold Lake Highway, then ride across Gold Lake Highway to the start of the lookout road.

2 WATSON LAKE & FIBREBOARD FREEWAY LOOP

Northstar-at-Tahoe, off Highway 267 near Truckee

Total distance: 9.2 miles   **Biking time:** 2.5 hours

Type of trail: Dirt roads

Type of bike: Mountain bike

Steepness: Steep sections   **Skill level:** Moderate

Several ski resorts around Lake Tahoe have jumped on the mountain biking bandwagon, opening up their ski hills to bike riders in the off-season in order to produce year-round income. Northstar-at-Tahoe was the first and is still the best of the lot, with more than 100 miles of bike trails and multiple chairlifts that carry bikers and their wheels high up the mountainside. Northstar reigns as the largest mountain bike park in Northern California.

But be advised: Easy riders should not throw away big bucks on the multi-ride ticket. Many of the park's trails are far from easy, with bumpy Tahoe-style rocks that jar your brains and sandy patches that make your wheels grind to a halt. You probably won't want to ride a whole bunch of different trails here, especially in one day. But one fun, easy loop trip to a mountain lake can be ridden by buying only the cheaper single-lift ticket.

Watson Lake

Besides saving money and enjoying a nice bike ride, you can have a picnic lunch at the lake and hike around a bit.

Exactly what route you take depends on which chairlifts are running when you go, but usually the trip requires a lift up the Echo chair from the village to mid-mountain, followed by a .25-mile bike ride over to either Vista Express lift or Lookout lift, where you'll be carried higher up the mountain. (Your bike usually rides on the chair immediately behind you or in front of you—the chairs have bike racks on their backsides.) After your second chairlift, make your way over to a trail called Tryumph (their spelling), also called Road 500. Tryumph runs across the backside of Mount Pluto and has many nice open views to your right. It climbs almost imperceptibly for 1.6 miles until you reach a gate. Pass through it and head downhill until the trail dead-ends at Fibreboard Freeway (Road 100).

Just off your loop and less than a mile to the right is Watson Lake. Keep an eye on your trail map and watch for two signed turns. After the first right turn, go left at the next intersection (.25 mile farther) rather than continuing straight on Fibreboard, and ride downhill to the lake's edge in .7 mile.

You'll probably see a few other cyclists at the lake, and possibly some cars that have driven in on Forest Service roads from the other side of the mountain. The lake is wide, pretty, and shallow—the kind of place where kids like to look for frogs, and usually find them. Some folks fish here, with mixed success, but most just have lunch and walk along the shore.

After your lake visit, backtrack up the trail and pick up the Fibreboard Freeway, turning right to complete your loop. This road is less rocky than other park trails, with smoother gravel and fewer big rocks, so you can just cruise along without having your eyes continually glued to the ground ahead of your front tire.

A three-mile stint on Fibreboard Freeway brings you to Road 300, where you turn left and ride past Northstar Reservoir, continuing until you junction with Roads 500 and 501, which bring you back to the top of Echo lift. There you pick up Village Run to cruise back downhill to the village.

Note that a bike park map is essential for your trip, since there are so many trails and possible routes in the park. They're available for free when you buy your ticket. A staff member can outline the Watson Lake loop for you.

Options

An easier route is to ride to the picnic area at the caboose at Sawmill Flat, which has a view of Northstar Reservoir and surrounding mountains. The caboose is used as a warming hut during ski season but is closed in summer. It's a three-mile round-trip.

Information and Contact

The bike park is open daily mid-June–Labor Day and weekends only in September and early October, weather permitting. Call to confirm exact opening and closing dates. Helmets are required for all riders. The fee is $20 for an adult single-ride ticket, $33 for an adult multi-ride ticket, $14 for a child single-ride ticket, and $20 for a child multi-ride ticket. Bike rentals are available. Bike park maps are free. For more information, contact Northstar-at-Tahoe, P.O. Box 129, Truckee, CA 96160, 530/562-1010 or 800/466-6784, website: www.northstarattahoe.com.

Directions

From Tahoe City, drive northeast on Highway 28 for seven miles to Highway 267 and turn left. Drive six miles to the left turnoff for Northstar-at-Tahoe. Drive up the hill to Northstar Village and park in the lot. Walk your bike to the bike shop in the village, buy your lift ticket and get a trail map, then carry your bike up the stairs and around the back of the village to get on the chairlift.

3 TRUCKEE RIVER RECREATION TRAIL

Tahoe City Parks and Recreation, off Highway 89
near Tahoe City

Total distance: 11.2 miles   **Biking time:** 1.5 hours

Type of trail: Paved bike trail

Type of bike: Road bike or mountain bike

Steepness: Mostly level   **Skill level:** Easiest

Of the many Tahoe-area paved bike paths, Truckee River Recreation Trail is far and away the most scenic and well loved. On summer weekends, it can be difficult negotiating your way amidst all the other bikers, in-line skaters, walkers, and baby strollers on the trail. Nonetheless, whether you're a novice rider or Lance Armstrong, you shouldn't miss this fun cruise. The trail parallels the Truckee River for 5.6 miles, keeping the water in sight and never more than a few feet away.

During peak vacation season, your best bet is to ride at the edges of the day—early in the morning or just before sunset—to avoid most of the trail traffic. On one beautiful September evening, the trail was peaceful enough that I was able to spot a beaver swimming in the Truckee and dozens of Canada geese.

The route parallels Highway 89 north of Tahoe City, but it was ingeniously

The Truckee River Recreation Trail is one of Tahoe's most scenic pathways.

built so that much of its path is 15–20 feet below the highway embankment. Because of this, the sight and sound of cars are no distraction and the river takes center stage. In the spring, the Truckee River can be a raging torrent of snowmelt, while in the fall, it's more of a lazy stream, often lined with big Canada geese flipping their tail feathers in the air as they dunk their heads in the water, and anglers making short casts into the stream. The river is tamest right by Tahoe City and gets wider and stronger as you ride toward Squaw Valley. There are plenty of little cutoffs from the trail where you can walk your bike down to the river, and the last section of trail has a nice picnic area by the water.

The trail used to end at Alpine Meadows ski area but in 1999 was extended to run another mile to the entrance to Squaw Valley, crossing picturesque Midway Bridge along the way. Food and shops are available at both ski resorts. A common practice is to ride to River Ranch Inn at the Alpine Meadows turnoff and have lunch on the riverside deck. In the summer, mountain bikers can ride to Squaw Valley Ski Resort and buy a ticket for the lifts. Squaw Valley metamorphoses from a ski resort to a mountain bike park in the warm months of the year. Road bikers can also extend their trip at Squaw. A two-mile-long paved trail runs beside Squaw Valley Road, with views of the meadow and surrounding peaks.

Options

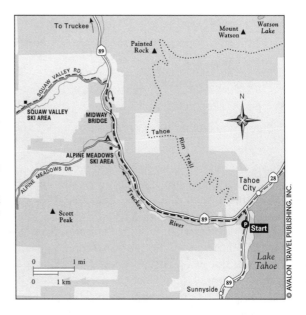

After you return to the trailhead parking area in Tahoe City, you might want to check out the other paved trails that start there. North Shore Trail travels east to Dollar Hill (2.5 miles one-way, with access to Lake Forest Beach and Pomin Park). Or ride south on West Shore Trail (nine miles one-way to Sugar Pine Point). West Shore Trail, despite its terrific lakeshore views, has one major drawback: It crosses Highway 89 dozens of times. Use caution if you ride it.

Information and Contact

There is no fee. For more information and a free map of Tahoe City area bike paths, contact Tahoe City Public Utility District Parks and Recreation, 221 Fairway Drive, Tahoe City, CA 96145, 530/583-3796, ext. 29, website: www.tahoecitypud.com.

Directions

From Tahoe City at the junction of Highways 89 and 28 drive .25 mile south on Highway 89 to the sign for the recreation trail parking area on the right. Turn right (west) and park.

4 BLACKWOOD CANYON

Tahoe National Forest, off Highway 89 near Tahoe City

Total distance: 4.0 miles   **Biking time:** 1.0 hour

Type of trail: Dirt roads

Type of bike: Mountain bike

Steepness: Rolling terrain   **Skill level:** Moderate

Bikers tend to be a little cynical about off-highway-vehicle riders, since the noise of screaming gas engines isn't usually appealing to those who ride under their own muscle power. But at Blackwood Canyon, bikers have the North Tahoe Trail Dusters off-highway-vehicle club to thank for the Blackwood Middle Fork Trail. When the Forest Service wanted to close down the trail, members of the club volunteered to maintain it and keep it open. So, if you ride at Blackwood Canyon, you'll have to be a little tolerant if you hear the wail of an engine somewhere off in the distance. Of course, you can always show up after Labor Day, in which case you'll probably have the whole place to yourself.

A watershed restoration project is in process along Blackwood Creek. The canyon has had a long and unhappy history of flooding, grazing, logging, and gravel mining, all of which took their toll on the stream and surrounding lands. In the 1960s, this beautiful canyon was nothing more than

Blackwood Canyon, Tahoe National Forest

a quarry pit, as miners pulled out gravel for Tahoe's roads and driveways. The Forest Service is in the process of reclaiming the land, and the flow of Blackwood Creek has been returned to its original channel. Today, it's a strong-running, clear stream.

Starting at the off-highway-vehicle camping area, the trail runs level for two miles through a dense mixed forest, with spectacular displays of wildflowers in the late spring and early summer. Then it begins to climb toward Barker Peak, elevation 8,166 feet, and I do mean climb, as in millions of switchbacks and a heady grade. It would be wise to turn around before the switchbacks. You'll pass another logging road off to your right (15N41, North Fork Trail), but ignore it and stay to the left on Middle Fork Trail (15N38). The trail surface is a little rocky, typical for North Tahoe, and you may have to walk across some of the creek crossings, whether they're wet or dry.

After riding the canyon's dirt trail, you can go back and ride around on the level part of paved Barker Pass Road (the road you drove in on). Although Barker Pass Road also climbs to Barker Peak, paralleling Middle Fork Trail, the 2.2-mile stretch from the off-highway-vehicle camp to Highway 89 is almost completely level.

Options

An option is to ride on paved Barker Pass Road only, which is smoother and easier to ride. The road is designated a "multipurpose" road for use by cross-country skiers, cyclists, in-line skaters, skateboarders, and yes, cars. But cars are usually in the minority.

Information and Contact

There is no fee. For more information, contact Lake Tahoe Basin Management Unit, 35 College Drive, South Lake Tahoe, CA 96150, 530/573-2600, website: www.fs.fed.us/r5/ltbmu.

Directions

From Tahoe City, drive 4.2 miles south on Highway 89 to Forest Service Road 03, Barker Pass Road, at Kaspian Picnic Area. Turn right (west) and drive two miles to Blackwood Canyon OHV area. Turn right on the dirt road to the parking area.

5 GENERAL CREEK LOOP

Sugar Pine Point State Park, off Highway 89 on Lake Tahoe's west shore

Total distance: 5.8 miles

Biking time: 1.5 hours

Type of trail: Dirt double-track

Type of bike: Mountain bike

Steepness: Rolling terrain

Skill level: Easiest

Cross-country skiers and easy mountain bike riders share an affinity for smooth dirt trails that roll for miles and miles, with no steep grades and no disagreeable obstacles to interrupt their momentum. At Sugar Pine Point State Park, both groups—skiers in the winter and bikers in the summer—find what they desire.

General Creek Loop is easy enough for families to ride, with an optional lock-up-your-bike-and-hike trip to a tiny, marshy lake. It makes a great morning or afternoon outing that is just long enough to satisfy your urge for fresh air and exercise without wearing you out. The trail is one of the first easy rides in the Tahoe area to open up after snowmelt, since it doesn't have a lot of creek crossings.

General Creek Loop offers easy riding through the sugar pines.

Start at campsite 149 in General Creek Campground. Heading straight past the first bridge sends you off counterclockwise around the loop. The trail is very smooth dirt and sand, with plenty of room for both hikers and bikers, and with only one hill, right at the beginning. It runs through a dense forest of sugar pines, Jeffrey pines, lodgepole pines, and firs on the north side of General Creek and open meadows on the south side. Cross-country skiing markers placed periodically along the trail assure that you are on the right track.

Head straight down the north side of General Creek (ignoring the left turn that goes over a bridge, which is your return route) and simply cruise along through the pines, with no turnoffs to distract you for a couple of miles until you reach the junction with the single-track trail to Lily Lake. Here, you can hike to the shallow lake, which is really more of a pond. Lock your bike to the trail marker, or to a pine tree if necessary—there are plenty of them around. (You are permitted to ride your bike on the first .5 mile of the one-mile single-track to Lily Lake, but the trail quickly becomes impossible to negotiate because of rocks, tree roots, and the like, so save yourself the frustration and ditch your bike here.)

True to its name, Lily Lake is completely covered with lilies. It covers a few acres but is very shallow, especially by late summer and fall, and is ringed by cottonwoods and aspen. In spring, wildflowers, corn lilies, and ferns in the meadow and surrounding forest can be quite lush. It's a peaceful spot in any season.

After your lake visit, return on the same single-track, then connect back to your loop, heading to the right and crossing a couple of bridges and a 100-yard-long boardwalk over a springtime marsh. Look for corn lilies and wildflowers here. The wooden planks deposit you onto a wide dirt trail that brings you back along the south side of General Creek. When you come to a trail junction with a bridge to your left and the dirt road continuing straight, go left to complete your loop, then head right, back to the campground.

Options

If after completing this short loop you want to do more easy riding, it's simple to connect to Lake Tahoe's West Shore Trail (paved). Just follow the park road out to Highway 89 and

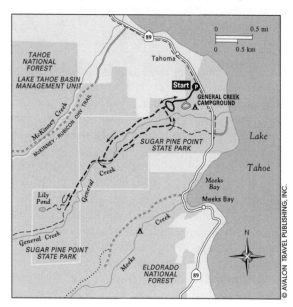

pick up the trail heading north. It crosses busy Highway 89 a few times, but it is almost completely level and leads to some interesting locations along the lakeshore. The trail extends all the way to Tahoe City, 10 miles north.

Information and Contact
A $6 day-use fee is charged per vehicle. A park map is available at the ranger kiosk. For more information, contact Sugar Pine Point State Park, P.O. Box 266, Tahoma, CA 96142, 530/525-7982 or 530/525-7232, website: www.parks.ca.gov.

Directions
From Tahoe City, drive nine miles south on Highway 89 to the General Creek Campground entrance on the right. Park in one of the day-use parking areas near the kiosk, then ride your bike down the park road to the campgrounds, staying right until you reach campsite 149 and the trail.

6 POPE-BALDWIN BIKE PATH
Lake Tahoe Basin Management Unit, off Highway 89 on Lake Tahoe's south shore

Total distance: 6.8 miles   **Biking time:** 1.5 hours

Type of trail: Paved bike trail

Type of bike: Road bike or mountain bike

Steepness: Mostly level   **Skill level:** Easiest

Truckee River Recreation Trail is the best paved bike path in North Tahoe (see the trail description in this chapter), and Pope-Baldwin Bike Path holds that honor in South Tahoe, outdistancing the competition by a long shot with some of the most stellar Lake Tahoe views imaginable. That, and it actually keeps you away from the road—far away, as in sometimes you can't even see it or hear it. Hallelujah.

The trail's west end is near Baldwin Beach, which can be your first stop if you are riding from the trail's west terminus at Spring Creek Road. A .5-mile cutoff from the bike path on Forest Service Road 13N05 brings you to the picnic area at Baldwin Beach, and a short walk takes you to spectacular white-sand beaches and lake views. Depending on how crowded it is, you may or may not want to hang around for long, so when you're ready, ride back to the bike trail and continue east.

Next stop is the bridge at Taylor Creek. If it's autumn, there's likely to be a crowd at the bridge, because this is where rainbow trout, brown trout, and kokanee salmon come to spawn each fall. On our trip, we saw hundreds of kokanees, bright red with green heads, laying their eggs and then slowly dying in the stream. The Forest Service has added more gravel to the streambed to make the spawning beds better for the eggs, which in a few short weeks will hatch small fry that make their way down Taylor Creek to Lake Tahoe.

It's a little sobering to watch fish meet their end, even as they are producing thousands of baby fish, so continue onward and turn left at the access road for Tallac Historic Site, which offers several historic mansions. Tour the houses and admire their opulence, or walk out to the small pier and listen to the water lapping on the shore. From the pier and its adjacent beach, you can gaze at miles and miles of Lake Tahoe and its dramatic mountain backdrops to the south and north.

Crowds gather at Taylor Creek Bridge to see the spawning kokanee salmon.

When you're ready, continue on the bike path, taking Forest Service Road 12N09 .5 mile to Pope Beach if you desire. Pope Beach has all the same amenities as Baldwin Beach: picnic area, swimming area, restrooms, and stellar lake views. The bike trail continues past the cutoff to Pope Beach for another .5 mile, leading almost, but not quite, into the town of South Lake Tahoe.

One tip to make your trip more enjoyable: In October, this trail is largely deserted, and the Forest Service often closes the access roads to Pope and Baldwin Beaches. Closes them to cars, that is—you can ride your bike right past the gates and down to the empty parking lots at the beaches, and see Lake Tahoe without the crowds.

Options

Mountain bikers have the option of crossing the highway where the bike path ends near South Lake Tahoe and picking up any of the myriad trails that wind into Forest Service land. Get a Forest Service map before attempting the ride, as most trails are not marked.

Information and Contact

There is no fee. For more information, contact Lake Tahoe Basin Management Unit, 35 College Drive, South Lake Tahoe, CA 96150, 530/573-2600, website: www.fs.fed.us/r5/ltbmu.

Directions

From Tahoe City, drive south approximately 25 miles on Highway 89 to the southern end of the lake, past Eagle Falls and Emerald Bay. Turn right on Spring Creek Road, which is Forest Service Road 13N07, shortly before Baldwin Beach on the left. Park in one of the sandy pullouts along the road. Walk your bike across Highway 89 to start on the bike route. (You can also park at Baldwin Beach or Tallac Historic Site and start riding from there.)

7 FALLEN LEAF LAKE ROAD

Lake Tahoe Basin Management Unit, off Highway 89 near
South Lake Tahoe

Total distance: 11.0 miles   **Biking time:** 1.5 hours

Type of trail: Paved road

Type of bike: Road bike or mountain bike

Steepness: Mostly level   **Skill level:** Easiest

Fallen Leaf Lake Road is an honest-to-goodness road, complete with car traffic and speed-limit signs, but it's as much like a paved recreation trail as any road could be. On summer days you'll find as many bikers and hikers on this lakeside route as automobiles. Due to the number of recreationists, plus the narrowness of the road, cars are forced to go slow, which makes the route safer for bikes than it would otherwise be. Still, I wouldn't recommend it for young children or

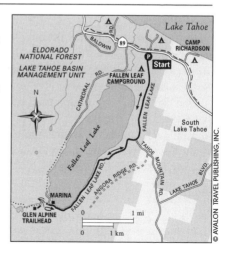

for bikers who are prone to attention deficits.

The road is an easy, level cruise that provides close-up views of large, 400-foot-deep Fallen Leaf Lake. In its final two miles, Fallen Leaf Lake Road is only 20 feet from the water's edge. Aside from the lake views, the ride's payoff is five miles out at a 100-foot cascade on Glen Alpine Creek, which roars with snowmelt into July. The road dead-ends .5 mile farther along at Glen Alpine Trailhead for Desolation Wilderness, a trailhead so popular that often there isn't enough parking.

Park in the pullout at the start of Fallen Leaf Lake Road (near its junction with

the end of Fallen Leaf Lake Road near Glen Alpine Trailhead

Highway 89) and start riding on the paved road. The first three miles pass by Fallen Leaf Campground and through a long stretch of forest. This may be the most peaceful part of the ride, before the road narrows to the width of one car and skirts the lakeshore, where a number of houses are located. You must watch for traffic entering and exiting driveways as you ride.

The final two lakeside miles bustle with activity from the houses, the Fallen Leaf Lake Store and Marina, the roadside waterfall, and the trailhead at Glen Alpine. But even with all the people sharing the narrow road, you still have plenty of chances to admire pretty Fallen Leaf Lake. Fortunately, on a bike, you are traveling at just the right speed to enjoy it.

Options
Mountain bikers can combine this ride with the following ride, Fallen Leaf Lake Trails.

Information and Contact
There is no fee. For more information, contact Lake Tahoe Basin Management Unit, 35 College Drive, South Lake Tahoe, CA 96150, 530/573-2600, website: www.fs.fed.us/r5/ltbmu.

Directions

From South Lake Tahoe at the northern junction of U.S. 50 and Highway 89, drive northwest on Highway 89 for three miles to the left turnoff for Fallen Leaf Lake (one mile past Camp Richardson Resort). Turn left on Fallen Leaf Lake Road and park in the dirt pullouts along the road.

8 FALLEN LEAF LAKE TRAILS

Tahoe National Forest, off Highway 89 near South Lake Tahoe

Total distance: 3.0 miles   **Biking time:** 1.0 hour

Type of trail: Dirt roads

Type of bike: Mountain bike

Steepness: Rolling terrain   **Skill level:** Moderate

People around the world rave about Lake Tahoe—sure, why not, it's North America's largest alpine lake and the 10th deepest lake on earth, as well as being clear blue and beautiful. But I like its smaller neighbor Fallen Leaf Lake at least as much, and maybe more. It's a lake of manageable size, for one thing, at approximately three miles long. And since much of its shoreline is privately controlled, it's never overcrowded. It's as deep blue as Tahoe, framed by groves of aspens that quake in the summer wind and turn golden in the fall chill. Combined with a backdrop of tall, craggy mountains, the scenery at Fallen Leaf Lake creates an impression that stays with you and keeps you coming back season after season.

The Forest Service has built an assortment of short trails that run from Fallen Leaf Campground to the lake, and partway around its northern border. Day-users can take the trail that begins on Fallen Leaf Lake Road, bypassing the campground and going straight to the lake. The route is single-track and sandy much of the way, but that's okay because it keeps your speed down, which is fortunate for the hikers who stroll around here. If you start from the day-use trailhead, you've got a decent hill to climb, over a ridge to the lake. Even if you have to walk your bike on some of the rockier, hillier parts, you'll be at the lake in less than 15 minutes.

Once you reach the lake's edge, there are several riding options. Short trails shoot off to the left and right. We took the trail to the right around the lake, followed it to the dam over Taylor Creek, then walked our bikes across the dam. From there, we took the trail a little farther to where it meets up with an old Forest Service road. We rode on that for a half mile or so, then turned around and rode back in the other direction. Follow the trails as you like, but when faced with a choice at a junction, try to stay near the lake's

riding through the aspens at Fallen Leaf Lake

edge, because the views are incredible. Fallen Leaf Lake's paths are some of the best in this book for simply looking out over gorgeous blue water.

In summer, expect company from hikers and bikers staying at the campground. The lake can also get noisy with boaters, especially on summer weekends, which can put a crimp in your pastoral, non-motorized biking experience. If you arrive in late September or October, though, the lake is likely to be still and quiet, delicately framed by bright fall leaves on the cottonwoods and aspens.

Options

You can combine this trip with a ride on Pope-Baldwin Bike Path (see trail description in this chapter). After riding around Fallen Leaf Lake, ride your bike on Fallen Leaf Lake Road from the day-use parking area back to Highway 89, where you can pick up the bike path across the road.

Information and Contact

There is no fee. For more information, contact Lake Tahoe Basin Management Unit, 35 College Drive, South Lake Tahoe, CA 96150, 530/573-2600, website: www.fs.fed.us/r5/ltbmu.

Directions

From South Lake Tahoe at the northern junction of U.S. 50 and Highway 89, drive northwest on Highway 89 for three miles to the left turnoff for Fallen Leaf Lake (one mile past Camp Richardson Resort). Turn left on Fallen Leaf Lake Road and drive .8 mile to the trailhead for Fallen Leaf Lake Trails.

9 ANGORA LAKES TRAIL

Tahoe National Forest, off Highway 89 near Fallen Leaf Lake

Total distance: 2.0 miles   **Biking time:** 1.0 hour

Type of trail: Dirt roads

Type of bike: Mountain bike

Steepness: Rolling terrain   **Skill level:** Easiest

Angora Lakes are probably the most popular destination for families with small children in the entire Lake Tahoe region. Kids are everywhere on this trail—on bikes, on their parents' shoulders, on their own two feet, and on top of the many boulders surrounding the trail. When you get to the upper lake, kids are everywhere there, too—on the beach, in the water, at the lemonade stand, and on the trail around the lake.

Granite-backed Upper Angora Lake

But show up after school starts in September, and it's a different story. Things quiet down quite a bit; in fact, there's hardly anyone around. This gives you some options: Take a family bike ride to Angora Lakes in the summer to give your kids instant companionship, or take a family bike ride to Angora Lakes in the fall to enjoy the scenery and the peace and quiet.

In any season, you get the same surroundings: Upper Angora Lake, at 7,280 feet in elevation, is a perfectly bowl-shaped lake in a glacial cirque basin, surrounded by pine forest and with lots of larger rounded boulders sprinkled around. The granite wall on the lake's far side is snow-covered most of the year, and during much of late spring and summer, a waterfall of snowmelt flows down its face.

The trail to the lakes is simple to follow, with no turnoffs to confuse you—just follow the dirt road as it curves up the hill for one mile. Keep your speed down and watch out for hikers and other bikers, especially little ones, on the trail. Ride by lower Angora Lake, which has a few private homes on its edge, and shortly you reach a log bike rack just before the upper lake and Angora Lakes Resort. Lock up your bike (the resort management insists on this) and explore. Built in 1917 on land leased from the Forest Service, Angora Lakes Resort has eight tiny cabins for rent right on the lakeshore, but they are so popular, it's almost impossible to get a reservation. No matter; the place is friendly toward day-users, too. They rent rowboats for a few dollars an hour and run a small refreshment stand, which pumps out lemonade by the gallon to thirsty bikers and hikers. A small sandy beach is popular for swimming and wading in summer, if you can stand the cold water.

Options
The dirt road that you drive in on is also suitable for riding, if you don't mind some car traffic. Some riders park their cars at the start of Road 12N14 and ride from there to Angora Lakes for a 6.6-mile round-trip.

Information and Contact
There is no fee. For more information, contact Lake Tahoe Basin Management Unit, 35 College Drive, South Lake Tahoe, CA 96150, 530/573-2600, website: www.fs.fed.us/r5/ltbmu.

Directions
From South Lake Tahoe at the northern junction of U.S. 50 and Highway 89, drive northwest on Highway 89 for three miles to the left turnoff for Fallen Leaf Lake (one mile past Camp Richardson Resort). Turn left on Fallen Leaf Lake Road and drive .8 mile to a fork in the road; stay left and continue .4 mile. Turn right on Forest Service Road 12N14, which alternates as paved and unpaved. Drive 2.3 miles, past Angora Fire Lookout, to the parking lot at road's end. The trailhead is on the left side of the farthest parking lot.

10 UNION VALLEY BIKE PATH

Eldorado National Forest, off U.S. 50 near Placerville

Total distance: 10.8 miles   **Biking time:** 1.5 hours

Type of trail: Paved bike trail

Type of bike: Road bike or mountain bike

Steepness: Rolling terrain   **Skill level:** Easiest

Sacramento Municipal Utility District, in conjunction with Eldorado National Forest, has built a terrific paved bike trail near Union Valley Reservoir in Crystal Basin Recreation Area. This two-lane, paved trail connects all the campgrounds on the east side of the giant reservoir, which is part of the water storage system for the city of Sacramento and a popular spot for boating and fishing. Although the bike path has a few short, steep grades, most children can complete this trail without any problems. A ride here is a perfect activity for families staying at the campgrounds at Union Valley Reservoir or nearby Ice House Reservoir. Don't forget to pack along your bikes when planning a vacation here.

The trail's two ends are at Jones Fork Campground, on the southeast end of the lake, and at Tells Creek, just north of Wench Creek Campground on the northeast end of the lake. One of the best places to start riding is about two-thirds of the way along the trail at Big Silver Campground, where there is a parking lot specifically for bike trail users. Just head out and back in both directions. You'll ride 1.8 miles northward and 3.6 miles southward. Views of the lake are excellent from most points along the trail. When you're not looking at the water, you're riding through a dense mixed conifer forest. Interpretive signs along the path explain the story of Union Valley and its use as an important water resource.

The trail crosses two impressively built bridges, including one over Big Silver Creek that is 109 feet long. It also passes by two campgrounds that are reserved for bikers, hikers, and boaters (no cars are allowed): Azalea Cove and Lone Rock. You might want to keep these lovely campgrounds in mind for a future trip.

If you get thirsty while riding this trail (it can get pretty hot and dry at this 5,000-foot elevation in summer), water is available at Sunset Boat Ramp and also at a few of the campgrounds. See? They've taken care of everything here. All you have to do is pedal and feel the wind in your hair.

Options

Mountain bikers can ride a 2.5-mile bike trail (dirt, not paved) at nearby Ice House Reservoir, which runs from Ice House Campground to Strawberry

Campground. The trail can be accessed from any of the campgrounds along Ice House Reservoir or from the intersection of Road 12N06 and Ice House Road (.2 mile north of the turnoff for Big Hill Lookout).

Information and Contact

There is no fee. A map of Crystal Basin Recreation Area and a brochure on the bike trails are available at the information station on Ice House Road (you pass it as you drive in). For more information, contact Eldorado National Forest, Pacific Ranger District, 7887 U.S. 50, Pollock Pines, CA 95726, 530/644-2349, website: www.fs.fed.us/r5/eldorado.

Directions

From Placerville, drive 21 miles east on U.S. 50 and turn left (north) on Ice House Road. Drive 16.2 miles on Ice House Road, past the turnoff for Ice House Reservoir, to Big Silver Group Campground on the left. Turn into the campground and you'll see a parking area for the bike trail.

11 BEAR VALLEY TO ALPINE LAKE

Stanislaus National Forest, off Highway 4 near Bear Valley

Total distance: 7.0 miles   **Biking time:** 1.5 hours

Type of trail: Dirt and paved bike trail

Type of bike: Mountain bike

Steepness: Rolling terrain   **Skill level:** Moderate

Beautiful Alpine Lake on Highway 4 is the centerpiece of Bear Valley Recreation Area. The granite-bound lake at elevation 7,300 feet is popular for trout fishing and has three Forest Service campgrounds near its lakeshore.

This newly constructed single-track trail is the non-highway route to Lake Alpine from Bear Valley, the big "town" in these parts. Although short, the trail includes a one-mile, heart-pumping climb. The trickiest part is finding the trail's start, which is just a few hundred feet east of Bear Valley on the south side of Highway 4. We had to ride up and down the highway a few times before we spotted it (apparently it is sometimes signed, sometimes not). Ride back out Bear Valley Road from where you parked your car, turn left on Highway 4, and pick up the single-track on the right side of the road in about 75 yards.

The trail parallels Highway 4 at first, then heads away from the road and uphill. It meanders through the forest, then meets up with a portion of the historic Emigrant Trail pioneer route. After skirting the south side of Silvertip Campground, the trail turns into a wide gravel path that leads downhill toward Lake Alpine. Turning left on a dirt road connects you to Lakeshore Trail, a paved bike trail that parallels the north shore of Lake Alpine. Lakeshore Trail runs smack in between the road and the lake, but the latter is so pretty, with its rocky shoreline and shady pine forest, that you won't even notice the nearby cars.

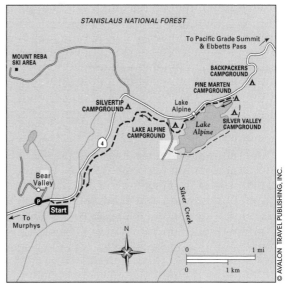

Options
The riding is so pleasant on this trail that I recommend an out-and-back, although you could easily turn this into a loop by heading back on Highway 4. Summer vacation traffic, especially on weekends, makes the loop option less appealing. You can also make a semi-loop by following the dirt trail and road on the back side of Lake Alpine (look for the trail at Pine Marten Campground), then returning on the single-track to Bear Valley.

Information and Contact
There is no fee. For more information, contact Calaveras Ranger District, Stanislaus National Forest, P.O. Box 500, Highway 4, Hathaway Pines, CA 95233, 209/795-1381, website: www.fs.fed.us/r5/stanislaus.

Directions
From Arnold, drive 29 miles east on Highway 4 to Bear Valley. Turn left on Bear Valley Road and park in any of the public parking areas near the shops.

Chapter 6

© ANN MARIE BROWN

San Francisco Bay Area

San Francisco Bay Area

Whether your tastes run to fat tires or skinny tires, the San Francisco Bay Area is an undisputed mecca for cyclists. Home to thousands of pairs of well-toned legs, closets full of black Lycra shorts, and more than 100 bike shops, the City by the Bay and its surrounding landscape afford a world of opportunities for mountain bikers, road cyclists, and recreational riders of all types, including those pulling Burley trailers or sporting training wheels, and even those who haven't been on a bike in decades but want to give the sport a try.

The Bay Area has all the right ingredients for cycling nirvana: hilly back roads, narrow and winding coastal Highway 1, world-famous landmarks like Golden Gate Bridge, and even Mount Tamalpais, the self-proclaimed birthplace of mountain biking. It was on Mount Tam's steep slopes that Gary Fisher, Joe Breeze, and others held the first formal off-road bike races in the late 1970s. Those first bikes were heavy, clunky, and downright dangerous, but a few years and a few modifications later, mountain bike fever caught on and an industry was born.

Several park agencies around the bay are particularly friendly to mountain bikers. We're fortunate to have the East Bay Regional Park

District, Golden Gate National Recreation Area, and Midpeninsula Open Space District on our side. Even Point Reyes National Seashore allows mountain bikes on many of its trails—a rarity in the national park system. Several state parks do as well: Mount Diablo, Mount Tamalpais, Big Basin Redwoods, Angel Island, McNee Ranch, Portola Redwoods, Henry Coe, and China Camp. A handful of these parks even allow bikers on some of their single-track trails, not just wide fire roads.

For those who prefer to ride on pavement, the San Francisco Bay Area is nationally recognized for its wealth of paved bike paths, most of which had their beginnings as railroad right-of-ways. More than a dozen of these paved recreation trails are described in this chapter.

With natural features such as towering redwood forests, teeming bay wetlands, and the rugged coastline south to Waddell Creek and north to the outer reaches of west Marin County, the San Francisco Bay Area is the most wild metropolitan area in the United States. Pedal your bike around this region, and you'll witness an urban wilderness like no other.

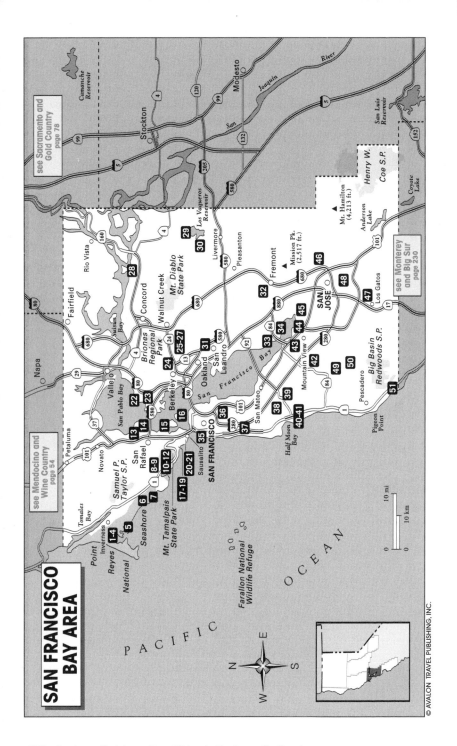

SAN FRANCISCO BAY AREA

1 MARSHALL BEACH TRAIL

Point Reyes National Seashore, off Highway 1 near Olema

Total distance: 2.4 miles   **Biking time:** 1.0 hour

Type of trail: Dirt double-track

Type of bike: Mountain bike

Steepness: Rolling terrain   **Skill level:** Easiest

Marshall Beach Trail is one of the best-kept secrets in Point Reyes. Few visitors know about Marshall Beach because the trailhead is situated on a dirt road to nowhere, at the northeastern tip of the Point Reyes peninsula. Although thousands of visitors pour into neighboring Tomales Bay State Park for its protected bay waters and stunning white beaches, few realize that right next door is Marshall Beach, with all the same advantages, but none of the crowds and no entrance fee.

On your first trip to the Marshall Beach trailhead, you may question if you are going the right way, because the road leads through cow country with no beach in sight. The paved road turns to dirt, and you keep driving along grassy coastal bluffs until you reach a nondescript trailhead sign. Then you start riding through cow pastures. Be sure to keep a vigilant lookout for meadow muffins—the stuff can stay on your tire treads for days.

Why are there cow pastures in a national park? Cattle and dairy ranches have been operating in Point Reyes since the 1850s. The 1962 law that authorized Point Reyes National Seashore made allowances so that the original ranch owners could continue operating within the park's boundaries. Ranching is considered part of the "cultural history" of the park. Currently, there are seven viable dairies in the park, milking about 3,200 cows and producing over five million gallons of milk each year. Just wave and smile at Bessie as you ride to the beach.

The ride is a simple out-and-back, with no trail junctions. Just cruise down the wide ranch road, which curves around the hillside and descends to the water's edge. You can practically coast all the way down, which means you'll face a healthy hill climb on the way back, ensuring your exercise for the day. You'll find no shade along the route, except for at the edge of Marshall Beach's cove, where windswept cypress trees stand guard. Thick lichen hangs from their branches.

Marshall Beach is a nearly perfect beach, with coarse white sand bordering azure blue Tomales Bay water. It's a small slice of paradise overlooking the hamlet of Marshall on the other side of the bay. The most common visitors to the beach are kayakers who paddle over from Marshall, Inverness, or

Tomales Bay State Park to the south. Other hikers are few. You can swim in the calm bay waters, which are protected from the wind by Inverness Ridge.

Essentials for this trip include a picnic, a bathing suit, a good book, and some binoculars for bird-watching. Settle in for a perfect afternoon, then drag yourself away—and back up the hill—when it's time to leave.

Options
Ride out and back from the trailhead on Marshall Beach Road, adding up to five miles to your trip.

Information and Contact
There is no fee. A free map of Point Reyes National Seashore is available at Bear Valley Visitor Center on Bear Valley Road. For more information, contact Point Reyes National Seashore, Point Reyes, CA 94956, 415/464-5100, website: www.nps.gov/pore.

Directions
From San Francisco, cross Golden Gate Bridge and drive north on U.S. 101 for 7.5 miles. Take the Sir Francis Drake Boulevard exit west toward San Anselmo and drive 20 miles to the town of Olema. At Olema, turn right (north) on Highway 1 for about 150 yards, then turn left on Bear Valley Road. Drive 2.2 miles on Bear Valley Road until it joins with Sir Francis Drake Highway. Bear left on Sir Francis Drake Highway and drive 5.6 miles, then take the right fork onto Pierce Point Road. In 1.2 miles, you'll see the entrance road for Tomales Bay State Park. Drive just past it to Duck Cove/Marshall Beach Road; turn right and drive 2.6 miles. The road turns to gravel and dirt; stay to the left where it forks. Park in the gravel parking area, being careful not to block any of the dirt roads that connect here.

---

2 ABBOTT'S LAGOON TRAIL
Point Reyes National Seashore, off Highway 1 near Olema

Total distance: 3.0 miles   **Biking time:** 1.0 hour

Type of trail: Dirt single-track

Type of bike: Mountain bike

Steepness: Mostly level   **Skill level:** Easiest

If the wind is howling and you've been nearly blown off your saddle on other rides at Point Reyes, drive over to the trailhead at Abbott's Lagoon for a trip through a sheltered watery paradise. The bike trail is not particu-

Abbott's Lagoon Trail

larly long, but it leads to Point Reyes Beach, where you can lock up your wheels and continue walking along the sand for miles. The result is a spectacular two-part trip: a ride through protected lagoons teeming with birdlife, then a windswept walk along the wide-open coastline.

Abbott's Lagoon is large—more than 200 acres—and joined by a spillway to two freshwater ponds. It is one of the many annexes of water that cradle the wide triangle of the Point Reyes peninsula. The lagoon is only partially connected to the ocean, so it is only rarely influenced by tides. This can occur when harsh winter storms break through the lagoon's western sand barrier and open it to the ocean. Eventually, sand accumulates and seals off the barrier once again, but the result is that the water in Abbott's Lagoon is brackish—a mix of saltwater and freshwater. This type of mixed-water environment is a haven for many species of birds, mammals, and plants.

You must ride slowly on this trail so as not to scare the wildlife or knock over any bird-watchers, who are sometimes oblivious to everything except what they see in their binoculars. Stay alert and keep your speed down. If you want to try your hand at bird identification, look for these common species: western grebes (large gray-and-white diving birds with a long, swanlike neck and yellow bill), pie-billed grebes (similar to western grebes but with a short, rounded bill and no white patch), coots (dark gray/black, hen-like birds that skitter across the water when they fly, dragging their feet), and caspian terns (like seagulls, but more elegant and angular, with large red bills). Posted signs warn you not to disturb the western snowy plover, a small, sand-dwelling bird that nests along the dunes of Point Reyes Beach. Because their population is in decline, their habitat is protected all along the Northern California coast.

The first 2,000 feet of trail is hard-packed for wheelchair use, and the rest of the route is wide, level single-track—very easy to ride. The trailside scenery is appealing right away, with a little bridge to cross and then a small pond on your left and the lagoon on your right. The sound of the ocean draws you straight ahead. A bucolic-looking white farmhouse, perched on a distant hillside over your right shoulder, watches over the whole scene.

Wildflower season, March–May, brings spectacular shows of poppies and lupines, but perhaps the best time to visit is on a crystal-clear day in winter, when the fog has vanished and the rich, primary colors of water, sky, and grasslands are thoroughly saturated.

If you want to walk along Point Reyes Beach, look for the bike-lock post at the end of the trail, next to a wooden bridge. Secure your bike and follow the foot trail that leads away from the lagoon and to the ocean in .2 mile.

Information and Contact

There is no fee. A free map of Point Reyes National Seashore is available at Bear Valley Visitor Center on Bear Valley Road. For more information, contact Point Reyes National Seashore, Point Reyes, CA 94956, 415/464-5100, website: www.nps.gov/pore.

Directions

From San Francisco, cross Golden Gate Bridge and drive north on U.S. 101 for 7.5 miles. Take the Sir Francis Drake Boulevard exit west toward San Anselmo and drive 20 miles to the town of Olema. At Olema, turn right (north) on Highway 1 for about 150 yards, then turn left on Bear Valley Road. Drive 2.2 miles on Bear Valley Road until it joins with Sir Francis Drake Highway. Bear left on Sir Francis Drake Highway for 5.5 miles, then take the right cutoff for Pierce Point Road. Drive 3.3 miles on Pierce Point Road to Abbott's Lagoon Trailhead on the left.

3 BULL POINT TRAIL
Point Reyes National Seashore, off Highway 1 near Olema

Total distance: 3.6 miles   **Biking time:** 1.0 hour

Type of trail: Dirt double-track

Type of bike: Mountain bike

Steepness: Mostly level   **Skill level:** Easiest

Bull Point is one of the largely forgotten Point Reyes trails, one that only the cows seem to know about. It's just far enough out on the peninsula that not many people bother to make the drive, and those who do are usu-

© ANN MARIE BROWN

Bull Point Trail

ally on their way to more glamorous destinations like Drake's Beach or Point Reyes Lighthouse.

But the trail is open to bikes and fun to ride, giving you the opportunity to pedal through a coastal prairie on your way to Drake's Estero. You ride on a wide strip of land between two arms of the *estero:* Creamery Bay and Schooner Bay, which was once the launching area for schooners carrying butter from Point Reyes dairies to dinner tables in San Francisco. Creamery and Schooner Bays, plus Barries and Home Bays, are the four fingers of the hand that is Drake's Estero—the Spanish word for estuary, a place where saltwater and freshwater mix. Most scholars believe that Sir Francis Drake landed here in 1579, although there are still a few holdouts who insist he landed in San Francisco Bay, near Larkspur Landing, or in one of a few other places in Northern California.

The trail begins on the left side of the parking lot at a cattle gate that you must close behind you. You're likely to ride past some grazing bovines on the first section of the route. The trail is an old ranch road that is rather indistinct at the trailhead, but gets more distinct as you ride, becoming easier to follow as it leads toward the bay. Riding here makes you feel like you're in a Merchant-Ivory film; backdrops of green pastoral countryside are interwoven with vistas of wide, blue water. No, this is not 19th-century England, but rather early-21st-century Point Reyes, although it's easy to mistake the two.

There are no trail junctions to confuse you; it's just a straight shot to the waterway across grassy coastal bluffs. The last 20 feet of trail, right before you reach the cliff's edge over the bay, are caved in, so be ready to put on the brakes at the land's edge. Looking toward the water, Creamery Bay is on your right and Schooner Bay is on your left. When the tide is low, you can see poles sticking out of the waters of Schooner Bay and gray mesh bags laying in the shallows and along the shoreline. The bags are filled with oysters, the property of Johnson's Oyster Farm across the bay. The farm is accessible by a side road off Sir Francis Drake Highway and might be worth a stop on your drive home.

As with all the bays, estuaries, lagoons, and ponds at watery Point Reyes, the coves here host thousands of migratory and resident birds. Elegant great egrets are among the most noticeable inhabitants. Their grand white plumage provides a stark contrast to the greens and blues of the landscape.

Information and Contact

There is no fee. A free map of Point Reyes National Seashore is available at Bear Valley Visitor Center on Bear Valley Road. For more information, contact Point Reyes National Seashore, Point Reyes, CA 94956, 415/464-5100, website: www.nps.gov/pore.

Directions

From San Francisco, cross Golden Gate Bridge and drive north on U.S. 101 for 7.5 miles. Take the Sir Francis Drake Boulevard exit west toward San Anselmo and drive 20 miles to the town of Olema. At Olema, turn right (north) on Highway 1 for about 150 yards, then turn left on Bear Valley Road. Drive 2.2 miles on Bear Valley Road until it joins with Sir Francis Drake Highway. Bear left on Sir Francis Drake Highway and drive 10.5 miles to the Bull Point parking area on the left side of the road. The trail leads from the left side of the parking area.

4 ESTERO TRAIL TO SUNSET BEACH

Point Reyes National Seashore, off Highway 1 near Olema

Total distance: 7.8 miles   **Biking time:** 2.0 hours

Type of trail: Dirt single-track and double-track

Type of bike: Mountain bike

Steepness: Rolling terrain   **Skill level:** Challenging

Of all the Point Reyes National Seashore bike trails in this book, Estero Trail is the most challenging, with the toughest hills and the roughest trail surface. But if you're prepared for the workout, it's an absolute must-do bike ride. To make your trip easier, plan your ride for a summer day or after a dry spell in winter, when there is no mud on the trail and the dirt is hard-packed.

Estero Trail crosses a bridge over Home Bay.

Estero Trail leads to paths that connect to either Sunset Beach or Drake's Head, both spectacular and distinct destinations. An out-and-back trip to Sunset Beach is slightly easier and shorter than the out-and-back to Drake's Head, so it's a better choice for novice riders. Estero Trail is quintessential Point Reyes, which means that it's full of good surprises. Riding here in the early morning, when the wildlife is abundant but people have not yet arrived, may produce a compelling desire to return again and again.

The trail leads from the left side of the parking lot and crosses a grassy hillside, providing little or no indication of what lies ahead. As you coast down the hard-packed trail, you round a corner and drop quickly into a stand of dense Monterey pines, the remains of an old Christmas tree farm. Another minute of riding, and surprise—the trail opens out to Home Bay. You ride across a causeway on the edge of the bay, with water (or mud-flats, if the tide is out) on either side of you.

You might want to stop for a moment along the causeway to gather some energy for your first hill climb. It comes up next as you rise above Home Bay. The incredible water views will comfort you as you work your way up the short but steep hill, then descend rapidly down the other side and cross another levee, in another protected cove.

Keep riding along and above the waters of Drake's Estero, ascending a total of three hills and continuing straight to the trail sign for Sunset Beach Trail at 2.4 miles. Here, the trail finally levels out and becomes less vulnerable to erosion. (Blame the cows who graze here for the rutted trail surface. Their heavy body weight and big hooves chew up the trail after wet weather.) The last 1.5 miles to the edge of Sunset Beach are the easiest miles of the day. The path dissipates at the edge of a large, quiet pond just before the beach. You'll have to stash your bike, or walk beside it, to continue the final yards to the breaking ocean waves where Drake's Estero empties into the sea. The sand spit that borders Limantour Estero is directly in front of you; often it is covered with barking harbor seals and sea lions.

Your chance of seeing wildlife along this route is excellent. In addition to the ever-present waterfowl, shorebirds, and pinnipeds, deer frequent this section of the park, including a small herd of nonnative white deer that were brought here by a rancher a generation ago. More common black-tail deer are also abundant, with the males bearing impressive racks in the wintertime.

Options

You can also ride Estero Trail for 2.4 miles to the left turnoff for Drake's Head. Turn left here and ascend a hill, then negotiate your way around a cattle corral and across the high coastal bluffs to an overlook above Limantour Estero. Drake's Head is a worthwhile destination for a picnic spot, but the ascent is more strenuous than on the trail to Sunset Beach.

Information and Contact

There is no fee. A free map of Point Reyes National Seashore is available at Bear Valley Visitor Center on Bear Valley Road. For more information, contact Point Reyes National Seashore, Point Reyes, CA 94956, 415/464-5100, website: www.nps.gov/pore.

Directions

From San Francisco, cross Golden Gate Bridge and drive north on U.S.

101 for 7.5 miles. Take the Sir Francis Drake Boulevard exit west toward San Anselmo and drive 20 miles to the town of Olema. At Olema, turn right (north) on Highway 1 for about 150 yards, then turn left on Bear Valley Road. Drive 2.2 miles on Bear Valley Road until it joins with Sir Francis Drake Highway. Bear left on Sir Francis Drake Highway and drive 7.5 miles to the left turnoff for the Estero Trailhead. Turn left and drive one mile to the trailhead parking area.

5 COAST TRAIL

Point Reyes National Seashore, off Highway 1 near Olema

Total distance: 5.8 miles   **Biking time:** 2.0 hours

Type of trail: Dirt double-track

Type of bike: Mountain bike

Steepness: Mostly level   **Skill level:** Easiest

If you have ever wanted to pack your panniers and ride your mountain bike to a campground that seems far removed from the hustle and bustle of the Bay Area, Coast Trail is your chance. Then again, if you have ever wanted to ride your bike to a windswept beach, then sit on the sand and look out to sea for an hour before getting back to San Francisco in time for dinner, Coast Trail is your chance for that, too. Coast Trail can provide both kinds of trip. It will be perfect either way.

Coast Trail is L-shaped and begins across from Point Reyes Hostel. It makes a beeline for the coast, then turns left (south) and runs parallel to the beach for another mile to Coast Camp. The trail is shadeless most of the way, except for a short section alongside a stream and its surrounding thicket of alders. In winter, the stream creates a few marshy areas, which are thick with cattails.

Riding is easy on this wide, dirt fire road, which heads slightly downhill on the way to the beach and slightly uphill on the way back, but with no real climbs to slow you down. It's the perfect trail for riding side by side with a friend and conversing, since there are no blind corners or narrow turns. In 1.8 miles, you reach the coast. A trail marker notes that you can walk to your right along the beach to reach the Limantour parking lot in less than a mile. Ride to the left instead, continuing along Coast Trail for 1.1 miles more to Coast Camp.

The trail continues beyond Coast Camp but isn't open to bikes, so lock up yours at the metal bike post next to the horse-hitching posts, and take the narrow foot trail by the camp restrooms to the beach. From there, you

Coast Trail

can walk as far as you like in either direction, either right toward Limantour Beach or left toward Sculptured Beach, with miles of uninterrupted sand in between.

To camp, you must make advance reservations; a camping permit is required. The campground has piped water, restrooms, and a few picnic tables—just about everything you need for a perfect overnight trip.

Information and Contact

There is no fee. A free map of Point Reyes National Seashore is available at Bear Valley Visitor Center on Bear Valley Road. For more information, contact Point Reyes National Seashore, Point Reyes, CA 94956, 415/464-5100, website: www.nps.gov/pore.

Directions

From San Francisco, cross Golden Gate Bridge and drive north on U.S. 101 for 7.5 miles. Take the Sir Francis Drake Boulevard exit west toward San Anselmo and drive 20 miles to the town of Olema. At Olema, turn right (north) on Highway 1 for about 150 yards, then turn left on Bear Valley Road. Drive 1.7 miles, then turn left on Limantour Road. Drive 5.8 miles to the left turnoff for Point Reyes Hostel. Turn left, drive past the hostel, and park in the lot on the right. Ride your bike past the hostel and take the dirt fire road just beyond it and across the road, signed "Coast Trail."

6 BEAR VALLEY TRAIL BIKE & HIKE

Point Reyes National Seashore, off Highway 1 near Olema

Total distance: 6.4 miles (plus 1.8-mile hike)　　**Biking time:** 2.0 hours

Type of trail: Dirt road

Type of bike: Mountain bike

Steepness: Rolling terrain　　　　　　　　**Skill level:** Easiest

Bear Valley Trail is far and away the most well known and busiest trail in Point Reyes, and for that reason you might think you should avoid it. But bypassing Bear Valley Trail is a big mistake. The trailside scenery is very beautiful. The trail's easy grade makes it suitable for a family biking trip. And arriving at the trailhead before 9 A.M. assures you of some solitude along the route, even on weekends. Winter is the best season to avoid crowds, and the trail is loveliest then anyway, when the streams are running full and the ferns are in full leafy display.

the final steps to Arch Rock on the Bear Valley Trail bike & hike

The trail is simple to follow. It begins as a wide dirt road just beyond Bear Valley Visitor Center and Morgan Horse Ranch. Several trails junction with Bear Valley Trail, but just stay on the wide main road and pedal your way through the mixed bay and Douglas fir forest, following the path of Bear Valley Creek. Ferns of many kinds adorn the creek's banks, including delicate five-finger ferns. You'll notice a bit of an uphill grade in the first mile, but the entire route never gains or loses more than 200 feet in elevation.

At 1.5 miles from the trailhead, you reach the edge of large Divide Meadow, a tranquil spot for a rest or a picnic on your return trip. Deer are often sighted here. Divide Meadow marks the divide in this valley: Bear Valley Creek, which flows north, is left behind, but soon the trail parallels Coast Creek, which flows south all the way to the sea. More forest, ferns, and lush streamside foliage keep you company as you forge onward. In spring, the buckeye trees along this stretch bloom with perfumed white flower clusters. Also in spring, the trail is bordered by a profusion of blue forget-me-nots and tasty miner's lettuce.

At 3.2 miles, you reach a junction of trails and a bike rack. You must leave your wheels (don't forget your bike lock), but the trip isn't over yet. Lock up your bike and continue on foot straight ahead on Bear Valley Trail to Arch Rock. Although at present you are deep in the forest, surrounded by alder, bay laurel, and Douglas fir, you will soon leave the shade. A half mile farther along, the trail opens out to coastal marshlands and chaparral, and the ocean appears straight ahead.

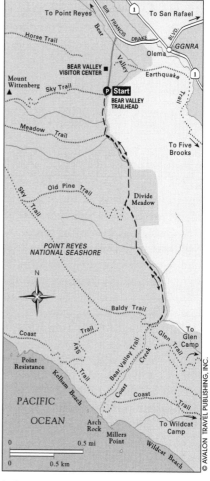

Nearing the sea, Bear Valley Trail splits off as it meets up with Coast Trail; bear left. The final steps are dramatic and memorable as you traverse the top of Arch Rock's precipitous, jade-green bluff jutting out into the sea. Coast Creek, the previously gentle stream you were following, now cuts a deep, eroded gorge on its way to the ocean. A spur trail leads down the edge of the gorge to the beach. Some visitors plan their trip so they can descend to the beach, then crawl through Arch Rock's tunnel at the mouth of Coast Creek during very low tides. But most are content to stay on top of Arch Rock and enjoy the view, which takes in numerous rock outcrops, the shoreline below, and the perpetually rolling surf.

Options

Even the youngest riders can make the trip as far as Divide Meadow, once the site of an old hunting lodge and now a grassy picnic area with tables and restrooms. This makes a three-mile round-trip.

Information and Contact

There is no fee. A free map of Point Reyes National Seashore is available at Bear Valley Visitor Center on Bear Valley Road. For more information, contact Point Reyes National Seashore, Point Reyes, CA 94956, 415/464-5100, website: www.nps.gov/pore.

Directions

From San Francisco, cross Golden Gate Bridge and drive north on U.S. 101 for 7.5 miles. Take the Sir Francis Drake Boulevard exit west toward San Anselmo and drive 20 miles to the town of Olema. At Olema, turn right (north) on Highway 1 for about 150 yards, then turn left on Bear Valley Road. Drive .5 mile and turn left at the sign for Bear Valley Visitor Center. Park in the large lot on the left, beyond the visitors center, and ride your bike past the gate on the wide dirt road, which is Bear Valley Trail.

7 OLEMA VALLEY TRAIL

Point Reyes National Seashore, off Highway 1 near Olema

Total distance: 7.4 miles   **Biking time:** 2.0 hours

Type of trail: Dirt single-track

Type of bike: Mountain bike

Steepness: Rolling terrain   **Skill level:** Moderate

There is only one important point to remember when riding Olema Valley Trail: Do not start from the well-known Five Brooks Trailhead, because the trail climbs like crazy within a mile of the parking area. Instead, start at the signed Olema Valley Trailhead, just two miles south of Five Brooks Trailhead. Then prepare to have a good time as you ride out and back in two directions through a level valley at the base of a forested ridge.

Okay, maybe there are two important points to remember. The other is to ride this trail in the dry season. In the rainy months, sections of the Olema Valley Trail are frequently submerged in marshy waters.

According to the Point Reyes park map, Olema Valley Trail appears to parallel the highway, but in fact it is far enough off the road that you rarely see or hear cars. Its trailhead is five miles from the main Point Reyes visitation areas, so you won't have to worry about having too much company, or running over any hikers, either. The level, somewhat bumpy single-track is great for easy biking, and your chances of seeing birds and deer, maybe even a bobcat or a fox if you're very fortunate, are excellent.

The signs are a bit confusing at the trailhead; although you will be riding on Olema Valley Trail, you must take Randall Spur Trail .5 mile to meet up with it. Do not ride on Randall Trail on the east side of Highway 1, which climbs a steep ridge; you want the level Randall Spur Trail on the west side of the highway. That taken care of, head across the meadow until you join Olema Valley Trail, where you can go left or right. Heading right, you'll ride 1.2 miles until the dirt single-track reaches some old, broken pavement. Traveling in this direction, you are mostly in the forest, cruising between big Douglas firs, California laurels, and live oaks. The wooded areas alternate with wide, wet meadows. The trail becomes narrow and eroded in places. Shortly after the stretch of broken pavement, the route climbs steeply to an intersection with Bolema Trail, then beyond to Five Brooks Trailhead.

If you're not in the mood for the climb to Five Brooks, turn around at the pavement and ride back to where Olema Valley Trail meets Randall Spur Trail. Then ride the opposite (southerly) direction on Olema Valley Trail. After an immediate short climb, the path leads along the meadow's edge for 2.5 miles to the trail's end at Highway 1 near Dogtown. Traveling in this direction, Olema Valley Trail is in open meadows for the whole distance.

Information and Contact
There is no fee. A free map of Point Reyes National Seashore is available at Bear Valley Visitor Center on Bear Valley Road. For more information, contact Point Reyes National Seashore, Point Reyes, CA 94956, 415/464-5100, website: www.nps.gov/pore.

Directions
From San Francisco, cross Golden Gate Bridge and drive north on U.S. 101 for 7.5 miles. Take the Sir Francis Drake Boulevard exit west toward San Anselmo and drive 20 miles to the town of Olema. At Olema, turn left (south) on Highway 1 and drive 5.5 miles to the trailhead for Randall Trail on the east side of the road and Olema Valley Trail on the west side of the road. (This trailhead is two miles past the Five Brooks Trailhead.) Park in the pullout, then begin riding on the west side of the road.

8 BOLINAS RIDGE TRAIL
Golden Gate National Recreation Area, off Sir Francis Drake Boulevard near Olema

Total distance: 7–10 miles   **Biking time:** 2.0 hours

Type of trail: Dirt road

Type of bike: Mountain bike

Steepness: Rolling terrain   **Skill level:** Moderate

The first time you ride Bolinas Ridge, you wonder how a trail could go up and down so much without ever leveling out. The path seems to have no pedal-and-cruise sections; you are either climbing up or coasting down the

© ANN MARIE BROWN
Open pasturelands line the northern edge of Bolinas Ridge near Olema.

whole way (more of the latter than the former). The ridge's roller-coaster grassland terrain is just plain fun, and scenic to boot: Its high points afford expansive views of Bolinas Lagoon to the south and Tomales Bay to the north. The trail is well-suited for all levels of riders; beginners can go out and back for a few miles, while more advanced riders can choose from a variety of loops.

The key is to start on the Olema side of Bolinas Ridge at the Sir Francis Drake Highway trailhead, rather than on the Mount Tamalpais side at the Bolinas-Fairfax Road trailhead. From the Olema side, less ambitious riders can pedal southward for a handful of miles as the trail climbs moderately. How far you go is up to you. The route carves through open pasturelands until the 5.4-mile mark, where it suddenly enters a thick Douglas fir and redwood forest. Say good-bye to the sun and the views, and hello to the refreshing woods. When you've had enough and are ready to turn around and head home, a fun descent awaits.

There are two factors to be prepared for: Number one, this is cow country, as in bovines everywhere, a regular cow-o-rama. Number two, because this is cow country, you must contend with a lot of cattle gates, which you must close behind you if you open them to ride through. Here's a little secret: The best way to get through the gates is not to open and close them; nor is it to lift your bike over the gate, set it down on the other side, then walk through the hikers' turnstile. The most efficient method is to lift your bike over your head (grab it firmly with both hands on the frame) and then walk through the turnstile with it. You and the bike arrive at the other side of the gate at the same time, and you get a five-second upper-body workout in the process, without straining your back.

The ride begins with a climb up to the ridge, and in about one mile, you pass the left turnoff for Jewell Trail, which connects Bolinas Ridge to Cross Marin Trail/Sir Francis Drake Bikeway (see the following trail description). Continue straight on Bolinas Ridge Trail, gliding up and down one hill after another. The trail surface varies greatly; although it is always a double-wide dirt path, it is sometimes smooth and sometimes eroded and rocky. Stick to the worn tire tracks in the roughest parts of trail, and keep in mind that the first half mile is the rockiest—it gets better after that. Give plenty of room to other trail users: equestrians, hikers, and mostly cows, who wander where they please along the trail. It's wise to keep your speed down, as the steepness of the downgrades can surprise you.

About the farthest most beginning riders would want to pedal on this trail is to the Shafter Trail junction, five miles out, with a total 1,000-foot elevation gain. Many will be content to turn around long before that; a good spot is near a tule-lined pond about 3.5 miles out. The return trip offers a good amount of downhill, and views are terrific all the way back. You can see for miles to the west, all the way out to Tomales Bay.

Options

Feeling ambitious? You can make a 15-mile loop by riding 6.2 miles out on Bolinas Ridge Trail, then turning right on Randall Trail. In less than two miles, you'll reach Highway 1, where you turn right and head back to Sir Francis Drake Boulevard and your car.

Information and Contact

There is no fee. A free map of Point Reyes National Seashore (which includes this section of Golden Gate National Recreation Area) is available at Bear Valley Visitor Center on Bear Valley Road. More information and a free map are also available from Golden Gate National Recreation Area, Building 1056, Fort Cronkhite, Sausalito, CA 94965, 415/331-1540, website: www.nps.gov/goga.

Directions

From San Francisco, cross Golden Gate Bridge and drive north on U.S. 101 for 7.5 miles. Take the Sir Francis Drake Boulevard exit west toward San Anselmo and drive 19.5 miles to the trailhead for Bolinas Ridge Trail on the left side of the road. If you reach the town of Olema and Highway 1, you have gone one mile too far. Park in the pullout alongside the road and lift your bike over the cattle gate.

9 CROSS MARIN TRAIL/ SIR FRANCIS DRAKE BIKEWAY

Golden Gate National Recreation Area and Samuel P. Taylor
State Park, off Sir Francis Drake Boulevard near Lagunitas

Total distance: 10.0 miles   **Biking time:** 2.0 hours

Type of trail: Paved bike trail and gravel double-track

Type of bike: Road bike or mountain bike

Steepness: Rolling terrain   **Skill level:** Moderate

Cross Marin Trail/Sir Francis Drake Bikeway is one trail with two names, under two different park jurisdictions. It's called Cross Marin Trail when it's on Golden Gate National Recreation Area land and Sir Francis Drake Bikeway when it's on Samuel P. Taylor State Park land. Two names, one trail.

The ride offers something for skinny tires and fat tires alike, with three miles of smooth pavement and another two miles of gravel and dirt suitable for mountain bikes. Two kinds of bikes, one trail.

The bike path is an old rail trail, built in 1874 by North Pacific Coast Railroad and abandoned in 1933. Samuel Taylor, the park's namesake, owned and operated a paper mill near the current park headquarters, and as he watched the narrow-gauge train with all its passengers chug by his mill, he got the bright idea to start an outdoor camping area right here along Lagunitas Creek (also called Papermill Creek). The trail's

The paved Sir Francis Drake Bikeway is bordered by an abundance of ferns.

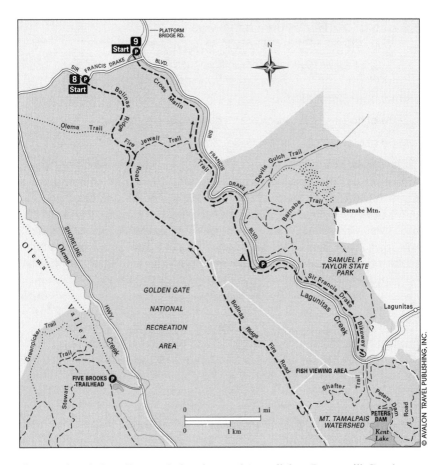

first section is heavily wooded as it travels parallel to Papermill Creek, then opens out to a broad meadow. The path then heads back into the trees, entering dense second-growth redwood stands surrounded by prolific sorrel and ferns.

At the state park border, your primeval redwood fantasy gets rudely interrupted by campgrounds, restrooms, and other indicators of civilization. Where the paved surface erodes to gravel and dirt past Redwood Grove Picnic Area, skinny tires must turn around, but mountain bikers should continue riding, crossing a footbridge over Sir Francis Drake Highway. The trail ends two miles later at the park boundary, where Shafter Bridge arches over Papermill Creek. In summer, some hard-core bikers walk their bikes across the creek and continue riding across Sir Francis Drake on fire roads that lead to Kent Lake, but in winter, the stream is often too high to ford.

By far the best time of year to ride this trail is in winter after a good rain, when the campgrounds are empty, the creek is running full, and the trees and ferns are dripping with moisture. Your solitude will be interrupted only by the occasional sight and sound of cars on Sir Francis Drake, rather than crowds of people at the campgrounds and picnic areas of Samuel P. Taylor. For much of the route, you ride along with a feeling of wonderment, amazed that these beautiful redwoods are accessible on a paved bike trail, so close to an urban area.

Options

A much more challenging option is to make a 13.4-mile loop out of this trip by crossing the creek at the trail's end. Carry your bike across the water, then climb uphill to Shafter Bridge. (If the stream is too high to ford, backtrack and ride on Sir Francis Drake Highway from the park entrance to Shafter Bridge.) Next comes a gnarly, 1.8-mile winding climb up Shafter Bridge Fire Road that slays even the best of 'em (1,100-foot gain). At the top, a heavenly, mostly downhill cruise on Bolinas Ridge Road awaits. Where the ridge trail ends at Sir Francis Drake Highway, cruise down the paved road back to your car.

Information and Contact

There is no fee if you park at Platform Bridge Road. A $6 per vehicle day-use fee is charged if you park in the paved parking areas at Samuel P. Taylor State Park. A trail map/brochure is available at the ranger kiosk at the park campground entrance. For more information, contact Samuel P. Taylor State Park, P.O. Box 251, Lagunitas, CA 94938, 415/488-9897 or 415/898-4362, or Golden Gate National Recreation Area, 415/331-1540, website: www.nps.gov/goga.

Directions

From San Francisco, cross Golden Gate Bridge on U.S. 101 and drive north for 7.5 miles. Take the Sir Francis Drake Boulevard exit west toward San Anselmo and drive 18.7 miles to the right turnoff for Platform Bridge Road, 3.4 miles past the main entrance to Samuel P. Taylor State Park. (If you reach the town of Olema and Highway 1, you have gone 1.8 miles too far.) Turn right on Platform Bridge Road and park in the pullout on the left. Begin riding on the paved connector path that leads from the pullout, cross a concrete bridge, ride about 30 yards, and then turn left immediately on the signed Cross Marin Trail.

10 KENT PUMP ROAD

Marin Municipal Water District, off Bolinas-Fairfax
Road near Fairfax

Total distance: 9.0 miles   **Biking time:** 2.0 hours

Type of trail: Dirt road

Type of bike: Mountain bike

Steepness: Rolling terrain   **Skill level:** Easiest

The Marin watershed lands offer several classic mountain bike rides—the kind of trails for which mountain bikes were invented. The Pine Mountain Loop is probably the most famous of those, complete with a downhill stint on Repack Fire Road, so named because after you ride it, you'll probably have to repack your bearings.

end of Kent Pump Road at Kent Lake

But if extensive bike repair does not interest you in the slightest, head out to the Marin watershed and ride Kent Pump Road, which is ever so much gentler and more forgiving. The ride is level, smooth, and easy, and best of all, it travels through a gorgeous watershed canyon all the way to 460-acre Kent Lake. The only way to reach Kent Lake is to hike or bike there, which greatly limits the amount of company you'll have.

A few notes for the start of this trail: First, be careful not to park in front of the gate at the trailhead, since this is a protection road. Second, because there is no turnstile, you must crawl under the gate with your bike, but it's easier than it sounds. Third, when you start riding, ignore the trail that leads immediately to the left. Stay straight on the main path.

Kent Pump Road is basically level, with only two short hills, one at the very beginning and one at trail's end at the lake. They are both short, manageable "ups" that are saved for the return trip. The trail surface is very smooth gravel, so smooth it might as well be pavement. The Marin Water District keeps the road well maintained. A ravine drops off steeply to the left, so it's best to stay far from the road's edge when riding, but be sure to stop, take a break, and look over the edge every now and then. The stream canyon is pristine and beautiful, with big mossy boulders and thick groves of trees draped with moss and lichens. You'll probably note many pleasant fragrances as you ride; the mix of firs, pine, and sage can be intoxicating.

The only major trail junction you pass is Old Vee Road, on your right at two miles; just keep straight, snaking your way deeper into the canyon. Kent Pump Road curves a lot; you may surprise a deer or two as you round the turns. The deer go bounding off down into the canyon, non-plussed by the near-vertical slope.

When you reach the southeast end of Kent Lake, continue straight past a sign reading "No Through Road in 0.5 Mile," ignoring two short right cutoffs. The route drops you at the lake's edge, where there's a small pumphouse. No water contact is permitted at Kent Lake, so forget swimming, but have a seat by the water's edge and listen to the birds calling and the woodpeckers pecking. Many dead trees poke out of the water—silent victims that were swallowed up when the lake was dammed. The woodpeckers make good use of them.

Information and Contact

There is no fee. For more information and a map, contact Marin Municipal Water District, 220 Nellen Avenue, Corte Madera, CA 94925, 415/945-1455, website: www.marinwater.org. Or phone Sky Oaks Ranger Station at 415/945-1181.

Directions

From San Francisco, cross Golden Gate Bridge and drive north on U.S. 101 for 7.5 miles. Take the Sir Francis Drake Boulevard exit west toward San Anselmo, then drive six miles to the town of Fairfax. Turn left by the "Fairfax" sign (on Pacheco Road), then turn right immediately on Broadway. Drive one block and turn left on Bolinas Road. Drive 7.8 miles on Bolinas Road to the dam at Alpine Lake. Park as close to the right (north) side of the dam as possible. The trailhead is on the right side of the dam, at the gated fire road.

11 LAKE LAGUNITAS LOOP

Marin Municipal Water District, off Bolinas-Fairfax
Road near Fairfax

Total distance: 2.0 miles   **Biking time:** 1.0 hour

Type of trail: Dirt single-track and dirt road

Type of bike: Mountain bike

Steepness: Mostly level   **Skill level:** Easiest

Probably the greatest compliment you can pay Lake Lagunitas is to say it's
a reservoir that somehow manages not to look like one. Surrounded by
oaks, madrones, pines, and firs, it appears to be an honest-to-goodness
lake, a water body that the earliest Marin inhabitants would have fished
and used as a water supply. It looks, well, natural.

It isn't, though. Lagunitas is a small, 22-acre reservoir, part of the
Mount Tamalpais watershed, managed by the Marin Municipal Water District. Its dam was built in 1873, making it the oldest of the five Marin
"lakes." Luckily, the Water District managers don't just horde water; they
also open up their lands and lakes for outdoor recreation, providing great
fishing, hiking, bird-watching, and bicycling opportunities.

From the parking lot by the often crowded picnic area, start riding on
the fire road near the restrooms, heading past a small abandoned house.
Your best bet is to ride clockwise around the lake, which means heading to
the left of the dam. Your ride gets interrupted almost immediately by signs
stating that you must walk your bike for a short stretch, which includes

Lake Lagunitas is the oldest of the reservoirs in the Mount Tamalpais Watershed.

carrying it up a few stairs. A couple more houses belonging to water district officials sit off to your left.

Where the single-track widens to a one-lane dirt road, the signs proclaim that you may ride again. Pedal underneath the canopy of oak trees near the lakeshore, which is crowded with reeds, tules, and cattails. Great views encompass the unmistakable profile of Mount Tamalpais. Various dirt roads come in from the left, but continue heading to the right to make a loop around the lake. Cross the East Fork of Lagunitas Creek (use the bridge, don't ride across the creek) and pedal along the shadier south side of Lagunitas. The oaks here are covered with moss all winter and mixed in with more conifers.

Cross two more forks of Lagunitas Creek, then reach the lake's pumphouse by Rock Springs/Lagunitas Road. To complete your circle, ride past the dam. The fire road continues straight and brings you down a steep hill to the opposite end of the parking lot from where you started.

If you can visit Lake Lagunitas on a weekday, you'll have the best experience and the least company. On a midweek afternoon, it's so quiet here that you can hear ducks splashing in the water 100 yards away.

Options
Rock Springs/Lagunitas Road leads off near the pumphouse and climbs more than 1,000 feet in 2.5 miles to reach Potrero Meadows. You can ride that trail as far as you like. (Bay Tree Junction is reachable in one mile, with a 600-foot elevation gain.) Many riders just circle the lake's perimeter twice, for a few more level miles.

Information and Contact
There is a $7 entrance fee per vehicle. For more information and a map, contact Marin Municipal Water District, 220 Nellen Avenue, Corte Madera, CA 94925, 415/945-1455, website: www.marinwater.org. Or phone Sky Oaks Ranger Station at 415/945-1181.

Directions
From San Francisco, cross Golden Gate Bridge and drive north on U.S. 101 for 7.5 miles. Take the Sir Francis Drake Boulevard exit west toward San Anselmo, then drive six miles to the town of Fairfax. Turn left by the "Fairfax" sign (on Pacheco Road), then turn right immediately on Broadway. Drive one block and turn left on Bolinas Road. Drive 1.5 miles to Sky Oaks Road, where you bear left. Drive straight .5 mile to the entrance kiosk, then continue and take the left fork signed for Lake Lagunitas. Park at the far end of the parking lot, then begin riding on the unsigned fire road that starts near the restrooms (to the left of the picnic area).

12 THREE LAKES LOOP

Marin Municipal Water District,
off Sir Francis Drake Boulevard in Ross

Total distance: 9.0–11.2 miles

Biking time: 2.0 hours

Type of trail: Dirt roads

Type of bike: Mountain bike

Steepness: Steep sections

Skill level: Moderate

Phoenix Lake is the most popular of the five lakes in the Mount Tamalpais watershed, but due to a cruel twist of fate, it also has the smallest parking lot, with space for only about 15 cars. This means that the hundreds of anglers, hikers, equestrians, baby-stroller pushers, and mountain bikers who want access to Phoenix Lake on summer weekends have to fight it out for a parking space. No street parking is available anywhere near the lake on weekends and holidays (the well-to-do residents

Phoenix Lake is one of three reservoirs visited on the Three Lakes Loop.

of Ross have made sure that their streets are clearly signed, and the No Parking rule is strictly enforced), so it's a good thing you're on two wheels. Unless it's a weekday, you must ride a short stretch on the street to gain access to this terrific lake-filled loop.

It's best to leave your car at the large parking lot at Ross Commons Park and pedal from there. A 1.1-mile ride brings you to the jam-packed parking lot at Natalie Coffin Greene Park. (If you can manage to park at Natalie Coffin Greene Park, your ride will be only nine miles instead of 11.2 miles.) Go around the gate and uphill to Phoenix Lake's dam. You've arrived at the first lake of the Three Lakes Loop. Ride around the right side of the lake, passing a log cabin built in 1893. At the four-way intersection known as Phoenix Junction, go right to climb uphill on Shaver Grade through dense redwoods. Stay on Shaver Grade until you reach the paved access road to Bon Tempe and Lagunitas Lakes, where you turn left. After briefly skirting the edge of Bon Tempe Lake, you face the best scenery of the day as you circle Lagunitas Lake, crossing three small bridges (see the previous trail description for directions and information on this two-mile stretch).

Too soon, you leave the water behind and face a climb up Lakeview Fire Road (go right). Don't forget to turn around and check out the trail's promised "lake view." A half mile later, you turn left for the final stretch of the loop on Eldridge Grade, one of the first wagon routes to the summit of Mount Tamalpais, built in 1889. Be cautious on the steep descent on this old, well-worn trail, which has been reduced to single-track in some stretches. It's the most challenging part of this entire ride, and it's all downhill.

Options
If you are not up for the length of this ride, just circle around Phoenix Lake for a shorter, easier trip.

Information and Contact
There is no fee. For more information and a map, contact Marin Municipal Water District, 220 Nellen Avenue, Corte Madera, CA 94925, 415/945-1455, website: www.marinwater.org. Or phone Sky Oaks Ranger Station at 415/945-1181.

Directions
From San Francisco, cross Golden Gate Bridge and drive north on U.S. 101 for 7.5 miles. Take the Sir Francis Drake Boulevard exit west toward

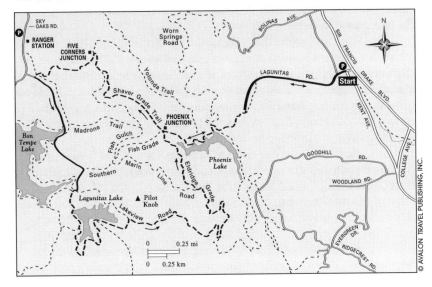

San Anselmo, then drive three miles to Lagunitas Road on the left, across from Marin Art and Garden Center. Turn left on Lagunitas Road and park at Ross Commons (junction of Lagunitas and Kent Roads). Or drive 1.1 miles on Lagunitas Road to the parking area for Natalie Coffin Greene Park, and see if you get lucky and snag one of only about 15 parking spots.

13 LAS GALLINAS WILDLIFE PONDS

Las Gallinas Valley Sanitary District, off U.S. 101 near San Rafael

Total distance: 6.5 miles   **Biking time:** 1.5 hours

Type of trail: Dirt double-track

Type of bike: Mountain bike

Steepness: Mostly level   **Skill level:** Easiest

Sometimes unlikely places make good bike riding. So it is at Las Gallinas Valley Sanitary District, where the important work of treating and disposing wastewater takes place, as well as the important work of preserving wetlands. At this wastewater reclamation project, you can find herons roosting in trees, a flock of white pelicans, and 3.5 miles of public access trails on the edge of San Pablo Bay.

The place may be alongside a sewage treatment plant, but it is still wildlife heaven out here. In a two-hour trip, I saw several big jackrabbits, a flock of Canada geese, three hawks, numerous turkey vultures, a great egret, and a great blue heron. And this wasn't even in autumn, which is the best season for spotting birds.

The reclamation project in northeast San Rafael includes a freshwater marsh, an irrigated pasture, storage ponds, and a saltwater marsh. Sure, there are electrical towers. Yes, there is a barbed-wire fence. But there is also uninterrupted San Pablo Bay shoreline with views of Mount Diablo to the east and Mount Tamalpais to the southwest. Plus, there's a great trail surface for easy bike riding—wide, smooth dirt and gravel—that makes the path accessible to anyone, even little kids.

Begin riding by the playing fields at McInnis Park, if you wish, or park right by the sanitary district buildings and start from there. A large sign-board by the bridge at the trail's start shows a map of the place and notes some of the wildlife you may see. Head straight toward the bay. You cruise along on top of gravel levees that separate the sanitary district's storage ponds from the saltwater marshes along the bay. These natural and man-made habitats encourage wildlife. To make things more appealing for the birds, sanitary district personnel have planted willow and acacia trees to

Las Gallinas Wildlife Ponds

encourage nesting on the storage ponds' small islands. They also plant fish in the ponds to provide food for herons, cormorants, and egrets.

The result of all these good works is that the Marin Audubon Society has observed more than 147 species of birds in the reclamation project area. Mallards, coots, and Canada geese nest and raise their young at the marshy pond. Cormorants, snowy and great egrets, night herons, great blue herons, long-eared owls, and red-shouldered hawks show up to fish or hunt for small mammals. Dozens of white pelicans frequent the marsh. Be sure to bring your binoculars for this ride, and stop your bike every now and then to listen to the variety of birdcalls.

When you reach the edge of the bay, turn left and follow Levee Trail for one mile to its end, then turn around and head back. At low tide, watch for shorebirds dipping their beaks in the mud at the edge of San Pablo Bay. On your return trip, be sure to circle around the freshwater ponds near the start of the trail and check out the resident population of ducks and coots.

Options
Skip the .5-mile ride from the McInnis Park playing fields to the reclamation project lands. Instead, park in the lot right next to the sanitary district buildings and start riding from there.

Information and Contact
There is no fee. For more information, contact Las Gallinas Valley Sanitary District, 300 Smith Ranch Road, San Rafael, CA 94901, 415/472-1734, website: www.lgvsd.org.

Directions

From San Francisco, cross Golden Gate Bridge and drive north on U.S. 101 for 11 miles to San Rafael. Take the Lucas Valley Road/Smith Ranch Road exit. Turn right on Smith Ranch Road and drive .75 mile to just before the entrance to John F. McInnis Park and Golf Course. Turn left and park in the pullout by the playing fields. Ride down the road for .5 mile to the entrance to the wildlife pond trails, just to the left of the Las Gallinas Valley Sanitary District buildings. (There is also a small parking lot for a few cars right by the entrance.)

14 SHORELINE TRAIL

China Camp State Park, off U.S. 101 near San Rafael

Total distance: 8.0 miles   **Biking time:** 2.0 hours

Type of trail: Dirt single-track

Type of bike: Mountain bike

Steepness: Mostly level   **Skill level:** Moderate

China Camp State Park is a rare bird in the California State Park system. One of only a handful of state parks that allow mountain bikes on single-track trails, China Camp also holds a scenic location on San Pablo Bay, with blue-water vistas from more than 1,500 shoreline acres. Bikers and hikers generally mind their manners and get along just fine here, although in recent years, the park has seen more bikers and fewer hikers, especially on weekends. China Camp has slowly evolved into a biker's park.

It's also a historic preserve, showcasing the remains of a Chinese shrimp-fishing village from the 19th century, where immigrants netted shrimp from the bay. Don't neglect visiting the historic buildings and experiencing the remarkable history of this area.

Saddle up and begin riding from the campground parking area (or from the entrance kiosk, if you parked along the road). You parallel San Pablo Bay as you ride east, heading for park headquarters in three miles, or China Camp Village and the park's eastern boundary in just over four miles. As the trail leads from the parking area, Jake's Island and Turtle Back appear off to your left, on the edge of the bay. These are shoreline hills that were once islands when bay waters were higher.

Stay on Shoreline Trail, roughly paralleling North San Pedro Road until the path heads inland through an oak and bay forest, then curves around into an open meadow and the park's group picnic area. Your single-track trail becomes a dirt road for a short distance, and you must head left, to-

High views of San Pablo Bay and Rat Rock can be seen from China Camp's trails.

ward the bay, not back into the forest. (You end up on Miwok Fire Trail for about 100 feet.) Then pick up the single-track again, continuing eastward with more bay views all the way to the park ranger's headquarters, a trailer along a service road.

From there, continue your trip on Shoreline Trail to China Camp Village in .7 mile; you have to cross North San Pedro Road. The historic village is worth a close look, so lock up your bike and explore around the pier and four remaining buildings filled with furniture and tools from the day-to-day life of the Chinese shrimp camp. A nice sandy beach to the west of China Camp Village is an excellent place for bird-watching, with great egrets fishing in the marshy edges of the bay.

If you ride to the far eastern boundary of the park (.2 mile farther, back on the south side of San Pedro Road), you rise up and above China Camp Village for a terrific view of Rat Rock (a tiny island) and the pier at China Camp. When you reach the park boundary sign, turn back and retrace your tire treads.

Options
Turn this into a loop trip by riding back to Back Ranch Meadows Campground on paved North San Pedro Road.

Information and Contact
A $6 day-use fee is charged per vehicle if you park at the campground; if you park along the road there is no fee. A trail map is available at park headquarters or the entrance kiosk. For more information, contact China

Camp State Park, 1455A East Francisco Boulevard, San Rafael, CA 94901, 415/456-0766 or 415/898-4362, website: www.parks.ca.gov.

Directions
From San Francisco, cross Golden Gate Bridge and drive north on U.S. 101 for 11 miles to San Rafael. Take the North San Pedro Road exit and drive east for 3.5 miles. Turn right at the sign for Back Ranch Meadows Campground and park in the campground parking lot. Shoreline Trail is on the bay side of the lot, signed as "No Dogs." You can also park along the road near Back Ranch Meadows Campground and begin your ride at the entrance kiosk.

15 TIBURON BIKE PATH
City of Tiburon, off U.S. 101 in Tiburon

Total distance: 4.6 miles   **Biking time:** 1.0 hour

Type of trail: Paved bike trail

Type of bike: Road bike or mountain bike

Steepness: Mostly level   **Skill level:** Easiest

Tiburon Bike Path provides the chance to pedal around some prime real estate along scenic San Francisco Bay—the type of property that 99.9 percent of us would never be able to afford in our wildest dreams. For easy riding with stunning bay views, you can't do much better than this old converted rail trail. The Northwestern Pacific Railroad used to travel this route, providing passenger and freight service from Corte Madera to Tiburon, and from there transporting railroad cars across the bay to San Francisco. The abandoned rail right-of-way was converted to a paved multiuse trail, which is well-loved by bicyclists, in-line skaters, walkers, and baby-carriage pushers. The entire route provides close-up bay views—the water laps within 20 feet of the trail at high tide—and glimpses of Sausalito, Golden Gate Bridge, and Mount Tamalpais.

The path begins in Blackie's Pasture, just outside the town of Tiburon, and ends where the paved, separate-from-traffic trail becomes a bike lane alongside busy Tiburon Boulevard, near the town center. The roadside bike lane is not recommended for families with small children since the traffic can be quite hectic, but the 2.3-mile bike path is safe from cars and an enjoyable ride, making a 4.6-mile round-trip.

The popular Blackie's Pasture trailhead is well known for its large statue of a horse, which was built to commemorate Blackie, who grazed in this

riding alongside the bay on the Tiburon Bike Path

pasture until his salad days ended at the ripe old age of 33, in 1966. Local admirers put up a gravestone, and later this handsome statue, in his memory. The trail leaves the parking lot and heads left, taking you past Richardson Bay Wildlife Ponds. These small bird ponds, managed by Richardson Bay Sanitary District, make good use of Tiburon's sewage. Huge cattails keep the ponds mostly hidden from view, but still you'll see many birds along the trail.

When you're not looking southward over the bay, your attention will often be captured by nearby human entertainment, which includes row-boaters and kayakers on the water, and joggers on the par course that borders part of this trail. You ride past some playing fields dotted with soccer players on weekend afternoons. Next to the fields is the only trail junction, but it's an easy choice: The upper route is closed to bikes.

The bike path offers plenty of opportunity for bird-watching, as long-legged types are perpetually digging in the bay mud for worms. Millions of migratory birds use the mudflats around San Francisco Bay as a safe haven and stopover on their long flights from cold climates to warm, and vice versa.

At the bike trail's end near downtown Tiburon, you can lock up your bike and explore the downtown on foot—there are plenty of restaurants and shops to visit—or just turn around and ride back to Blackie's Pasture.

Options
You can combine this ride with a trip on the Tiburon ferry to Angel Island, then ride your bike on Perimeter Trail (see the following trail de-

scription). Or, where the bike trail ends in downtown Tiburon, continue riding on Main Street as it becomes Paradise Drive, then ride a six-mile loop around the Tiburon peninsula by following Paradise Drive to Trestle Glen Drive (go left here to return to Blackie's Pasture).

Information and Contact

There is no fee. For more information, contact Department of Public Works, City of Tiburon, 1175 Tiburon Boulevard, Tiburon, CA 94920, 415/435-7399, website: www.tiburon.org.

Directions

From San Francisco, cross Golden Gate Bridge and drive north on U.S. 101 for six miles. Take the Tiburon/Highway 131/East Blithedale Avenue exit and drive east for 1.5 miles, then turn right at Blackie's Pasture Road and park in the large parking lot.

16 PERIMETER TRAIL

Angel Island State Park, in San Francisco Bay near Tiburon

Total distance: 5.5 miles   **Biking time:** 1.5 hours

Type of trail: Gravel and paved road

Type of bike: Road bike or mountain bike

Steepness: Rolling terrain   **Skill level:** Moderate

Perimeter Trail at Angel Island State Park is the most spectacular easy bike ride in the entire San Francisco Bay Area. This is high praise considering the Bay Area has plenty of first-rate rides, all perfect 10s in the scenery category. But what sets this trip apart is that Angel Island is an island, so going there adds an element of excitement that no mainland trail can provide. The 360-degree views alone are reason enough to make the journey.

What comes as a surprise to first-time visitors is how fun it is just getting to Angel Island—walking your bike up the ferry gangway, finding a spot on the ferry's top deck or inside the lower deck, smelling the salt air, and watching as you depart the mainland. No matter how crowded the boat is, everybody is always smiling.

In about 25 minutes from Tiburon or 40 minutes from San Francisco, your ferry docks at Ayala Cove. Claim your bike from the holding area, buy a park map at the dock, then ride to the right, past the island's café and mountain bike rental shop. The picnic area ahead will be packed with

Golden Gate Bridge views from Angel Island's Perimeter Trail

people, but ride past them and take the gravel trail on the left, which switchbacks gently up a hill to join the main Perimeter Trail.

Perimeter Trail is a partially paved road, with the pavement deteriorating to gravel and dirt in places. True to its name, the trail loops around the island's perimeter, so you can ride your bike in either direction. The route suggested here goes clockwise. Heading this way, first you gain views of Tiburon, then Richmond Bridge and the northern stretch of the bay. You have to keep analyzing and reanalyzing what you are looking at, because your perspective is so different from the middle of San Francisco Bay than it is from any of its edges. We landlubbers just aren't used to seeing the Bay Area this way.

Obviously, the views change as you move around the island. One of the best vistas is about two-thirds of the way around the loop, at an open stretch where you can see Bay Bridge and Golden Gate Bridge simultaneously, and everything in between and on either side, including Alcatraz, which is directly ahead. You're viewing the whole area from Berkeley to Sausalito, a 180-degree scene. On a clear day, it's stunning.

The wind can blow at Angel Island, and the fog can come in on a moment's notice, so come prepared with an extra jacket, even on sunny days. Usually the trail is windiest on the west side of the island, where you are facing the Golden Gate. The trail also has its only major hill heading in this direction, but the Golden Gate views make the ascent worth the effort.

There are all kinds of historical side trips possible on Perimeter Trail, since Angel Island has a long and varied history as a military outpost, a Russian sea otter hunters' site, and an immigrant detention

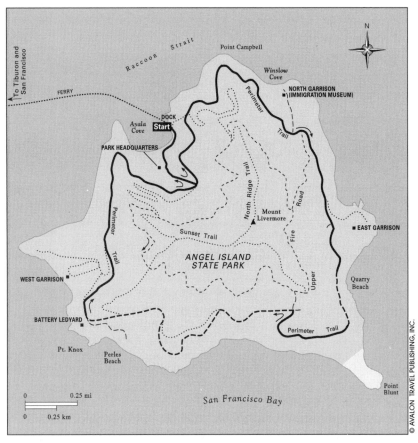

center. The visitors center near the picnic area at Ayala Cove is a treasure trove of information.

And if you forgot to pack along a picnic for your day at Angel Island, you don't have to go hungry. The café near the ferry dock serves surprisingly good food and has an outside deck where you can dine alfresco.

Options

Angel Island offers a second loop trail, "inside" the loop of Perimeter Trail and slightly higher in elevation. Riding both loops makes a 10-mile round-trip; turn right on Fire Road at Angel Island Fire Station. Get a park map for details.

Information and Contact

Phone the ferry companies listed below for current crossing fees; this charge includes your day-use fee at Angel Island State Park. A park map/brochure is available at the ferry landing on the island. For more information, contact Angel Island State Park, 415/435-1915 or 415/898-4362, website: www.angelisland.org.

Directions

Ferry service to Angel Island is available from Tiburon, San Francisco, Oakland/Alameda, and Vallejo. For Tiburon departures, phone Tiburon Ferry at 415/435-2131. For Oakland or Alameda departures, phone East Bay Ferry at 510/522-3300. For San Francisco departures, phone Blue & Gold Fleet at 415/773-1188. For Vallejo departures, phone Baylink at 707/64-FERRY (707/643-3779).

17 LAUREL DELL FIRE ROAD

Marin Municipal Water District, on Mount Tamalpais
near Mill Valley

Total distance: 6.5 miles   **Biking time:** 2.0 hours

Type of trail: Dirt road

Type of bike: Mountain bike

Steepness: Rolling terrain   **Skill level:** Moderate

Mount Tamalpais is known as the birthplace of mountain biking; geologically speaking, it is perfectly shaped for it. Years ago, those first mountain bikers took their old beach cruisers out of their garages, had someone drive them to the top of Mount Tam, then let 'em rip—all the way down to the bottom. Later, the idea came up to add gears to the bikes so they could climb back up the mountain.

Some of us think it was better in the old days, when mountain biking didn't include going "up." Laurel Dell Fire Road is the kind of trail for us. The fire road is a rolling track that laterals across the mountain, never gaining more than 300 feet. It cruises through a fir- and redwood-lined canyon, over a serpentine knoll, and into grassy hillsides just below the west peak of Mount Tam. If you like a ride that has a little bit of everything except a nasty climb, this one's for you.

The first section of trail drops 300 feet immediately, on its way to Laurel Dell, so right away you have a fun downhill through dense forest. Laurel Dell is a meadow and picnic area on your left; in winter, you'll probably have to cross a stream to reach it. In summer, the trail is dry. Next comes a series of short hills, one after another, providing a little interval training for your heart and lungs. Take a break from climbing any time you want and smell the Christmas-tree aroma of the dense fir trees.

Luckily, all the hard work takes place in the shade, and when you finally come out into the open, you're on top of a rocky ridge. Notice the green serpentine (California's state rock) and dry, acidic soil. Riding along the ridge, you get some great views down the north slopes of Mount Tam, especially right after you pass the right turnoff for Barth's Retreat. On clear days, you can make out the Fairfax golf course far below and the blue water of Bon Tempe Lake. The large mountain that stands out far to the north is Mount Saint Helena in Napa County.

Keep riding straight, heading into open meadows, to the end of Laurel Dell Fire Road at Potrero Meadows, where it joins with Lagunitas/Rock Springs Fire Road. Look up just before the junction of the two fire roads to spot the radar station buildings on top of the west peak of Mount Tam at 2,560 feet. If Potrero Meadows doesn't suit your rest-stopping fancy, ride to the left .25 mile on Lagunitas/Rock Springs Fire Road until you come to Rifle Camp, a great little forested picnic area with a restroom nearby. (Legend has it that the camp was named for an old rifle that was dug up there by a dog named Schneider.)

Lagunitas/Rock Springs begins to descend here, leading all the way to the lakes of the Mount Tamalpais watershed, so turn your wheels around and ride back to Laurel Dell Fire Road, then turn right and return the way you came. The way back is mostly downhill, except for a final .5-mile climb from Laurel Dell back to the parking area.

Options

There are numerous great add-on hikes for this trip, including Cataract Trail from Laurel Dell, leading northwest to a series of cascades. Bring a map and a bike lock and explore.

Information and Contact

There is no fee. For more information and a map, contact Marin Municipal Water District, 220 Nellen Avenue, Corte Madera, CA 94925, 415/945-1455, website: www.marinwater.org. Or phone Sky Oaks Ranger Station at 415/945-1181. Because this trip borders Mount Tamalpais State Park, rangers there can also help you. Contact Mount Tamalpais State Park, 801 Panoramic Highway, Mill Valley, CA 94941, 415/388-2070.

Directions

From San Francisco, cross Golden Gate Bridge and drive north on U.S. 101 for four miles. Take the Mill Valley/Stinson Beach/Highway 1 exit and continue straight for one mile to a stoplight at Shoreline Highway (Highway 1).

Turn left on Shoreline Highway and drive 2.5 miles, then turn right on Panoramic Highway. Drive .9 mile to a four-way intersection. Take the middle road (straight), continuing on Panoramic Highway for 4.3 more miles to Pantoll Road. Turn right on Pantoll Road and drive 1.4 miles to its intersection with Ridgecrest Boulevard. Turn left and drive 1.6 miles to a small parking area on the right. Park there and take the trail marked "Laurel Dell."

18 OLD STAGE ROAD: PANTOLL TO WEST POINT INN

Mount Tamalpais State Park, off Panoramic Highway near Mill Valley

Total distance: 4.0 miles   **Biking time:** 1.0 hour

Type of trail: Paved and dirt road

Type of bike: Mountain bike

Steepness: Rolling terrain   **Skill level:** Moderate

Take a ride through Mount Tamalpais history on this out-and-back on Old Stage Road. This view-filled bike ride follows the route used by passengers on the old Mount Tamalpais Scenic Railway, who got off the train to ride the stagecoach to Stinson Beach and Bolinas. The ride's end point is West Point Inn, which is as much a popular stopover for cyclists and hikers today as it was for train and stagecoach passengers 100 years ago.

Begin your ride at the large parking area by Pantoll Ranger Station. After a hasty and cautious crossing of Panoramic Highway, mount your bike and ride on paved Old Stage Road. The pavement soon turns to dirt, and the views of San Francisco and Marin start to amaze you. Old Stage Road's grade is remarkably gradual as it winds through myriad twists and turns.

In less than half an hour, you reach West Point Inn, which was built by the railroad in 1914 as a restaurant and stopover for railway passengers. After the rail days ended, the building came under the jurisdiction of Marin Water District, and it is now leased and operated by a nonprofit group. You can purchase drinks and snacks at the inn, which is open all day on weekends, afternoons only on weekdays (closed on Mondays). Restrooms and picnic areas are available all the time. A small sign on West Point Inn's front door conveys its philosophy: "You may use the parlor if you keep it tidy."

The inn has several bike racks and picnic tables, but the real draw is the great view from its deck, which takes in Mountain Home Inn down below, a wide expanse of the bay, Bay Bridge and Richmond Bridge,

The historic Old Stage Road provides views of Angel Island, southern Marin County, and a peek at the San Francisco skyline.

Larkspur Landing, and San Francisco. West Point Inn also has four cabins and seven rooms for rent, and although there is no electricity, there is propane for light, heat, and refrigeration. Despite the somewhat primitive amenities, the inn is wildly popular, and it is difficult to get a weekend reservation here.

From West Point Inn, you can hike Nora Trail to Matt Davis Trail, which has great views in either direction, or Old Railroad Grade to the east, heading toward Mountain Home Inn.

Options

Combine this ride with the one in the following trail description for an eight-mile round-trip. Make a hard left turn in front of the inn and continue uphill on Old Railroad Grade. Turn right onto the pavement when Old Railroad Grade ends near the East Peak loop.

Information and Contact

A $6 day-use fee is charged per vehicle. A trail map/brochure is available at the ranger station. For more information, contact Mount Tamalpais State Park, 801 Panoramic Highway, Mill Valley, CA 94941, 415/388-2070, website: www.parks.ca.gov. For information about West Point Inn, phone 415/388-9955.

Directions

From San Francisco, cross Golden Gate Bridge and drive north on U.S. 101 for four miles. Take the Mill Valley/Stinson Beach/Highway 1 exit and continue straight for one mile to a stoplight at Shoreline Highway (Highway 1). Turn left on Shoreline Highway and drive 2.5 miles, then turn right on Panoramic Highway. Drive .9 mile to a junction of roads. Continue straight 4.3 miles farther to Pantoll Ranger Station and the parking lot on the left. You must walk your bike across Panoramic Highway to access the start of Old Stage Road.

19 OLD RAILROAD GRADE: EAST PEAK TO WEST POINT INN

Mount Tamalpais State Park, off Panoramic
Highway near Mill Valley

Total distance: 4.0 miles   **Biking time:** 1.0 hour

Type of trail: Dirt road

Type of bike: Mountain bike

Steepness: Steep sections   **Skill level:** Moderate

If you've heard the war stories about the Old Railroad Grade on Mount Tamalpais, you may approach the trail with some trepidation. If you've been told that Old Railroad Grade is long, rocky, and steep, you've been told the truth. But the key is to ride only a section of it, not the whole eight miles from the bottom of the mountain to the top. The best place to start is at the summit, the 2,571-foot East Peak of Mount Tam. Since you are going for a bike ride that is famous for its spectacular views, you might as well begin with a doozy.

At the parking area, take a look around before you mount your bike. From near the mountaintop visitors center, views spread east across the bay and south to San Francisco and its bridges. All of Marin County and San Francisco stretches out below you. If you want to go even higher and see even more, hike up the stairs to the closed fire lookout perched above the visitors center, or walk the one-mile Verna Dunshee Trail, which loops around the peak. Bike racks, picnic tables, and restrooms—all the bicyclist's basic necessities—are located by the visitors center.

When you've been adequately awed by the view, mount your bike and ride out of the parking lot, picking up Old Railroad Grade on the left side of East Ridgecrest Boulevard, just past the paved loop at East Peak. (You

Mountain bikers use historic West Point Inn as a rest stop on the ascent of Mount Tamalpais.

passed the trail on your way in.) Old Railroad Grade is not your average rail trail; it was part of Mount Tamalpais Scenic Railway, which was known as the "Crookedest Railroad in the World," with 281 turns and curves. Even with all those switchbacks, the trail is as steep as a ski slope in many spots. It's also somewhat rough and rocky, so prepare to brake a lot and keep your speed down, or risk losing your balance on the rocky surface. This is a great place to practice your downhill riding skills. Stay alert for people coming the other way around the curves, as the route is popular with bikers, and if you have kids with you, be sure they stay on the inside track, hugging the mountain. The outside track has some steep and dramatic drop-offs.

You won't pedal at all on the short, sweet trip down to West Point Inn, but that means the trip uphill will be a lot more time- and energy-consuming. Enjoy the free ride while you have it. For more information on your destination at West Point Inn, see the previous trail description.

Options
Combine this ride with the previous ride, continuing from West Point Inn to Pantoll Ranger Station.

Information and Contact
A $6 day-use fee is charged per vehicle. A trail map/brochure is available at the visitors center. For more information, contact Mount Tamalpais

State Park, 801 Panoramic Highway, Mill Valley, CA 94941, 415/388-2070, website: www.parks.ca.gov.

Directions

From San Francisco, cross Golden Gate Bridge and drive north on U.S. 101 for four miles. Take the Mill Valley/Stinson Beach/Highway 1 exit and continue straight for one mile to a stoplight at Shoreline Highway (Highway 1). Turn left on Shoreline Highway and drive 2.5 miles, then turn right on Panoramic Highway. Drive .9 mile to a four-way intersection. Take the middle road (straight), continuing on Panoramic Highway for 4.3 more miles to Pantoll Road. Turn right on Pantoll Road and drive 1.4 miles to its intersection with Ridgecrest Boulevard. Turn right on Ridgecrest Boulevard and drive 2.9 miles to the East Peak parking area. Ride your bike out of the parking lot loop and pick up Old Railroad Grade on the left.

20 TENNESSEE VALLEY TRAIL

Golden Gate National Recreation Area,
off U.S. 101 near Mill Valley

Total distance: 4.0 miles   **Biking time:** 1.5 hours

Type of trail: Paved and dirt road

Type of bike: Mountain bike

Steepness: Rolling terrain   **Skill level:** Easiest

On weekends, the Tennessee Valley Trailhead in Mill Valley is busier than a shopping mall at Christmas. The parking lot is filled with a mix of bikers, walkers, and runners, all wanting to get a piece of the scenery at Tennessee Valley Beach and/or its surrounding ridges and hillsides.

And no wonder; there's something for everyone here. Biking families and novice riders enjoy the easy, wide dirt road that rolls gently out to Tennessee Beach, a black-gravel pocket beach framed by jagged bluffs on both sides. The path is amazingly easy and scenic. Bring a picnic and a bike lock (a bike rack is provided) for the picturesque beach. And for the best experience, visit here on a weekday, or very early in the morning on weekends, before the crowds arrive.

The trail begins as a paved route by Miwok Stables, where horses can be rented and riding lessons are held. Shortly, the pavement forks left and the main trail continues straight as a wide dirt road. The mostly level path follows a creekbed between tall grassy ridges lined with coastal chaparral. Rabbits, deer, and bobcats are often seen in the early morning. Your destination

Tennessee Valley Beach, Golden Gate National Recreation Area

is two miles away at Tennessee Cove. The cove, beach, and trail are all named for the 1853 steamship *Tennessee,* which wrecked in dense fog on its way to San Francisco while carrying cargo, mail, and 600 passengers. Fortunately, all lives were saved.

While Tennessee Beach is the trail's prime attraction, a bird-filled, blue lagoon along the way is a close runner-up. The trail forks shortly before the lagoon; bikers must stay on the wide road to the right while hikers take the single-track to the left. The trails rejoin .5 mile later as they near Tennessee Beach.

At the beach, rolling waves crash on dark sands, pelicans soar overhead, and an offshore rock is battered by breakers. Although Tennessee Beach is a great spot for surf-watching, don't think about swimming here, even on the rare days when the air and sun are warm enough to tempt you. The surf is extremely treacherous. If you tire of reposing on the beach and wish to see the world from a pelican's perspective, a short trail leads up the northwestern bluff nearly 200 feet to an overlook at an old military bunker.

The ride back has a bit more climb to it, including one pretty good hill that comes as a surprise after all the level pedaling you've been doing. Still, six-year-olds can manage it, although the tricycle set often dismounts and walks on the way home.

Options

For more ambitious riders, several mountain biking loops are possible from Tennessee Valley Trailhead. For a 5.3-mile loop, follow Tennessee Valley Trail to .5 mile before the beach, then make a short but strenuous climb up Coastal Trail. At the summit, catch your breath and enjoy the views, then climb more gently on Coyote Ridge Trail. A final right turn and a downhill stint on Miwok Trail bring you back to the trailhead. Note that this loop is substantially more challenging than the out-and-back on Tennessee Valley Trail.

Information and Contact

There is no fee. A free map/brochure is available by contacting Golden Gate National Recreation Area, Building 1056, Fort Cronkhite, Sausalito, CA 94965, 415/331-1540, website: www.nps.gov/goga.

Directions

From San Francisco, cross Golden Gate Bridge and drive north on U.S. 101 for four miles. Take the Mill Valley/Stinson Beach/Highway 1 exit and continue straight for .6 mile to Tennessee Valley Road on the left. Turn left and drive two miles to the trailhead.

21 MILL VALLEY/SAUSALITO BIKE PATH

Marin County Parks, off U.S. 101 in Mill Valley and Sausalito

Total distance: 7.0 miles   **Biking time:** 1.5 hours

Type of trail: Paved bike trail

Type of bike: Road bike or mountain bike

Steepness: Mostly level   **Skill level:** Easiest

People love paved bike paths that are separated from car traffic. The better the trail's scenery, the more people love it. That is why Mill Valley/Sausalito Bike Path is packed with people on weekend afternoons, while other Marin County bike paths see comparatively little use. If you are choosing between riding along the bay's tidal waters or riding around a shopping center and freeway, it's not a difficult choice.

Mill Valley/Sausalito Bike Path gives you a good tour of the area, starting from Sycamore Park near downtown Mill Valley and running all the way into central Sausalito. Sycamore Park is like a train depot for bikes, with trails running in three directions and bikers milling about. Although there are three trail options here, for recreation purposes there is really only one way to go, which is south to Sausalito.

So southward we go, paralleling the edge of Bothin Marsh and Richardson Bay for three-plus miles to Harbor Drive in Sausalito. Unfortunately, the trail also parallels U.S. 101 for a mile of the route near Manzanita

riding past the mud flats during low tide on the Mill Valley/ Sausalito Bike Path

Junction in Marin City, but keep your eyes on the bay to your left and don't look at the freeway over your right shoulder. You ride underneath the freeway near Manzanita Junction.

Despite how built-up this urban corridor is, nature manages to thrive on the edges of the bay. During a low tide, you will view the mudflats close up. Bird-watching is often excellent. Two wooden bridges carry the trail across sections of the marsh, where you can see egrets, herons, and sandpipers by the dozens. During a high tide, the bay water is pretty and blue, but there are fewer birds. Mount Tamalpais is behind you; you get a fine view of its outline on your return trip.

Just before Manzanita Junction, there is one paved turnoff from the trail, which leads to the right toward Tennessee Valley Road and Tamalpais Junction. Some riders use this route to access the Tam Junction neighborhood, or to continue biking on Tennessee Valley Road and connect to dirt trails there. Continue straight instead. The main part of the bike path ends in 1.5 miles at Harbor Drive, near the bike store in Sausalito and Waldo Point Harbor. If you wish, you can keep riding into town along sidewalks and side roads.

Options
Bikers who don't mind riding with auto traffic can combine this ride with a trip across Golden Gate Bridge, by following Bridgeway Avenue through Sausalito and to the base of the bridge. The road turns into Second Street,

then South Street, climbing uphill. At the top of the hill, the road turns right and becomes Alexander Drive, which leads to the bridge.

Information and Contact
There is no fee. For more information, contact Marin County Open Space District, 3501 Civic Center Drive, Room 415, San Rafael, CA 94903, 415/499-6387, website: www.marinopenspace.org.

Directions
From San Francisco, cross Golden Gate Bridge and drive north on U.S. 101 for six miles. Take the Tiburon/Highway 131/East Blithedale Avenue exit, then turn left and drive west on East Blithedale. Turn left on Camino Alto and then left again on Sycamore Avenue. Follow Sycamore Avenue to its end at the park.

22 POINT PINOLE ROAD & BAY VIEW TRAIL
Point Pinole Regional Shoreline, off I-80 near Richmond

Total distance: 6.0 miles   **Biking time:** 2.0 hours

Type of trail: Dirt double-track and paved bike trail

Type of bike: Road bike or mountain bike

Steepness: Rolling terrain   **Skill level:** Easiest

Point Pinole Regional Shoreline is a little park with a big heart, a place of tranquility not far from the urban bustle of the East Bay. Few visitors other than avid anglers and dog walkers make the trip to the tip of Point Pinole, but those who do are surprised at how much their four-dollar park admission can buy. In addition to inspiring bay views, a fascinating history, and good pier fishing, the park offers volleyball courts, picnic areas, and more than 12 miles of winding dirt trails suitable for mountain biking. A paved bike trail provides options for those on skinny tires.

Don't be put off by the drive into the park. Point Pinole Regional Shoreline has some odd neighbors, including Chevron's oil refineries and a juvenile detention center. The Southern Pacific Railroad runs right along the park boundary. But once you're inside the gates of Point Pinole, all is peaceful. You won't find much in the way of crowds at this park, even on weekends.

You will find plenty of scenery. The main draws are the wide-open bay views, which you get from just about everywhere in the park. Skinny-tire riders can ride up and back on the paved bike path, checking out the bay views first over their left shoulder and then over their right shoulder. The path makes a straight shot right up the narrow peninsula to a .25-mile-long pier that juts out into the bay. You can ride your bike to the very end of the pier, then pause for a moment to smell the salty air and admire the views of Mount Diablo on your right and Mount Tamalpais on your left. Looking back toward the shoreline from the end of the pier, you'll see rugged cliffs that rise 100 feet above the bay. Point Pinole is the only place on this side of the bay that has shoreline cliffs; everywhere else, the water's edge is surrounded by flatlands.

© ANN MARIE BROWN

bay views from the trail at Point Pinole Regional Shoreline

Fat-tire riders should start out on the paved path as well, then veer off on any of several double-track dirt trails. Bay View Trail is the best of the lot, leading along the western edge of the peninsula with great views of Mount Tamalpais, Richmond Bridge, and the East and West Brothers Islands. Marsh Trail is another favorite, providing views to the north of Napa, San Pablo Bay, and Carquinez Bridge. Most of the park's landscape is made up of grasslands and eucalyptus groves, but there is also a large salt marsh, which Marsh Trail borders.

Start riding from the parking lot, picking up the paved bike trail near the ranger kiosk. At a small mound planted with flowers, a plaque marks the site of Giant Powder Company (1892–1960). When terrible explosions ruined its San Francisco and Berkeley factories, Giant Powder moved to remote Point Pinole to manufacture dynamite. It built a thriving company town and railroad here.

Ride left, over a railroad bridge and through a picnic area planted with palm trees and eucalyptus (a funny-looking combination). Beyond the volleyball courts and playing fields, you're on your way to more remote land as you ride along the peninsula's length. Pass a paved loop with a bus shelter; shuttle buses ride this route every 30 minutes. Continue out to the pier's end, where there are Plexiglas shelters for anglers to hide behind when the wind howls.

Road bikers should just turn around at the pier and ride back to the parking area, but mountain bikers can return to just north of the shuttle bus stop and pick up Bay View Trail, leading west across the bluffs for a longer return loop. The wide dirt trail skirts the edge of Point Pinole's peninsula and supplies continual views of San Pablo Bay. To the southwest, plumes of gas and steam rise from Chevron's oil refineries. To the west, Mount Tamalpais looms over Marin County. In the foreground are miles of open bay water, interrupted only by the San Rafael–Richmond Bridge and the East and West Brothers Islands. A few duck blinds dot the shoreline. Seabirds gather on the mudflats during low tide.

Another way to loop back is to pick up Marsh Trail from just south of the shuttle bus stop. Pedal along the edge of Whittell Marsh and connect to Cook's Point Trail to return. The Bay View loop and the Marsh Trail loop, plus the paved out-and-back trail, add up to about six miles.

Options
Ride just the paved trail out to the pier for a three-mile round-trip. Be sure to go to the end of the pier to check out the great views.

Information and Contact
A $4 entrance fee is charged per vehicle. A free map is available at the entrance kiosk. For more information, contact East Bay Regional Park District, 2950 Peralta Oaks Court, P.O. Box 5381, Oakland, CA 94605-0381, 510/237-6896, 510/562-7275, or 510/635-0135, website: www.ebparks.org.

Directions
From I-80 in Richmond, take the Hilltop Drive exit west. Turn right on San Pablo Avenue, then left on Richmond Parkway. Follow Richmond Parkway to the Giant Highway exit. Turn right and drive .75 mile to the park entrance on the left.

Or, from U.S. 101 in Marin, take San Rafael–Richmond Bridge east (I-580), then take the first exit east of the bridge, for Castro Street and Richmond Parkway. Drive 4.3 miles on Richmond Parkway to the Giant Highway exit. Take the exit and drive .5 mile, then turn right on Giant Highway. Drive .75 mile to the park entrance on the left.

23 WILDCAT CREEK TRAIL

Wildcat Canyon Regional Park, off I-80 near Richmond

Total distance: 8.0 miles

Biking time: 2.0 hours

Type of trail: Dirt double-track

Type of bike: Mountain bike

Steepness: Rolling terrain

Skill level: Easiest

Wildcat Canyon Regional Park is an oasis of wild land amid urban sprawl, a treasure of open space and a safe haven for wildlife and plant life. It is well-loved but not overused by its neighbors, and it offers East Bay residents 10 miles of mostly dirt trails for mountain bike riding, horseback riding, dog walking, and exploring. While hikers and hill-loving mountain bikers may take to the higher ridges of the park for stunning East Bay views, easy-biking enthusiasts can have a great morning or afternoon riding Wildcat Creek Trail along the park's nearly level canyon.

Bunny-rabbit fans, take note: You are likely to see literally hundreds of furry hoppers on this trail, especially if you ride in the morning before the sun gets too hot. They scurry across the trail as you round almost every curve. Birdlife is plentiful too.

But the thing you will notice the most, the one natural element that really stands out, is the huge collection of cardoon thistle plants that line the grasslands. These giant, nonnative thistles-on-steroids are everywhere, pok-

Eucalyptus trees and grasslands border the Wildcat Creek Trail.

ing up through the tall grass. Entire armies of them stand in loose formations on the hillsides.

From the parking lot, the first mile of Wildcat Creek Trail alternates as pavement and dirt, then it becomes dirt only. The trail is part of an old roadbed that was abandoned because it lies along an earthquake fault and didn't hold up well against the forces of entropy. Wildcat Creek's canyon is forested on one side and has open hillsides on the other. Creekside trees include alders, willows, and California bays. The hillsides are a mix of native and nonnative grasses, studded with those ubiquitous thistles.

The ride is an easy roller coaster, with only one big hill by the trail spur to Rifle Range Road. You come around the corner and you think, oh boy, do I have to climb that (?!), but it's not as bad as it looks. Just sweat it out and keep pedaling until you come to Tilden Nature Area. The trail becomes even smoother here, and the dirt surface more hard-packed. A small pond shows up on your right, as well as several trail spurs that are clearly marked "No Bikes."

Ride all the way through the nature area to the parking lot just before the visitors center. Lock up your bike there or walk it through the visitors center yard, where there is a miniature farm. If you ever wanted to pet a cow, here's your chance. They even have pony rides. When you've seen enough, turn around and ride back.

Options
If you're up for some hill climbing, connect this trail to the paved Nimitz Way Bike Trail (see the following trail description) by taking either the Havey Canyon Trail or Conlon Trail cutoff. Both are opposite Rifle Range Road, and both involve a challenging climb to gain the ridge.

Information and Contact
There is no fee. A free map is available at the trailhead. For more information, contact East Bay Regional Park District, 2950 Peralta Oaks Court, P.O. Box 5381, Oakland, CA 94605-0381, 510/635-0135 or 510/562-7275, website: www.ebparks.org.

Directions
From I-80 heading north in Richmond, take the Amador/Solano exit and drive three blocks east on Amador. Turn right on McBryde Avenue and drive .5 mile to the entrance to Wildcat Canyon Regional Park. (Bear left where the road forks.) The trail begins on the far side of the parking lot and is paved at the start. (Heading south on I-80, take the McBryde Avenue exit and go east.)

24 NIMITZ WAY BIKE TRAIL

Tilden Regional Park, off Highway 24 near Berkeley

Total distance: 7.5 miles   **Biking time:** 1.5 hours

Type of trail: Paved bike trail

Type of bike: Road bike or mountain bike

Steepness: Rolling terrain   **Skill level:** Easiest

It's a rare bike trail that can bridge the philosophical gap between fat-tire riders and skinny-tire riders, a trail that all kinds of bikers love equally. Nimitz Way, a paved bike route along the tip-top of San Pablo Ridge, gives skinny-tire riders the wildland experience of mountain biking, and a feeling of being far away from the suburbs below. And the trail gives fat-tire riders the cheap and easy thrill of gliding along on pavement while they cruise up and down the ridge.

Start at the well-marked gate by the Inspiration Point parking lot, a regular Bike City on weekends. This entire region is well loved for biking, with dozens of possible rides starting from one staging area. Its popularity is no surprise—if you think the view is good from Inspiration Point, wait till you head out on the trail. The vistas keep changing as you pedal: There's San Pablo Reservoir, and behind it Briones Reservoir, plus looming Mount Diablo—all on your right. Then there's San Francisco Bay, Golden Gate Bridge, and Angel Island on your left. At every turn in the trail, over every hill, you get a slightly different twist on the view: Richmond Bridge drops into sight, the Gold Coast comes into frame up ahead, then San Francisco disappears and the Brothers Islands come into view. Suddenly, Napa and Carquinez Strait show up to the north. And so it goes.

You just cruise along on pavement, stopping when you want to enjoy the sights from your top-of-the-ridge perch. Benches sit at strategic points along the trail. They are dedicated to bygone Nimitz-lovers whose names are engraved on tiny plaques.

You confront only one steep hill, right before the pavement ends at 3.8 miles; it will make you say a hearty hello to your cardiovascular system. Where the paved trail ends, skinny-tire riders must turn around and head back, but mountain bikers can continue riding on the dirt trail, which leads through a cattle gate and along San Pablo Ridge 1.5 miles more to the end of San Pablo Ridge Trail in Wildcat Canyon Regional Park. Then ride back or connect to other trails there.

Don't forget to bring along a jacket, even on warm days, because it can be quite windy on top of the ridge. And, as always, be prepared to share the trail with hikers and lots of other bikers. Keep your speed down, and call out when you need to pass.

Options
If you have a mountain bike, continue on dirt on San Pablo Ridge Trail. You can ride three miles out and back or make a five-mile loop back to the pavement by riding along San Pablo Ridge, turning left on Belgum Trail, left again on Wildcat Creek Trail, then left on Conlon Trail to head back to Nimitz Way. This involves some sizable ascents and descents.

Information and Contact
There is no fee. A free map is available at the trailhead. For more information, contact East Bay Regional Park District, 2950 Peralta Oaks Court, P.O. Box 5381, Oakland, CA 94605-0381, 510/635-0135 or 510/562-7275, website: www.ebparks.org. Or phone Tilden Regional Park at 510/544-2711.

Directions
From I-580 in Oakland, take Highway 24 east. Go through the Caldecott Tunnel and exit at Orinda. Turn left on Camino Pablo. Drive north for two miles, then turn left on Wildcat Canyon Road. Drive 2.4 miles to the Inspiration Point parking lot. The trail begins at the far edge of the parking lot.

25 LAFAYETTE RESERVOIR
East Bay Municipal Utility District, off Highway 24 near Lafayette

Total distance: 3.0 miles   **Biking time:** 1.0 hour

Type of trail: Paved bike trail

Type of bike: Road bike or mountain bike

Steepness: Mostly level   **Skill level:** Easiest

Lafayette Reservoir is like San Pablo Reservoir's kid brother. It is often overshadowed by the larger, older reservoir's reputation for excellent boating and fishing. But both of these East Bay watershed lakes are open to many kinds of recreation, including biking on paved trails along their edges. The foothill scenery at both lakes makes the riding pleasant and pastoral, with plenty of wildlife to watch and the option of bringing along your spinning rod to fish from shore.

But a real downer at San Pablo Reservoir is that every year November–mid-February, the place is closed down. That's usually just about the

Lafayette Reservoir

time you want a paved trail to ride on, when all the dirt trails in the Bay Area have turned to mud. So that's also about the time that people get around to appreciating Lafayette Reservoir, which stays open year-round and, unlike San Pablo, is rarely overcrowded.

The managers at Lafayette have done several things right. Since the paved bike trail around the lake is short—just a three-mile loop—they instituted a rule that makes it safe for all kinds of trail users. Biking is permitted only on Tuesday and Thursday afternoons, from noon until closing at dusk, and on Sunday mornings, from opening (about 7 A.M., but the time varies with the season) until 11 A.M.

Visiting here on a Sunday morning is just about perfect. You can ride the loop one or more times, then take your family out on the lake in a rental pedal boat or rowboat before the afternoon crowds show up. In summer, the reservoir is open until 8:30 P.M. on Tuesdays and Thursdays, perfect for an after-work ride.

The bike trail begins at the parking area over the dam, and you can ride in either direction. The south and east edges of the lake are the most undeveloped and offer pleasant riding through acres of grasslands and a mixed forest, plus plentiful lake views interrupted only by the occasional picnic area or fishing dock. Several hiking trails branch off from the paved trail, but these are closed to bikes.

The best time to visit Lafayette Reservoir is unquestionably in winter and spring, when the air is cool, the hillsides are green, and the wildflowers pop out among the grasses.

Options

Bring a bike lock with you so you can sample some of Lafayette Reservoir's hiking trails, which rise into the hills above the edge of the lake.

Information and Contact

A $6 fee is charged per vehicle for all-day entrance to the park, or you can park in metered parking spots for $1 per hour (quarters only, two-hour limit). A free map is available at the visitors center. For more information, contact Lafayette Reservoir at 925/284-9669. Or contact East Bay Municipal Utility District, P.O. Box 24055, Oakland, CA 94623, 510/287-0407, website: www.ebmud.com/services/recreation.

Directions

From I-580 in Oakland, take Highway 24 east toward Walnut Creek. Go through the Caldecott Tunnel and exit at Acalanes Road/Mount Diablo Boulevard. Veer right, then continue straight on Mount Diablo Boulevard for one mile to the reservoir entrance on the right. Drive up the hill and park on top of the dam. Start riding near the restrooms, to the right of the metered parking spots.

26 LAFAYETTE-MORAGA REGIONAL TRAIL

East Bay Regional Park District, off Highway 24 near Lafayette/Moraga

Total distance: 15.5 miles   **Biking time:** 2.5 hours

Type of trail: Paved bike trail

Type of bike: Road bike or mountain bike

Steepness: Mostly level   **Skill level:** Easiest

When a lot of people live together in a small space, and when suburbs grow so large that they connect town to town without any buffer of open land in between, one of the smartest things that city planners can do is open up spaces where folks can get a little fresh air and sunshine—places that are protected from cars, traffic, and urban noise. Lafayette-Moraga Trail is such a place, an open corridor between two East Bay cities on which all users under their own power—whether that means a bicycle, in-line skates, hiking boots, or a wheelchair—are welcome.

The Lafayette-Moraga Regional Trail was opened in 1976 as one of America's first 500 converted rail trails.

Riding here is not exactly a trip to the wilderness, but you will see plenty of deciduous trees on the first half of the trip, and plenty of foothills and grasslands on the second half. Squirrels are omnipresent along the trail—not plain old Bay Area gray squirrels, but cute and chubby red squirrels with shiny, rust-colored coats. We saw a few busily burying nuts in flower beds. Their genetic instinct was preparing them for the long, hard, snowbound winter that will never come to sunny Moraga.

A paved-over portion of the old San Francisco–Sacramento Railroad, Lafayette-Moraga Trail is bordered by suburban neighborhoods and open-space lands. The trail retains some of its history, proudly displaying signs of its railroad past with white train-crossing markers at every intersection in the first few miles out of Lafayette.

The trail is well used and well loved by East Bay residents, despite the fact that it crosses many roads. Fortunately, only one of them is subject to much serious auto traffic; it is near the trail's midpoint at Lafayette Community Center, where a spur trail goes straight ahead to the center. You should continue right, crossing St. Mary's Road. Be very careful as you cross, because the cars come quickly around a curve.

After Lafayette Community Center your surroundings become more rural, you see less of parallel St. Mary's Road, and you leave most of the houses behind. The trail passes St. Mary's College, with its pretty white church tower and green playing fields. Shortly thereafter you come to

Moraga Commons, a town park with a play area, restrooms, par course, and the like. The park also has an interesting waterfall sculpture and a sign that notes that Lafayette-Moraga Trail was opened in 1976 and dedicated in 1992 as one of America's first 500 rail trails.

The final section of trail leads out to the country, from Moraga Commons to Valle Vista Staging Area on Canyon Road. At Valle Vista, several East Bay Municipal Utility District trails lead off in all directions, but bikes are not permitted on these routes, so turn your wheels around.

Options

Ride just to Moraga Commons, where kids can take a break in the play area, then turn around. This is a 12-mile round-trip, requiring about 1.5 hours to ride.

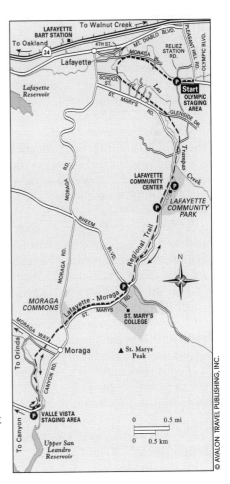

Information and Contact

There is no fee. A free map is available at Moraga Commons or Lafayette Community Center. For more information, contact East Bay Regional Park District, 2950 Peralta Oaks Court, P.O. Box 5381, Oakland, CA 94605-0381, 510/562-PARK or 510/635-0135, website: www.ebparks.org.

Directions

From I-580 in Oakland, take Highway 24 east toward Walnut Creek. Go through the Caldecott Tunnel and take the Pleasant Hill Road exit south. Drive .7 mile to Olympic Boulevard. Turn right on Olympic Boulevard; the parking lot is on your right in about 50 yards. Another parking area lies shortly beyond it.

27 IRON HORSE REGIONAL TRAIL TO DANVILLE

East Bay Regional Park District, off I-680 near Walnut Creek/Danville

Total distance: 10.0 miles   **Biking time:** 1.5 hours

Type of trail: Paved bike trail

Type of bike: Road bike or mountain bike

Steepness: Mostly level   **Skill level:** Easiest

The East San Francisco Bay Area has an abundance of paved bike paths, which is a great boon for its cities and citizens, but sadly, many of them leave something to be desired in the aesthetics department. Contra Costa Canal Trail, Alameda Creek Trail, and Iron Horse Regional Trail, for example, are all easily accessible trails that extend more than 10 miles one-way, but they are truly suburban pathways. The landscape that surrounds them is a far cry from the great outdoors. Ride the wrong stretch of these trails and you can find yourself in the middle of a huge industrial complex, or underneath a freeway cloverleaf, or in a residential neighborhood where you have to cross streets every two minutes. Your trip can feel more like work than a weekend excursion.

So, before you ride, get informed. Here's the scoop on one of the most popular East Bay paved bike trails, San Ramon Valley Iron Horse Regional Trail: At present, it runs 12.7 miles between Concord and Dublin, but someday it will run all the way from Livermore to Suisun Bay, a distance of 33 miles. Iron Horse Trail is a trail-in-progress, following the route of the 1891 Southern Pacific Railroad. When the railroad was abandoned in 1977, various citizen and government groups worked together to preserve the right-of-way and develop a recreational trail.

The trail is as much as 75 feet wide in places (you could drive a tank on it—maybe two tanks side by side), and there are stretches without a single tree or bush in sight. Unless you are a big fan of concrete and corporate business parks, it's best to avoid much of this trail, unless you are commuting and need to get somewhere. Instead of riding the whole thing, stick to the scenic five-mile stretch from Walnut Creek to Danville. The remaining seven miles from Danville to San Ramon are straight as an arrow, shadeless, often too hot, and as dull as dishwater.

But from Walnut Creek to Danville, the ride is a perfect family bicycling jaunt. On a nice Sunday, you'll see more bikes pulling baby trailers on this trail than probably anywhere else in the Bay Area, plus the usual collection of dog walkers, in-line skaters, and kids on tricycles being closely followed by their parents.

The trail begins officially at Newell and Broadway Avenues in Walnut Creek, although many people start .5 mile farther at the Park and Ride at Rudgear Road and I-680, or on any of the little side streets that cut off Danville Boulevard, which runs parallel to the trail. The first mile has far too many road intersections to cross, but at least they're quiet residential streets with little car traffic. After passing through the Alamo Square shopping area at 2.5 miles, the trail gets noticeably more scenic. The landscape becomes greener and shadier as you draw closer to the town of Danville. A city parking lot at Prospect Avenue is your destination. You can lock up your bike here and explore the cute old railroad town.

Beyond Prospect Avenue, Iron Horse Trail crosses Danville Boulevard (in a somewhat treacherous manner), passes under I-680 (in a rather ugly manner), then continues south to Pine Valley Road in San Ramon, with endless vistas of concrete buildings. This is why Prospect Avenue in Danville is a great turnaround point, with many shops in the town center open for brunch, coffee, or snacks.

Options
You can ride a full 25 miles out and back on this trail, traveling all the way from Walnut Creek to San Ramon, but don't expect to be awed by the scenery.

Information and Contact
There is no fee. A free map is available by contacting East Bay Regional Park District, 2950 Peralta Oaks Court, P.O. Box 5381, Oakland, CA 94605-0381, 510/562-PARK or 510/635-0135, website: www.ebparks.org.

Directions
From I-680 in Danville, take the Rudgear Road exit and park at either the Park and Ride lot (east side of the freeway) or the Staging Area (west side). Note that Danville Boulevard runs parallel to the bike path. At any of the streets that intersect Danville Boulevard between Rudgear Road and Danville, you can drive one block west and reach the bike path. Along most of these streets there is parking for a few cars right next to the bike trail.

28 EASTERN CONTRA COSTA REGIONAL TRAILS

East Bay Regional Park District, off Highway 4 near Antioch

Total distance: 17.0 miles   **Biking time:** 2.5 hours

Type of trail: Paved bike trail

Type of bike: Road bike or mountain bike

Steepness: Mostly level   **Skill level:** Easiest

East Bay Regional Park District deserves high praise and loud applause for the number of paved multiuse trails it has made available for public use. Many of its trails serve as important corridors for bicycle-riding commuters. All of them are heavily used by recreationists who seek a safe place to ride bikes, push baby strollers, jog, walk dogs, and so on.

Marsh Creek Regional Trail is no exception. It's the hub of a system of trails that runs through eastern Contra Costa County. Currently, Marsh Creek Trail runs 6.5 miles from the town of Oakley to Creekside Park in Brentwood. In Oakley, it connects with Big Break Regional Trail, which runs 2.5 miles along the Big Break shoreline of the San Joaquin Delta. At Cypress Road in Oakley, Marsh Creek Trail also connects with a section of 15-mile-long Delta De Anza Regional Trail. Still under construction, the latter path will someday make most of Contra Costa County accessible by paved multiuse trail, running a full 25 miles across the county.

But the thorough coverage and usefulness of the trails in eastern Contra Costa County are not their only selling points. If you stick to Marsh Creek Trail and Big Break Trail, the paved paths are also surprisingly scenic and interesting. Pedal both trails out and back for a 17-mile round-trip that feels like a ride in the country.

You can start your trip at one of several points. If you don't live in the area, you might want to begin near the junction of Highway 4 and Cypress Road in Oakley, where Delta De Anza Regional Trail and Marsh Creek Regional Trail intersect. Ride north along Marsh Creek Trail, heading for the San Joaquin Delta and Big Break Regional Trail. The path leads through farmlands, heading almost to the wave-lapped delta's edge. You are likely to see birds and other wildlife; we saw hundreds of coots, a great blue heron, and numerous ground squirrels. Although the trail never quite touches the shoreline, you ride close enough to sense it and smell it. Where Big Break Trail ends rather abruptly in a suburban neighborhood, simply turn around and ride back to join Marsh Creek Trail.

Marsh Creek Trail, Eastern Contra Costa Regional Trails

To continue on your trek, cross Cypress Road at the traffic light (near where you parked your car), then stay on Marsh Creek Trail all the way to Brentwood. Marsh Creek flows with a surprising amount of water, especially in winter and spring, and it attracts white egrets by the dozens. They take their fishing seriously. South of Cypress Road, the Marsh Creek Trail crosses only a few roads; the intersections are mostly in quiet neighborhoods. (Look before you cross.) For the most part, the trail makes a pleasant path through peaceful farmlands and suburbs.

Options

Ride a section of Delta De Anza Regional Trail as well. The trail currently runs just over 15 miles, heading west from Oakley.

Information and Contact

There is no fee. Free trail maps are available at signposts along the trail. For more information, contact East Bay Regional Park District, 2950 Peralta Oaks Court, P.O. Box 5381, Oakland, CA 94605-0381, 510/562-PARK or 510/635-0135, website: www.ebparks.org. Or phone East Contra Costa County Regional Trails Office at 925/625-5479.

Directions

From Antioch, take Highway 4 east for five miles toward Oakley (Highway 4 becomes Main Street). In Oakley, turn left on Cypress Road. There is a parking pullout on the left, next to the bike trail.

29 ROUND VALLEY REGIONAL PRESERVE

East Bay Regional Park District, off I-580 near Livermore

Total distance: 10.8 miles | **Biking time:** 2.0 hours

Type of trail: Dirt double-track

Type of bike: Mountain bike

Steepness: Rolling terrain | **Skill level:** Moderate

If you ever start to feel like the East Bay is too crowded, too congested, and has too much concrete, take a trip a little farther east to the back side of Mount Diablo. Here, on the far eastern edge of the San Francisco Bay Area, just before the bay's geography converges with that of the San Joaquin Valley, are wide-open spaces, spring wildflowers, and stately oak trees.

You'll find all this and more at Round Valley Regional Preserve, the 2,000-acre home of nesting golden eagles, burrowing owls, chubby ground squirrels, and the endangered San Joaquin kit fox. The bike riding here is mellow and easy, unless of course you show up at midday in August, when it can be more than 100 degrees.

From the preserve staging area, the trail starts out with a long bridge over Marsh Creek. At the far side of the bridge, a right turn puts you on Miwok Trail. Immediately, you face the only real hill of the day; the remaining miles of this ride are mostly level.

In .5 mile, the wide dirt road meets up with Round Valley Creek. If you've timed your trip for the wet season, the stream will run cool and

The riding is easy on the ranch roads at Round Valley.

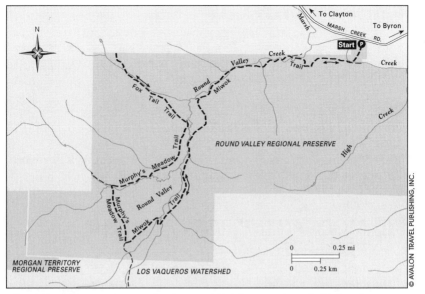

clear alongside you for much of your ride. The remains of old farming equipment lie scattered along the dirt trail; this land was farmed by the Murphy family from 1873–1988, when it was donated to East Bay Regional Park District. Prior to the Murphys' ownership, the Round Valley area was home to Native Americans, who probably used the land as a meeting and trading place between San Joaquin Valley tribes and East Bay hill tribes.

Stay on Miwok Trail through the entire length of the preserve, then turn right on Murphy's Meadow Trail. You'll loop back on the far side of Round Valley Creek. At a junction with Fox Tail Trail, follow Fox Tail Trail uphill for a short out-and-back excursion. Head for the top of the hill and a wide view of rolling hills and vast, unpopulated parkland. What a fine spot for a picnic lunch.

The best time to ride here? Unquestionably, it's in spring, when the grassy hills of Round Valley turn a brilliant green and are sprinkled with grassland wildflowers. The small miracle of Round Valley Creek flows with unmodulated passion from March–June, when it drops to meager pools along the streambed.

Options
Riders looking for more mileage can follow Miwok Trail out of the park, through a 1.6-mile stretch of Los Vaqueros watershed, and into the east side of Morgan Territory Regional Preserve, where most trails are open to mountain bikes. Get a map of the area from East Bay Regional Park District before you go.

Information and Contact

There is no fee. Free trail maps are available at the trailhead parking area. For more information, contact East Bay Regional Park District, 2950 Peralta Oaks Court, P.O. Box 5381, Oakland, CA 94605-0381, 510/562-PARK or 510/635-0135, website: www.ebparks.org.

Directions

From I-580 in Livermore, take the Vasco Road exit and drive north 13 miles. Turn left (west) on Camino Diablo Road and drive 3.5 miles. Where Camino Diablo ends, continue straight on Marsh Creek Road for 1.5 miles to the Round Valley parking area on the left.

30 MORGAN TERRITORY REGIONAL PRESERVE

East Bay Regional Park District, off I-580 near Livermore

Total distance: 7.0 miles **Biking time:** 2.0 hours

Type of trail: Dirt double-track

Type of bike: Mountain bike

Steepness: Rolling terrain **Skill level:** Moderate

Morgan Territory—even the name sounds wild, like a holdover from the Old West. If you're wondering if anything wild could still exist in Contra Costa County, wonder no more. Come to Morgan Territory and rediscover the wild East Bay.

The drive to the trailhead is a trip in itself. Follow narrow, winding Morgan Territory Road north of Livermore to the preserve's main trailhead. Try not to get so wowed by the views that you drive right off the curvy, narrow road.

At the trailhead parking lot, you've climbed to 1,900 feet in elevation. (Okay, so your car has done the work.) Ideally, you've planned your visit for the cooler months of the year, because the open hills around Livermore bake in the summer. If you're riding in the warm season, make sure it is *very* early in the morning. Pick up a free trail map at the trailhead (the preserve has an overabundance of trail junctions) and follow Volvon Trail uphill and through a cattle gate. This first climb allows for no warm-up, but fear not, the trail gets mellower at the top. (To skip this first hill, take the dirt road to the right of the parking lot; it has a mellower grade and soon meets up with Volvon Trail.)

After .5 mile on Volvon Trail, bear right on Blue Oak Trail and prepare

Morgan Territory Regional Preserve

yourself for a few glimpses of the San Joaquin Valley far to the east. When you aren't facing east, you have great views of Mount Diablo to the west. The dirt road rolls gently up and down small hills; you just glide along. The only difficulty for mountain bikers is the ruts and holes caused by the trampling feet of cattle. The roads are roughest in spring, after they've been wet from winter rains. If rough surfaces spoil your biking fun, wait to ride at Morgan Territory until fall, when the road has been smoothed out by dry air and frequent spring and summer bicycle use.

True to its name, Blue Oak Trail features some magnificent oak trees, interspersed with rocks covered with colorful lichens. Dozens of spots invite you to throw down your bike, wander among the trees, and spread out a picnic.

Stay on Blue Oak Trail for 1.3 miles until you reach a cattle gate and a portable toilet. Continue through the gate and turn right on Valley View Trail. (The trail straight ahead will be the return of your loop.) A quick and steep descent on Valley View Trail leads you to remarkable views of the San Joaquin Valley. After relishing the vista, turn right on Volvon Loop Trail to start your return, climbing back up to the cattle gate and portable toilet. From here, you have an easy ride on Volvon Trail all the way back to the trailhead parking lot.

A few tips for making your biking trip to Morgan Territory ideal: One, pick a cool day. Two, make sure you carry one of the park's free maps, because trail junctions are plentiful. And three, bring plenty of water and a suitable picnic to spread out under the shade of the biggest oak you can find.

Options

This trip is a figure-eight loop; to cut it short, just ride half of the figure eight. Turn around when you reach the cattle gate and toilet at the junction of Blue Oak, Volvon, and Valley View Trails. Ride back on Volvon Trail for a four-mile loop.

Information and Contact

There is no fee. Free trail maps are available at the trailhead parking area. For more information, contact East Bay Regional Park District, 2950 Peralta Oaks Court, P.O. Box 5381, Oakland, CA 94605-0381, 510/562-PARK or 510/635-0135, website: www.ebparks.org.

Directions

From I-580 in Livermore, take the North Livermore Avenue exit and turn north. Drive north for four miles, then turn right on Morgan Territory Road. Drive 5.6 miles to the entrance to Morgan Territory Preserve on the right. (The road is narrow and steep.)

31 LAKE CHABOT WEST & EAST SHORE TRAILS

Anthony Chabot Regional Park, off I-580 near San Leandro

Total distance: 8.5 miles   **Biking time:** 1.0 hour

Type of trail: Paved bike trail

Type of bike: Road bike or mountain bike

Steepness: Rolling terrain   **Skill level:** Easiest

Surprise—the paved trail at Lake Chabot is a roller-coaster ride. Lakeside trails are usually level and somewhat predictable, but the West and East Shore Trails around Lake Chabot never stop turning, twisting, climbing, and diving. You're either braking hard or pedaling hard the whole way, but rarely just coasting. The trail provides more of a workout than many paved trails, yet at the same time it is not too difficult for kids or not-so-fit adults.

You can customize the Lake Chabot trails according to your desires and abilities. Mountain bikers in decent shape may want to ride the entire 14-mile Lake Chabot Loop, which combines the paved West and East Shore Trails with several dirt fire roads. Easy bikers will get the most out of the trip by starting their ride at San Leandro's Chabot Park, just outside the border of Anthony Chabot Regional Park, where

This easy, paved stretch is part of a longer loop around Lake Chabot.

West Shore Trail begins. From there you can ride out and back for an 8.5-mile trip on West and East Shore Trails. Those seeking an even easier, shorter ride may want to park at Lake Chabot Marina, the midway point on the paved trail, and ride only East Shore Trail, which is less hilly than West Shore Trail.

Both trails skirt the lake's edge, sometimes rising up along its steep walls, sometimes tracing just a few feet from the water. After the initial steep hill climb from Chabot Park to Lake Chabot's dam, the lake is always within view. Some riders bring their fishing rods with them on the trail; shorefishing prospects for trout, bass, and catfish are excellent. A Lake Chabot fishing permit and a California Fish and Game license allow you to drop a line in anywhere you please.

A few paths branch off from the main trail, but if you stay along the water's edge, you'll do fine. One important junction is .5 mile in at the top of the hill by the dam, where you must stay right on West Shore Trail. Otherwise, just ride until the paved trail ends at a gate two miles beyond Lake Chabot Marina. Then turn your bike around and ride back, or take a park map with you to continue following the dirt loop (see Options, below).

If you want to turn your bike ride into a day at the park, the marina has boats for rent, plus a small café that sells hot dogs and coffee along with the Power Bait. A large picnic area lies near the marina, and several hiking trails branch off from the paved bike trails.

Options

The paved East Shore Trail ends at the dirt Cameron Loop, and mountain bikers can continue to the left on Cameron to connect with Live Oak, Towhee, and Brandon Trails, then loop back to Chabot Park and the West Shore Trail on Goldenrod and Bass Cove Trails. The 14-mile route is a great place to work on improving your mountain biking skills. Strong beginners can manage it.

Information and Contact

There is no fee for parking at San Leandro's Chabot Park on Estudillo Avenue (see Directions, below). If you park at Lake Chabot Marina, a $4 fee is charged per vehicle. A free park map is available at Lake Chabot Marina. For more information, contact East Bay Regional Park District, 2950 Peralta Oaks Court, P.O. Box 5381, Oakland, CA 94605-0381, 510/562-PARK or 510/635-0135, website: www.ebparks.org. Or phone Lake Chabot Marina at 510/582-2198.

Directions

From Oakland, drive east on I-580 and take the Dutton/Estudillo Avenue exit in San Leandro. Drive .5 mile, then turn left on Estudillo Avenue and drive .4 mile. Bear right at the Y junction with Lake Chabot Road and drive 2.5 miles to a T junction. Turn left, then left again into the marina. Alternatively, to start your ride at Chabot Park in San Leandro, follow the directions above but bear left at the "Y" with Lake Chabot Road. Bear right at the next junction, then turn right into Chabot Park. The paved trail begins just inside the gates, on the left.

32 ALAMEDA CREEK TRAIL

Fremont to Coyote Hills Regional Park, off I-680 in Fremont

Total distance: 24.0 miles   **Biking time:** 2.5 hours

Type of trail: Paved bike trail

Type of bike: Road bike or mountain bike

Steepness: Mostly level   **Skill level:** Easiest

Alameda Creek, the largest stream in Alameda County, was once a valuable resource to the Ohlone Indians who settled along its banks. Today, Alameda Creek Trail follows the creek from the mouth of Niles Canyon in Fremont 12 miles westward to San Francisco Bay.

The trail is actually two parallel trails on the south and north banks of

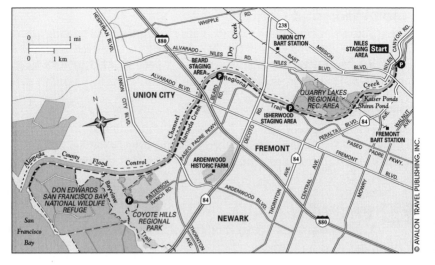

the creek. The south-side trail (paved) is for bikers, hikers, and runners, and the north side (unpaved) is for equestrians, too. The south-side trail, described here, accesses Coyote Hills Regional Park, where more riding possibilities are available.

Everything is in place here to make your ride easy. Unlike some trails in the East Bay's impressive system of paved recreation paths, Alameda Creek Trail is uninterrupted by street intersections, so you have 12 miles of worry-free riding in both directions. Mileage markers are installed along the trail, and water and restrooms are available at several points. Even when the afternoon westerly wind comes up from the bay, it will be at your back for the slightly uphill ride home.

Alameda Creek Trail passes under highway overpasses and alongside neighborhood backyards, so it isn't exactly a nature trail, although you will probably spot birds along the narrow-channeled creek. If you're clamoring for something more, well, natural, add on a ride in Coyote Hills Regional Park, a bayside park with an abundance of wildlife and fascinating Native American history (see Options, below).

Options

Where Alameda Creek Trail ends near the edge of the bay at Coyote Hills Regional Park, skinny-tire riders are restricted to adding 3.5 paved miles on the park's Bay View Trail (see the following trail description), but mountain bikers can pedal around on the numerous dirt trails that roll up and down Coyote's rounded hills. Those who enjoy steep ups and fast downs should not miss Red Hill Trail, but the park has many other trail options for mountain bikers.

Information and Contact

There is no fee. Free trail maps are available at the trailhead parking area. For more information, contact East Bay Regional Park District, 2950 Peralta Oaks Court, P.O. Box 5381, Oakland, CA 94605-0381, 510/562-PARK or 510/635-0135, website: www.ebparks.org.

Directions

From I-680 in Fremont, take the Mission Boulevard exit and drive west to Highway 84/Niles Canyon Road. Turn right, then right again on Old Canyon Road. The staging area is on the left.

33 BAY VIEW TRAIL

Coyote Hills Regional Park, off Highway 84 near Newark

Total distance: 4.5 miles   **Biking time:** 1.0 hour

Type of trail: Paved bike trail

Type of bike: Road bike or mountain bike

Steepness: Rolling terrain   **Skill level:** Easiest

Driving across Dumbarton Bridge from San Francisco's South Bay to the East Bay, you notice a few things. Huge electrical towers straddle the blue-gray bay waters. An old railroad bridge parallels Dumbarton Bridge, a dismantled relic from an earlier era. The bay itself seems impossibly expansive in contrast to the density of the cities and freeways that surround it. But then urban-weary eyes come to rest on the soft green knolls of Coyote Hills Regional Park, just ahead and to your left as you cross the bay. The park's tule marshes, creeks, and acres of grasslands beckon you to pull off the freeway and explore.

A 1,000-acre patch of open space along the bay's edge, Coyote Hills was the homeland of Ohlone Indians for more than 2,000 years. They fished bay waters for food and cut willow branches along the creeks to build their homes. Today, the park is a wildlife sanctuary, both a permanent home and a temporary rest stop for thousands of resident and migratory birds. As a bonus, the park has a paved bike trail that skirts the base of its hills, providing a great 3.5-mile loop trip with marsh and bay views. A .5-mile extension up a long hill and a connection to Alameda Creek Trail offer more miles of riding possibilities.

Start your trip at the Quarry/Dairy Glen Trail parking lot and pick up paved Bay View Trail across the road. (It actually begins by the entrance kiosk, but there is no parking there.) Riding to your left, you immediately

Don't forget your binoculars when you ride at bird-filled Coyote Hills Regional Park.

pass Alameda Creek Ponding Area, usually covered with waterbirds, and a wooden hiker's boardwalk over the marsh. Watch for car traffic as you pass the visitors center; for a few hundred yards, the trail follows directly alongside the park road. Then continue past a connecting route to Alameda Creek Trail.

Bay View Trail contours around the park's hillsides, with plenty of curves but little climbing. At a sharp left curve, you pass a wooden overlook above the bay, with stairs that descend to a hiking trail along a levee. Here, your bay views begin to open up, and they remain wide open as you ride southward along the water. On a clear day, the sparkle of sunshine on the bay is a glorious sight.

Making a long loop around the bay's edge, you come around to a junction with Meadowlark Trail, a paved path that goes up a steep hill to some water district buildings and TV towers. If you want a quick but tough workout, ride up Meadowlark Trail for great views of the bay and flatlands below. You'll probably need at least one rest stop along the way—although it's short, it's very steep. Then have fun cruising back down to rejoin the Bay View Trail loop. You pass plenty of dirt trail junctions, many of which are open to bikes. Apay Way Trail leads to the Don Edwards San Francisco Bay National Wildlife Refuge visitors center (see the following trail description). Nike Trail and Red Hill Trail climb to the higher areas of the park for panoramic views and a close-up look at some odd rock formations—outcrops of reddish-gold chert that were once part of the ocean floor.

Binoculars are an excellent accessory for this trail. If you have children with you, ask them to watch for white great egrets and count how many they can see. Two of the largest egret nesting colonies in Northern California are located in neighboring Don Edwards San Francisco Bay National Wildlife Refuge. Their numbers are plentiful at Coyote Hills.

Options
Bay View Trail connects with 12-mile-long Alameda Creek Trail via a short dirt trail. Ride the loop as described above, then pick up the connector trail near the visitors center that leads to Alameda Creek Trail. This is the north end of the paved trail, so you can ride southward on pavement or northward along a gravel levee into Don Edwards San Francisco Bay National Wildlife Refuge.

Information and Contact
A $4 entrance fee is charged per vehicle. A free map is available at the entrance kiosk and parking areas. For more information, contact East Bay Regional Park District, 2950 Peralta Oaks Court, P.O. Box 5381, Oakland, CA 94605-0381, 510/562-PARK or 510/635-0135, website: www.ebparks.org.

Directions
From Highway 84 westbound in Fremont, take the Paseo Padre Parkway exit, turn right (north), and drive one mile to Patterson Ranch Road. Turn left and continue to the first parking lot on the left (before the visitors center), which is signed "Quarry/Dairy Glen Trails."

34 TIDELANDS LOOP & NEWARK SLOUGH TRAIL
Don Edwards San Francisco Bay National Wildlife Refuge, off Highway 84 near Newark

Total distance: 7.0 miles   **Biking time:** 2.0 hours

Type of trail: Dirt double-track

Type of bike: Mountain bike

Steepness: Rolling terrain   **Skill level:** Easiest

To combine a perfectly easy mountain bike ride with some bayside nature lessons, saddle up to ride at Don Edwards San Francisco Bay National Wildlife Refuge. Riding a bike is the perfect way to see the refuge, because the place is big—over 20,000 acres of open space, the nation's largest urban wildlife refuge. If you walk, you can't get very far. If you ride, you can combine Tidelands Loop with Newark Slough Trail for a seven-mile loop along a combination of slough, mudflats, wetlands, and levees.

Start your trip by stopping in at the refuge visitors center. It's loaded with exhibits and information about bayside habitats and the plants and animals that make the bay their home. Then start riding by the visitors center parking lot, climbing the short but steep paved road to access Tidelands Loop. This is the only hill you will see all day.

The view from the top is worth the effort, anyway. From an overlook just above the visitors center, gaze across the expanse of the South Bay. The most noticeable landmark is Dumbarton Bridge and its thousands of perpetually streaming cars. With all the traffic and industrial areas around this part of the bay, the wildlife refuge feels like an oasis for human beings as well as for wildlife.

Keep riding, using 1.3-mile Tidelands Loop to get to the longer Newark Slough Trail. One loop connects to the other via a wooden bridge over the slough. Tidelands Loop is well marked, but Newark Slough Trail has little to identify it except small, brown hiker signs. All the trails at the refuge are open to bikes, so just ride as you please on the level, gravel double-track. You can't get lost, because the visitors center buildings can be seen from almost everywhere on the trail.

Newark Slough Trail makes a wide loop, just over five miles in length. After crossing the wooden slough bridge, ride clockwise (to your left), heading south toward Marshlands Road (the road you drove in on). Then ride west along the slough and finally northward, looping back by Dumbarton Bridge. Near Marshlands Road and Thornton Avenue you may see canoeists or kayakers putting in at a launch ramp on the slough, then paddling through the shallow waters.

The ride is all about the senses—smells, sounds, and sights. Close to the visitors center, the odor of anise and sage prevails, while out along the tidelands, you'll notice only the scents of the bay. On the northern part of the loop, your ears pick up the rush of cars on the highway, while a mile or so southward, only the sounds of birds and lapping water are heard. The farther you travel on the loop, the greater variety of birds you will see, including willets, avocets, sandpipers, ducks, and snowy egrets. Winter is the best time for viewing large flocks and for seeing occasional visitors, like Canada geese. Don't forget your binoculars, and keep on the lookout for small ground mammals like rabbits and red foxes, which also inhabit the marshes.

Options

You can also ride from the visitors center parking lot along the three-mile paved road that leads to the pier alongside Dumbarton Bridge. (You may share the road with a few cars.) Ride out of the parking lot the way you drove in, then turn left at the sign for the pier, staying in the bike lane.

Information and Contact
There is no fee. For more information and a map, contact Don Edwards San Francisco Bay National Wildlife Refuge, P.O. Box 524, Newark, CA 94560, 510/792-0222 or 510/792-4275, website: http://desfbay.fws.gov.

Directions
From U.S. 101 south, take the Highway 84 East exit. In just under one mile, turn right at the stoplight to continue on Highway 84 across Dumbarton Bridge. Take the Thornton Avenue exit and turn right at the stop sign. Drive .5 mile and turn right at the Don Edwards San Francisco Bay National Wildlife Refuge sign (Marshlands Road), then follow the signs to the visitors center parking lot. Ride your bike on the gravel trail to the right of the wooden stairs, then turn left on the paved road that goes to the visitors center. You'll see signs for Tidelands Loop along this road.

35 COASTAL TRAIL & GREAT HIGHWAY BIKE PATH
Golden Gate National Recreation Area, off Highway 1 on the San Francisco coast

Total distance: 8.0 miles   **Biking time:** 2.0 hours

Type of trail: Dirt double-track and paved bike trail

Type of bike: Road bike or mountain bike

Steepness: Rolling terrain   **Skill level:** Easiest

What is the wildest place in San Francisco? While some might argue for the South of Market nightclubs, I vote for Land's End Coastal Trail. It's hard to believe you can find a city trail that seems this natural and remote, but here it is. The path delivers million-dollar views of crashing surf, offshore outcrops, Golden Gate Bridge, and the Marin Headlands.

In its entirety, Coastal Trail is 11 miles long, although not all of it is contiguous, and some of it follows city streets. This ride follows two sections of Coastal Trail that are open to bikes; first the Land's End stretch, and then the bike path along the Great Highway and Ocean Beach. Pick a clear day, when the wind is light, and prepare to see some of San Francisco's finest scenery.

Golden Gate Bridge views from Adolph Sutro's rail trail

The ocean views from the parking lot are a satisfying first impression. As you strap on your bike helmet, watch for a Golden Gate–bound freighter or the spout of a gray whale, and lend an ear to the chorus of barking sea lions. Then take the trail from the north end of the lot that dips into a canopy of cypress trees. Ignore the spur trails on the left; take the right fork to connect to the wide main trail, which is the remains of the roadbed for Adolph Sutro's 1888 steam train.

Sutro was a San Francisco entrepreneur who wanted to make his Cliff House Restaurant and adjoining bathhouse more accessible to working-class folks. He built the railroad and charged people only a nickel to ride. Unfortunately, numerous landslides made maintaining the railway too expensive, and in 1925, it was closed down.

Today, the former rail trail supplies postcard views of the Golden Gate Bridge, Marin Headlands, Pacific Ocean, and San Francisco Bay. The trail is lined with windswept cypress trees, which have taken on strange, stiff forms, as if they've been hair-sprayed into shape. If you look closely at the ocean waters below the trail, you might spot the remains of several Golden Gate shipwrecks. Point Lobos and Mile Rock, two submerged rocks, have taken many casualties off Land's End. Today, both rocks are marked with buoy signals.

A half mile in, at a right fork, a gated road heads uphill to the Palace of the Legion of Honor art museum. You can ride right up to it or continue straight on Coastal Trail, following the San Francisco shoreline on top of 300-foot cliffs. Your total stint on Sutro's rail trail will be only about a mile; beyond that, you reach a fence at Painted Rock Cliff and a trail that is signed for hikers only, leading uphill. Turn around and retrace your tire tracks, but stay to the left on the trail (instead of taking the right spur to the Merrie Way parking area). Ride to the junction of Point Lobos Avenue, El Camino del Mar, and 48th Avenue, which is about 100 yards uphill from Merrie Way. Use the crosswalk to cross the road, then continue on the rail trail into Sutro Heights Park, the remains of Sutro's estate. Pedal the short loop around the park and be sure to stop at the far end, just below a rock parapet that was built in the 1880s as a viewing platform. You are directly above Cliff House, looking out toward Farallon Islands. On a clear day, it's a world-class view.

From Sutro Heights Park, walk your bike across Point Lobos Avenue again, then head downhill past the Merrie Way parking lot and Cliff House Restaurant. You might want to walk your bike on this short downhill stretch, because the area is often crowded with tourists. When you are beyond the crowds, mount your bike and ride along Ocean Beach on the wide concrete path. At Lincoln Avenue, the concrete ends, so cross over to the inland side of the Great Highway (use the crosswalk and walk your bike), then cross Lincoln Avenue (using the crosswalk again). At the southeast corner of the Great Highway and Lincoln Avenue intersection, pick up the paved Great Highway bike path.

Now follow the paved trail for two miles to its end. Although you are on the inland side of the highway, your ocean views are still good, and they become progressively better as you ride south on the trail. When you reach Sloat Boulevard, the trail abruptly ends, so turn your wheels around and ride back to Cliff House, then dismount and walk uphill on the sidewalk to the Merrie Way parking area.

Options

If you just want to ride along Ocean Beach and on the paved bike path, it's easier to park alongside Ocean Beach in any of the parking spots south of Cliff House. Start riding from there for a six-mile round-trip completely on pavement.

Information and Contact

There is no fee. A free map is available by contacting Golden Gate National Recreation Area, Fort Mason, Building 201, San Francisco, CA 94123, 415/561-4700. For more information, contact the Presidio Visitor Center at 415/561-4323 or Fort Funston Ranger Station at 415/239-2366, website: www.nps.gov/goga.

Directions

In San Francisco, head west on Geary Boulevard to 48th Avenue, where Geary becomes Point Lobos Avenue. Continue on Point Lobos Avenue for 150 feet to the Merrie Way parking lot on the right, just above Louis' Restaurant. The trail leads from the north side of the parking lot.

36 SADDLE & OLD GUADALUPE TRAILS

San Bruno Mountain State & County Park, off U.S. 101
near Brisbane

Total distance: 2.5 miles   **Biking time:** 1.0 hour

Type of trail: Dirt double-track

Type of bike: Mountain bike

Steepness: Rolling terrain   **Skill level:** Easiest

Everyone who works in an office in Brisbane, South San Francisco, or Daly City should make a lunch-hour trip to San Bruno Mountain State and County Park. A 10-minute drive from the freeway will make you feel like you've gotten away from it all.

The park is a happy surprise for first-time visitors. You can drive up and down U.S. 101 all your life and never get an inkling that this terrific open space is so close by, and so accessible. The park is at about 1,200 feet in elevation, high above the Cow Palace, that huge entertainment arena that houses everything from monster truck shows to well-bred-cat competitions. It overlooks Candlestick Park and the business complexes at Sierra Point and Oyster Point along U.S. 101. Surprisingly, San Bruno Mountain's quirky surroundings simply add to its charm.

Saddle and Old Guadalupe Trails take you on an easy tour of the northeast side of the park, providing a mix of city and bay views and grassy hill-

Saddle Trail, San Bruno Mountain State and County Park

sides brimming with wildflowers. The latter are particularly important here, because San Bruno Mountain is the habitat of the mission blue butterfly, which thrives on three kinds of native lupine. The mission blue is an endangered species that lives only on San Bruno Mountain and in Golden Gate National Recreation Area.

San Bruno Mountain is also home to another endangered butterfly, the San Bruno elfin, as well as rare plants, including Montara manzanita (found nowhere else in the world) and Franciscan wallflower. The 2,700-acre park is carefully managed with a habitat conservation plan to protect the precious species. This is basically a legal agreement between the public and local developers, who would prefer to grow housing tracts on the mountain's hillsides. Although developers have contested the conservation plan in court several times, it has always been upheld.

Meanwhile, bicyclists and walkers are allowed to share the hillsides with butterflies and wildflowers. Because Saddle and Old Guadalupe Trails make a 2.5-mile loop around the mountainside, your views change with almost every minute of your ride. The trail is hard-packed gravel, easy enough for even the most novice mountain biker, and marked with little jogger signs that note your mileage. Riding the loop counterclockwise, in the first .5 mile you round a bend and see Oyster Point and Sierra Point far below you and to the south. Then you reach a strategically positioned bench with a wide-angle view of Twin Peaks, San Francisco's downtown, the Cow Palace, Candlestick Park, Bay Bridge, and the East Bay hills. You can hear the freeway, but perched up high in this oasis, you feel oddly separate and remote from it.

As you continue riding northward, you lose your southern Bay vistas, but the view of San Francisco gets clearer. A grassy knoll at about 1.3 miles offers a terrific view of the city, where you can even see the tip of the cross on Mount Davidson, a San Francisco landmark.

As the trail begins to loop back to your left, you pass a junction with an unmarked trail that leads to a day camp and group picnic area. After a long spell of seeing only low coastal scrub, nonnative gorse bushes, and grasslands, trees are now visible on the trail, a mix of nonnative pines and eucalyptus. Keep riding straight to the junction with Old Guadalupe Trail, where you turn left to close out the loop. Old Guadalupe is a bumpy paved trail, shaded by eucalyptus trees.

When you return to the picnic area, you'll find plenty of bike posts for locking up your wheels, so you can explore hiking trails on foot. A park map, available at the entrance kiosk, details all the options.

Information and Contact
A $4 park entrance fee is charged per vehicle. Free maps are available at

the entrance kiosk. For more information, contact San Bruno Mountain State and County Park, 555 Guadalupe Canyon Parkway, Brisbane, CA 94005, 650/992-6770, website: www.parks.ca.gov or www.eparks.net.

This park is currently closed Tues–Thurs.

Directions

From U.S. 101 south of San Francisco, take the Brisbane/Cow Palace exit and drive 1.8 miles on Bayshore Boulevard, heading toward the Cow Palace. Turn left (west) on Guadalupe Canyon Parkway and drive 2.3 miles to the park entrance. Turn right and drive past the kiosk, then park in the first parking lot, near the picnic area. Follow the paved trail to the far side of the picnic area, on the right. The trail turns to gravel double-track and is signed "Saddle Trail."

37 SWEENEY RIDGE PAVED TRAIL

Golden Gate National Recreation Area, off I-280
near San Bruno

Total distance: 4.4 miles   **Biking time:** 2.0 hours

Type of trail: Paved bike trail

Type of bike: Road bike or mountain bike

Steepness: Steep sections   **Skill level:** Easiest

A clear day is a crucial requirement for a bike ride on Sweeney Ridge Trail, because you won't want to miss the breathtaking views of the bay and coast from the top of the ridge.

An abundance of energy is a second crucial requirement, because the paved trail ascends rather steeply over its two-mile stretch. Fortunately, there's plenty to look at while you wait for your heart rate to slow down. As you ride uphill, your vista expands. First you see the open areas around San Andreas Lake, then the prominent landmarks of South San Francisco and the northern peninsula, and finally the incredible 360-degree panorama from the top of Sweeney Ridge. This vista takes in the Pacific coastline and San Francisco Bay, as well as the landmass to the east, north, and south.

It was here, at the 1,200-foot summit on top of Sweeney Ridge, that Gaspar de Portola and the Portola Expedition spotted San Francisco Bay on November 4, 1769. A stone monument commemorates their discovery. Near it is a second monument in memory of Carl Patrick McCarthy, who was instrumental in obtaining protective status for Sweeney Ridge. Carved on this granite marker are all the major landmarks you can identify from

on top of Sweeney Ridge

the ridge, including Mount Tamalpais, Mount Diablo, Mount Hamilton, Montara Mountain, Point Reyes, Farallon Islands, and Point San Pedro.

The paved trail is simple to follow. Starting from the parking area, it slowly winds its way uphill. About two-thirds of the way up a yellow line bisects the trail. That's the "fog line," designed to aid bikers and hikers when visibility is bad. At the start of the fog line, the trail enters into its steepest stretch.

After panting your way to the top of the ridge, you reach a major junction of trails. Straight ahead a wooden bench overlooks the Half Moon Bay coast. Go left for a short distance to see the Portola monument. Then take the paved ridge trail to the right, which stays pleasantly level for .25 mile and offers more nonstop views. The trail ends at the abandoned buildings of an old Nike missile site.

A highlight on this trail is the amount of wildlife you are likely to see, especially on an early morning trip. On our way up the ridge, we spotted deer, hawks, and numerous bunnies. The terrain surrounding the trail is mostly coastal scrub and grasslands, so April–June, the hillsides bloom with Douglas irises and purple nightshade.

Options
From the junction of trails at the top of Sweeney Ridge, mountain bikers can take either of the dirt roads; they lead south along the ridge or west

toward Pacifica. Remember that it's all downhill from Sweeney Ridge, so unless you plan on making a loop, you'll have to climb back up to this junction to return on the paved trail to the parking area.

Information and Contact

There is no fee. A free map is available by contacting Golden Gate National Recreation Area, Fort Mason, Building 201, San Francisco, CA 94123, 415/561-4700. For more information, contact the Presidio Visitor Center at 415/561-4323 or Fort Funston Ranger Station at 415/239-2366, website: www.nps.gov/goga.

Directions

From I-280 in San Bruno, take the Sneath Lane/San Bruno Avenue exit and head west. Drive 1.9 miles on Sneath Lane to the trailhead parking area.

38 SAWYER CAMP RECREATION TRAIL
San Mateo County Parks, off I-280 near Hillsborough

Total distance: 12.0 miles   **Biking time:** 2.0 hours

Type of trail: Paved bike trail

Type of bike: Road bike or mountain bike

Steepness: Rolling terrain   **Skill level:** Easiest

On weekends, it's hard to find a parking place at the trailhead for Sawyer Camp Recreation Trail, but it's not without good reason. The paved six-mile trail is long enough to make you feel like you're going somewhere and diverse enough to provide both scenic views and interesting history. It's also managed properly, so that even with the trail's many and varied users, everybody has fun.

Sawyer Camp Trail is well loved by bicyclists, walkers, joggers, in-line skaters, baby-stroller pushers, and scooter riders. Due to its popularity, bicyclists must keep their

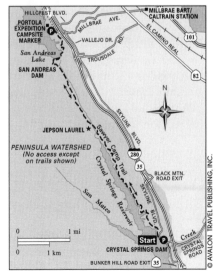

Cyclists share Sawyer Camp Trail's six-mile length with joggers and other users.

speed down; a posted speed limit of 15 miles per hour is enforced. At both ends of the trail, the limit drops to five miles per hour.

The trail travels the length of Lower Crystal Springs Reservoir, then leads through marshlands to southern San Andreas Lake, continuing to the dam at San Andreas and slightly beyond to Hillcrest Boulevard in Millbrae. Interpretive signs along the trail explain everything from the geology of the area (the trail parallels nearby San Andreas Fault) to the trail's history (the path was paved in 1978 through the cooperative efforts of San Mateo County, the California Department of Parks and Recreation, and the San Francisco Water Department).

A highlight is the Jepson laurel tree 3.5 miles from the trail's start. The tree was named for noted California botanist Willis Jepson. At more than 600 years old and 55 feet tall, the Jepson laurel is the oldest and largest living California laurel tree.

The ride is an easy cruise. You probably won't even shift gears until you get past mile marker 4.5, where you reach the first small grade. Much of the trail is heavily shaded by Monterey cypress, Monterey pines, and various kinds of eucalyptus. The marshy area in between Lower Crystal Springs Reservoir and San Andreas Lake is an excellent area to spot deer and other wildlife.

Near San Andreas Lake's dam, a plaque on a boulder notes that this spot was Captain Gaspar de Portola's first camp after his discovery of San Francisco Bay on November 4, 1769. The trail ends shortly beyond the dam with a short but steep hill climb to trail's end at Hillcrest Boulevard and I-280.

Options

Mountain bikers can connect this trail with San Andreas Trail for another five miles of riding. Ride under the freeway at Hillcrest Boulevard, turn left and ride north on the frontage road, then turn left on Larkspur. Cross back under the freeway to pick up San Andreas Trail.

Information and Contact

There is no fee, but donations are accepted. For more information, contact San Mateo County Parks and Recreation, 455 County Center, Fourth Floor, Redwood City, CA 94063, 650/363-4020, website: www.eparks.net.

Directions

From I-280 in San Mateo, take the Highway 92 exit west, then turn right (north) immediately on Highway 35. Drive .5 mile to Crystal Springs Road and the trail entrance.

39 CAÑADA ROAD BICYCLE SUNDAYS

San Mateo County Parks, off Highway 92 near Woodside

Total distance: 8.0 miles   **Biking time:** 1.5 hours

Type of trail: Paved road (closed to cars)

Type of bike: Road bike or mountain bike

Steepness: Mostly level   **Skill level:** Easiest

Cañada Road Bicycle Sunday has become a ritualized event on the San Francisco peninsula. Every Sunday, the San Mateo County Parks Department closes off Cañada Road to cars, and the four-mile stretch from Edgewood Road to Highway 92 becomes a parade of bicyclists of all shapes and sizes.

Cañada Road is a great ride even with cars, so it's a stellar ride without cars. It provides great views of Upper Crystal Springs Reservoir and the eastern slopes of Montara Mountain, along with just the right amount of mileage to give you that good feeling of having gotten some fresh air and exercise.

Cañada Road is closed to cars 9 A.M.–3 P.M. every Sunday November–March, and 9 A.M.–4 P.M. every Sunday April–October. The only exceptions are on winter holiday Sundays and during inclement weather. Phone the Cañada Road hotline for an update on closures at 650/361-1785.

Cañada Road is scenic, smoothly paved, and free of cars on Bicycle Sundays.

The route traverses peninsula foothill country lined with grasslands and oaks, but its most striking feature is its views of Upper Crystal Springs Reservoir, the hidden paradise of the San Francisco watershed. Public access to this lovely body of water is strictly forbidden, but Cañada Road provides many long looks at it.

The road also leads past Pulgas Water Temple. This Romanesque structure is where the San Francisco Water District celebrates the terminus of the Hetch Hetchy aqueduct, bringing water over 200 miles by canal and tunnel from Yosemite. Good for San Francisco, bad for Yosemite. A growing force of people believe that the reservoir at Hetch Hetchy Valley should be drained so the landscape can return to its once pristine state as a near twin to Yosemite Valley. Visit Hetch Hetchy once and you get their point. In the meantime, Pulgas Water Temple is worth a look—it is a big swimming pool with Roman pillars and expensive landscaping.

Options
Less than .5 mile from Pulgas Water Temple is Filoli Estate, a historic 1917 mansion and 16 acres of spectacular formal gardens. Tours are available by reservation on some Sundays. Phone Filoli at 650/364-2880 for information.

Information and Contact
There is no fee. For more information, contact San Mateo County Parks and Recreation, 455 County Center, Fourth Floor, Redwood City, CA 94063, 650/363-4020, website: www.eparks.net.

Directions

From I-280 near San Carlos, take the Edgewood Road exit. Turn west and drive .5 mile to the intersection of Edgewood Road and Cañada Road. Park alongside the road.

40 RANCH TRAIL

Burleigh Murray Ranch State Park, off Highway 1
near Half Moon Bay

Total distance: 4.0 miles   **Biking time:** 1.0 hour

Type of trail: Dirt double-track

Type of bike: Mountain bike

Steepness: Mostly level   **Skill level:** Easiest

This easy bike trip is a ride through Half Moon Bay history. It's a great place to introduce kids or beginning riders to mountain biking. Burleigh Murray Ranch State Park may be one of California's newest state parks, but more than 100 years ago, its land was home to a bustling dairy farm, owned by an artisan named Robert Mills. Mills leased the land to recently immigrated English, Irish, Italian, and Portuguese farmers, who ran successful dairy businesses. Mills built a giant dairy barn on the property, plus a ranch house and other outbuildings.

English bank barn, Burleigh Murray Ranch

Mills's still-standing barn is the showpiece of this park. It is an English bank barn, one of only two in the United States. Built in 1889, the barn was two stories high and 200 feet long, built into the hillside so the upper story could easily be loaded by wagon. The barn could hold 100 cows. Today, the barn is a favorite spot for photographers, who like to shoot its rustic weathered wood and the rusted farm implements found around its foundation. A beautiful old stone wall lines the barn's southern side.

Mills and his heirs leased the property to immigrant farmers for more than a century. In 1979 it was donated to the state to preserve its natural and cultural heritage. The park's 1,300 acres are bisected by Mills Creek, an alder-shaded stream canyon. In early and mid-spring, ceanothus bushes bloom with fragrant white and blue flowers. In late spring and summer, orange sticky monkeyflower is on display.

Mountain bikers will find the riding blessedly easy, with only a 200-foot elevation gain over the entire course of the trip. The trail is short—only four miles round-trip—so you might as well bring your binoculars, camera, and a picnic, and take your time.

The trail runs right alongside Mills Creek, which is bordered by a dense mass of blackberry bushes, poison oak, willows, and alders. It passes a few of the old ranch buildings, crosses the stream twice, and then reaches the remarkably large barn at one mile out. The trail ends at a set of wooden water tanks at two miles out. Along the way, you pass a couple of picnic areas—one by the barn and one in a stand of eucalyptus trees along the trail.

One further note of historical interest: As you drive in or out of the park on Higgins Purisima Road, be sure to check out the historic James Johnston House, a huge white farmhouse plainly visible on the hillside. It was built in 1853 and was the center of cultural and social life in Half Moon Bay in the late 19th century. Johnston House is considered to be the earliest American home still standing along the coast of San Mateo County. It is often open for tours on Sunday afternoons.

Options

If you don't mind some car traffic, you can ride out and back as far as you wish on Higgins Purisima Road. This beautiful rural road has some challenging ups and downs, but they aren't outside of the ability range of most strong beginners.

Information and Contact

There is no fee. For more information, contact California State Parks, San Mateo sector, 650/726-8819, website: www.parks.ca.gov.

Directions

From the junction of Highway 1 and Highway 92 in Half Moon Bay, drive south for 1.2 miles and turn east on Higgins Purisima Road (by the firehouse). Drive 1.6 miles to the park entrance on the left.

41 HALF MOON BAY BIKE PATH

Half Moon Bay State Beach, off Highway 1 in Half Moon Bay

Total distance: 5.0 miles   **Biking time:** 1.0 hour

Type of trail: Paved bike trail

Type of bike: Road bike or mountain bike

Steepness: Mostly level   **Skill level:** Easiest

The popular coastal resort town of Half Moon Bay is almost as famous for fog as it is for its annual pumpkin festival, but when you visit here in winter, you'll find neither one. By the end of November, the pumpkin fields have been rototilled and the fog has disappeared from the coast, leaving crystal-clear days for bicycling on Half Moon Bay Bike Path. The trail is only 2.5 miles long, but you can ride it in both directions and combine it with a trip to the beach.

The route starts at the state beach parking lot at Francis Beach, then runs north along the coast until it dead-ends at Mirada Road in Miramar. The first mile of the trail runs parallel to an equestrian trail (the routes are divided by a fence), so you might be accompanied by riders on horseback. After crossing two wooden bridges over a coastal marsh, the horse trail and bike trail briefly merge, then separate again. The paved path passes by three state park beach areas: Francis, Venice, and Dunes beaches, each with a parking lot and public access. Although swimming is not recom-

Half Moon Bay Bike Path

mended at Half Moon Bay because of cold water and rip currents, hiking and picnicking on the beach are great year-round activities.

For those who enjoy ocean views, Half Moon Bay Bike Path is bicycling heaven. As you ride, you are treated to nonstop views of seagulls and sand, plus an occasional kayaker gliding by on the waves or a surf fisherman poised on the beach. Numerous turnouts along the trail allow you to leave your bike and walk out on the coastal bluffs.

Because it's short and completely flat, this coastal ride is perfect for children. The trail sees frequent use by tricycles and training wheels.

Options
You can lock up your bike at either end of the trail and walk on Francis Beach or Miramar Beach.

Information and Contact
A $6 day use fee is charged per vehicle. For more information, contact California State Parks, San Mateo sector, 650/726-8819, website: www .parks.ca.gov. Or phone Half Moon Bay State Beach at 650/726-8820.

Directions
From the junction of Highway 1 and Highway 92 in Half Moon Bay, drive south on Highway 1 for .5 mile and turn right (west) on Kelly Avenue. Drive .5 mile to the beach park on the right. The bike trail is on your right as you enter the parking areas.

42 CORTE MADERA TRAIL
Arastradero Preserve, off I-280 near Palo Alto

Total distance: 5.0 miles   **Biking time:** 2.0 hours

Type of trail: Dirt double-track

Type of bike: Mountain bike

Steepness: Rolling terrain   **Skill level:** Easiest

Arastradero Preserve is a Palo Alto city park, a favorite of locals but little known outside of the immediate area. The easily accessed preserve is popular with a variety of trail users, including plenty of dog walkers, hikers, and mountain bike riders.

Because of the pedestrians, we bikers must mind our manners on the trails. A ranger here told me that this park has few conflicts between bikers and hikers because it has a neighborhood-like atmosphere and most

Corte Madera Trail

visitors are very tolerant and aware. Bikers should also note that while the park's main trail, Corte Madera Trail, is usually open year-round, some of the other trails (Meadowlark and others) are closed during the winter months when the trails are wet. Check the City of Palo Alto website (address below) for an update on trail closures during the rainy season.

Start riding out of the east side of the parking lot, paralleling Arastradero Road for a few hundred yards, then crossing the road and picking up Corte Madera Trail, the main access trail into the park. As you ride through grassy foothills, heading toward Arastradero Lake, consider your options: For the easiest ride, head out and back on Corte Madera Trail, riding around the west side of the lake to the southern border of the park. For a tougher climb but a killer view, veer to the right on the wide, unmarked trail at the lake's northwestern border, then connect with Meadowlark Trail and follow it to the left all the way to the highest point in the park (a mere 770 feet in elevation). There you'll find a horse paddock and Casa de Martinez, a closed-to-the-public ranch house. From this high point, you can see parts of the Stanford University campus, San Francisco and its bay, and many wealthy-looking Palo Alto hillside homes. The view is surprisingly pretty, especially when the park's rolling hills are green and the sky is filled with puffy white clouds.

To return from the top of Meadowlark, your best bet is just to turn around and ride slowly back downhill (it's quite steep, so take it easy). Experienced riders like to ride the single-track on Acorn Trail back down to Corte Madera Trail, making a loop out of the trip.

Get a park map at the parking lot to help plan your ride, but keep in mind that neither the hill on Meadowlark nor the single-track on Acorn Trail is for the faint of heart. Parents riding with children and novice riders should stick to the out-and-back on Corte Madera Trail, then take a break on the return trip at Arastradero Lake, a big pond circled by tules. Fishing from shore is permitted at the little lake.

Options
A five-mile trip is possible by riding both Corte Madera Trail and Meadowlark Trail, but if you ride only Corte Madera Trail, your trip will be 2.5 level miles.

Information and Contact
There is no fee. A free map of Arastradero Preserve is available at the trailhead. For more information, contact Arastradero Preserve, c/o City of Palo Alto, 250 Hamilton Avenue, Palo Alto, CA 94301, 650/329-2423, website: www.city.paloalto.ca.us or www.arastradero.org.

Directions
From I-280 in Palo Alto, take the Page Mill Road exit and head west for .25 mile to Arastradero Road. Turn right and drive .4 mile to the parking area on the right.

43 DUMBARTON BRIDGE RIDE
Don Edwards San Francisco Bay National Wildlife Refuge, off Highway 84 near Menlo Park

Total distance: 4.0 miles   **Biking time:** 1.0 hour

Type of trail: Paved bike trail

Type of bike: Road bike or mountain bike

Steepness: Rolling terrain   **Skill level:** Easiest

When you're driving on Dumbarton Bridge, it's hard to notice much besides the traffic, concrete, and urban sprawl on either end of the bridge's span. But when you ride your bike on Dumbarton Bridge, the scene around you looks completely different. The natural world of the bay and its environs suddenly becomes more obvious than the man-made world.

From the highest point on Dumbarton Bridge, all of the Bay Area's highest peaks are in view: Mount Hamilton (4,209 feet), Mount Diablo (3,849 feet), Mount Tamalpais (2,571 feet), and Montara Mountain (1,898 feet). The tidelands below the bridge may be either high water or mudflats, depending on the tidal flow, but they are fascinating to view in any stage.

At the spot where Dumbarton Bridge crosses the bay, the west and east shores are only one mile apart, making your ride over water fairly short. As you ride, you'll see another bridge just to the south of Dumbarton that was the first bridge built across the bay, in 1908. Called Dumbarton Cutoff, it carried Southern Pacific freight trains across the water until 1982.

Two piers alongside Dumbarton Bridge are also a part of history; both Ravenswood Pier on the west side (where you start your ride) and Dumbarton Pier on the east side were sections of the first Dumbarton Bridge, built for auto traffic in 1927. Present-day Dumbarton Bridge was constructed right alongside the remains of the old bridge.

From Dumbarton Bridge, your riding options are wide open. The trail along the south side of the bridge accommodates riders traveling in either direction. On both sides of the bay the trail connects to an array of other trails. On the East Bay side, you can continue riding in San Francisco Bay National Wildlife Refuge or Coyote Hills Regional Park. On the peninsula side, a paved bike trail leads north to Bayfront Park, completely separate from car traffic.

Options

Add on a trip on the paved recreation trail to Bayfront Park, or ride the three-mile-long pier on the East Bay side of the bridge. After exiting Dumbarton Bridge, the bike trail joins with the pier, which sees some car traffic but has a wide bike lane. The path leads along the bay to the Don Edwards San Francisco Bay National Wildlife Refuge headquarters.

Information and Contact

There is no fee. A free map of the Don Edwards San Francisco Bay National Wildlife Refuge is available by contacting the refuge at P.O. Box 524, Newark, CA 94560, 510/792-4275 or 510/792-0222, website: http://desfbay.fws.gov.

Directions

From U.S. 101 near Palo Alto, take the Willow Road exit (Highway 84 east). In .8 mile, turn right at the stoplight to head for the Dumbarton Bridge entrance. Watch for the signs for Ravenswood/Don Edwards San Francisco Bay National Wildlife Refuge on the right, and just before getting on the bridge, bear right into the parking area for Ravenswood Pier. Drive .2 mile, paralleling the bridge approach, then park in the lot. Ride your bike back along the access road and pick up the trail signed "Dumbarton Bridge to Fremont."

Mountain View Shoreline Park, off U.S. 101 near Mountain View

Total distance: 8.0 miles   **Biking time:** 2.0 hours

Type of trail: Dirt double-track and paved bike trail

Type of bike: Road bike or mountain bike

Steepness: Mostly level   **Skill level:** Easiest

Okay everybody, let's saddle up and go ride our bikes on top of a garbage dump. I realize it doesn't sound very appealing, but this place is a whole lot better than it sounds.

At Mountain View's Shoreline Park, trails run all over the place. My favorite route starts by Lakeside Cafe, where mountain bikers can get off pavement quickly and be free from most of the pedestrians. Those with skinny tires can ride here, too, even though much of the trail is dirt, because it is completely smooth and hard-packed.

As you ride, try to keep in mind that this well-groomed park was built on domestic garbage landfill, which raised the height of the land about 15 feet, just enough to avoid bayside high tide and flooding problems. From 1970 to 1983, the city of San Francisco dumped its garbage here at Shoreline, while engineers figured out how to use its byproduct, methane gas, to

egrets and coots at Palo Alto Baylands

generate electricity. The power generated every day at Shoreline supports the park's maintenance and operation.

Meanwhile, bikers and other trail users cruise around on the surface of that landfill, following trails along the bay's edge. From the café parking lot, ride around the back side of Shoreline Lake and then to the left, heading north along the bay. Shoreline Lake is a 50-acre artificial salt lake, often crowded with small-craft sailors and sailboarders on summer afternoons. The bike trail runs on a bluff above it, between the lake and the bay's edge. The trail is paved for the first .25 mile, then becomes a very wide dirt path as it curves around Charleston Slough.

Although you will see many trail spurs, stay on the wide main path and remain as close to the bay as possible. You start seeing signs for Palo Alto Baylands within the first mile of this trail, and after three miles you cross a bridge, walk your bike through a turnstile, and see Palo Alto Baylands Interpretive Center ahead of you, across a marsh.

To get to the interpretive center, stay on the wide dirt trail that leads away from the bay, heading past the interesting sculptures at Bixby Landfill Park (they look like odd-sized telephone poles). The trail dumps you out on a road, where you ride the bike lane to your right for 100 yards to the access road for Palo Alto Baylands, then turn right again. You could ride Baylands Trail, which starts from the interpretive center, but it's better to lock up your bike and walk. There is much to be seen at a slower pace, including tons of birdlife and jackrabbits, and small planes taking off and landing at Palo Alto Airport.

Riding back to Shoreline Park from Palo Alto Baylands, you gain a long-distance view of Moffett Field Air Station and Shoreline Amphitheatre. When you return to the parking area, you can buy a snack at the café, hang out on the patio, and watch sailboarders on the lake practicing their waterstarts, while pelicans dive in between them.

Options

You can ride from Shoreline Park southward for three-plus more miles on the perfectly paved Stevens Creek Trail, although the scenery leaves something to be desired. The first mile is pleasant as you ride past a golf course and along the Mountain View marshlands, but soon the trail turns inland and becomes remarkably straight and monotonous, eventually crossing under U.S. 101 into Mountain View.

Information and Contact

There is no fee. A free map of Shoreline Park is available at the entrance gate. For more information, contact Shoreline Park, City of Mountain View, 500 Castro Street, P.O. Box 94041, Mountain View, CA 94041, 650/903-6300, website: www.ci.mtnview.ca.us.

Directions

From U.S. 101 in Mountain View, take the Shoreline Boulevard exit and go east, toward the bay. Drive 1.2 miles to the entrance gate for Shoreline Park. Continue past the entrance gate to the sign for "Bicycle Use Parking." Turn right and park there, or continue on the park road to Lakeside Cafe, next to the sailing lake, and park in the large lot there.

45 ALVISO SLOUGH TRAIL

Don Edwards San Francisco Bay National Wildlife Refuge, off Highway 237 near Sunnyvale

Total distance: 8.5 miles   **Biking time:** 2.0 hours

Type of trail: Dirt double-track

Type of bike: Mountain bike

Steepness: Mostly level   **Skill level:** Easiest

The first time I tried to ride at Alviso Slough was just after a few days of rain, on a gorgeous sunny day when the bay was sparkling in all its majesty. I headed out from the dirt trail, happy to be outside and looking forward to a solid eight-mile loop trip. The trail looked damp but firmly packed, with no visible puddles or soft spots. But after riding only a couple hundred feet, so much mud caked up under my front fork that the wheel wouldn't turn. I scraped the mud off, walked my bike to what looked like firmer ground, and tried again. A quarter mile farther, same problem.

This was some kind of super-mud, more powerful and sticky than ordinary mud. I wound up walking my bike back to my car, with the stuff caking up on my shoes as well as my wheels. At least I learned from the experience: Ride Alviso Slough Trail only after a period of dry weather. If you ride it after a rain, you'll have mud pies for dinner.

So, assuming it's been dry for a while, drive over to Alviso Marina at the very southern tip of San Francisco Bay, the point where the East Bay and the South Bay meet and shake hands. Alviso Slough is part of Don Edwards San Francisco Bay National Wildlife Refuge. There are all kinds of critters to be seen here, particularly wetlands birds like egrets and herons, plus lots of ground squirrels darting about. The trail, which is built on a levee, is bordered by still waters, salt marshes, rich mudflats, and the slough itself. Much of the land is leased to Cargill Salt Company, which uses the salt marshes to manufacture—you guessed it—salt.

The ride is an easy-to-follow loop, leading along Alviso Slough to the edge of the bay and Coyote Creek, then cutting across the salt marsh to loop back to the parking area. A 1.5-mile trail spur leads across the railroad tracks to Alviso Slough Environmental Education Center, which is open on weekends 10 A.M.–5 P.M. This is a great place to get educated on the natural history of the bay.

If you're wondering about the worn-looking boats slowly decomposing in the marsh by the Alviso parking lot, they remain from the days when Alviso was a working marina, before this part of the bay filled in with silt. Alviso, a 130-year-old town, was once one of the busiest ports on the bay.

Information and Contact
There is no fee. A free map of Alviso Slough is available by contacting Don Edwards San Francisco Bay National Wildlife Refuge, P.O. Box 524, Newark, CA 94560, 510/792-4275 or 510/792-0222, website: http://desfbay. fws.gov. Or contact Alviso Environmental Education Center at 408/262-5513.

Directions
From U.S. 101 in Sunnyvale, take the Highway 237 exit east. Follow Highway 237 for 4.5 miles to the Gold Street exit. Take Gold Street all the way toward the bay, then turn left on Elizabeth Street. Drive two blocks and turn right on Hope Street. The Alviso Slough parking lot is at the intersection of Hope and Elizabeth Streets. The trail leads from the right (south) side of the parking lot.

46 PENITENCIA CREEK TRAIL
Alum Rock Park, off U.S. 101 near San Jose

Total distance: 4.0 miles   **Biking time:** 1.0 hour

Type of trail: Dirt double-track and paved trail

Type of bike: Mountain bike

Steepness: Mostly level   **Skill level:** Easiest

For those who regularly commute down U.S. 101 in the South Bay, San Jose can seem like just another series of off-ramps and on-ramps, yet another place where the traffic comes to a dead halt as too many people try to merge and exit the freeway. But if all the gray concrete, metal bumpers, and highway dividers are making you nuts, a trip to Alum Rock Park can be just the antidote you need—a refreshing visit to a shady, tree-filled canyon nestled within the lower mountains of the Diablo range.

Alum Rock's claim to fame is that it is California's first and oldest park,

bridge over Penitencia Creek, Alum Rock Park

dedicated in 1872. From 1890 to 1932, the area was a health resort, offering visitors the chance to take a dip in 27 separate mineral springs. Even today, the smell of sulphur is present in the park, and you can see the rock pools where bathers once lolled in the waters. A steam railroad was built in 1890 to transport visitors from downtown San Jose uphill to the park.

The abandoned rail bed is the basis for Penitencia Creek Trail, which travels along year-round Penitencia Creek. The creek is lined with ferns in winter and wildflowers in spring, and shaded year-round by big-leaf maples, alders, oaks, and bays. This means a bike ride here is possible even in the heat of summer. Late fall and winter are still the best times to visit, however, when the park is uncrowded and the deciduous trees put on a nice display of color.

The easiest parking is at the end of the park road, across the creek from the park visitors center. From there, ride to the east (left), crossing Penitencia Creek and heading deeper into its canyon. Simply turn around at the bike trail's end and ride in the opposite direction. The first mile is perhaps the most interesting, as you pedal past the mineral springs and beautiful old rock bridges and structures along Penitencia Creek. The park looks genuinely old, as few places do in California. It isn't hard to imagine early-20th-century ladies and gentlemen strolling through these grounds, taking their "cures" in the magic waters.

Continue riding past the picnic areas (the trail turns from pavement to dirt) to the place where Penitencia Creek joins with Aguague Creek; only hikers may continue on the route. Walk across the bridge and take a peek at the creek confluence, a tumbling jumble of miniature waterfalls after winter rains. Then ride back along the creek trail, keeping the stream on your right, heading past the visitors center and other park facilities to a bridge that crosses over the main park road. Beyond the bridge, a trail branches off to the left, then shortly thereafter another trail branches off to the right, leading uphill toward Eagle Rock and connecting to North Rim Trail, which loops back to the parking area in 1.5 miles. Riders who don't want to do any climbing can just turn around at the North Rim Trail intersection and ride back along the creek for a four-mile round-trip.

Options
Instead of riding out and back along the level creek trail, loop back on North Rim Trail, which proceeds along the higher north side of the canyon.

Information and Contact
A $6 entrance fee is charged per vehicle. A free map of Alum Rock Park is available at the visitors center. For more information, contact Alum Rock Park, 16240 Alum Rock Avenue, San Jose, CA 95127, 408/259-5477 or 408/277-2757, website: www.ci.san-jose.ca.us.

Directions
From I-680 in San Jose, take the Berryessa Road exit and go east. Turn right on Capitol Expressway and drive south. Turn left on Penitencia Creek Road and proceed to the Alum Rock Park entrance.

47 LOS GATOS CREEK TRAIL
Vasona Lake County Park, off Highway 17 near Los Gatos

Total distance: 9.0 miles   **Biking time:** 1.5 hours

Type of trail: Dirt double-track and paved bike trail

Type of bike: Road bike or mountain bike

Steepness: Rolling terrain   **Skill level:** Easiest

Here's a family outing that includes plenty of options for your kids besides just fresh air and a bike ride. Vasona Lake County Park is ideally suited for family fun, with a section of the nine-mile long Los Gatos Creek Trail running through it, plus a miniature train, carousel, and children's play area.

Los Gatos Creek Trail is the main attraction for bike riders, and the section that runs from Vasona Lake County Park to Lexington Reservoir is one of the loveliest stretches of the entire route. The problem with the rest of the trail is that its northern section runs parallel to Highway 17 and is completely exposed to the busy freeway and backsides of housing tracts.

Los Gatos Creek Trail

But from Vasona Lake to Lexington Reservoir, the trail is largely shaded by trees and protected from the highway's sights and sounds. It provides a quick, easy escape from the urbanization of the South Bay.

Park near the children's playground and ride out of the parking lot to pick up the bike trail on the playground's far side. Right away, you'll notice an abundance of birds—ducks, coots, and Canada geese especially—and bird lovers who come to feed them crumbs of bread. You might choose to ride to your right first for a quick tour around the edge of Vasona Lake, but turn around when you reach the dam because the real fun is in the other direction, heading southward.

Heading south from the park, you parallel the narrow-gauge railroad tracks. Cross over the creek at the railroad crossing and check out the depot for Billy Jones Wildcat Railroad (remember, you have to be 38 inches tall to ride) and the old-fashioned carousel. On summer weekends, you can hear its nostalgic music from the trail.

Back on the main trail, ride with the creek on your right and Highway 17 on your left for just over a mile. The trail changes from pavement to wooden planks as you near Forbes Mill Footbridge; here you must walk your bike on the Highway 17 overpass. On the far side, the trail turns right and deposits you at the former Forbes Flour Mill. Today, a museum of local history is housed in the beautiful 1854 stone building built by James Forbes.

Skinny-tire riders will have to turn around here for a six-mile round-trip, as the trail changes to dirt and becomes a bit more rugged as it ascends to the dam at Lexington Reservoir. Fat-tire riders can ride up the left or right side of the spillway to get to the top of the dam, but either way, it's a good climb. At the top, stop and catch your breath as you gaze at the huge, 475-acre reservoir, which is popular with sailboaters, anglers, and rowing teams. It is quite pretty when the reservoir is filled with water, which unfortunately is not all the time.

On your ride back, make a stop in Old Town Los Gatos, walking through the big wooden doors on the western side of Forbes Mill Footbridge. Its small shopping district has a candy store that comes highly recommended.

Options

Want more mileage? Los Gatos Creek Trail continues as a paved, separate-from-cars trail for 4.6 more miles from Vasona Lake northward to Blackford Elementary School near the Campbell/San Jose border.

Information and Contact

A $5 entrance fee is charged per vehicle. A free map of Vasona Lake County Park is available by contacting Santa Clara County Parks and Recreation Department, 298 Garden Hill Drive, Los Gatos, CA 95030, 408/355-2200, website: www.parkhere.org. Or contact the Vasona Lake County Park Office at 408/356-2729.

Directions

From U.S. 101 in San Jose, take I-880 south toward Santa Cruz. I-880 becomes Highway 17; continue on Highway 17 to Los Gatos. Take the Lark Avenue exit and go east, then turn right on Los Gatos Boulevard and right again on Blossom Hill Road. Continue to the park entrance on the right side of the road. Park in the lot nearest the children's play area. The bike trail is on the far side of the play area.

48 COYOTE CREEK TRAIL

Coyote Hellyer County Park, off U.S. 101 near San Jose

Total distance: 13.6 miles   **Biking time:** 2.0 hours

Type of trail: Paved bike trail

Type of bike: Road bike or mountain bike

Steepness: Mostly level   **Skill level:** Easiest

Think of San Jose, and you probably think "industrial parks." It's true, San Jose has more than its share of these mammoth concrete complexes, but it also has peaceful farmlands, orchards, and gurgling creeks. Coyote

Creek Trail passes by all of it on its 14.7-mile length from Coyote Hellyer County Park south to Anderson Lake County Park. This makes a level, 29.4-mile round-trip on a paved recreation trail. If you simply want to crank out some level miles on your bike without worrying about cars or trail junctions, this is a good place to do it, and it's close to home for millions of Bay Area residents. The ride suggested here follows the first 6.8 miles of the trail from Coyote Hellyer south to Metcalf Road. But if you're feeling energetic, you can always just keep on riding.

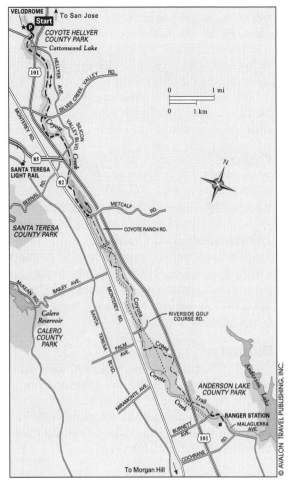

The trail begins at Coyote Hellyer County Park, home of the only velodrome in Northern California. Bike races are usually held on Friday nights in summer. The open-air velodrome was built in 1962 as a training site for the Pan American Games. Pick up the bike trail from the parking lots right next to the velodrome.

In the trail's first half mile, you ride past small Cottonwood Lake on the left, a popular spot with shore fishermen. The lake, which was developed out of an old rock quarry, is stocked with rainbow trout. Shortly beyond it, the trail crosses under U.S. 101 to its east side.

As you ride, ignore the numerous side bridges over Coyote Creek that access San Jose neighborhoods. Stay on the main path, which for a paved trail is a bit rough in places. You have to put up with the steady hum of road noise from U.S. 101 and Monterey Highway, which are never far away. But you also have the fine companionship of shady sycamores, cottonwoods, and live oaks along Coyote Creek, plus occasional scrub jays and ground squirrels.

At nearly six miles, the trail crosses U.S. 101 again, now back on its west side. Shortly thereafter, the trail reaches a levee along a dam on Coyote Creek. Here or soon beyond is a good place to turn around. At 6.8 miles, the trail reaches busy Metcalf Road, which you must cross if you want to continue southward.

Options

Continue riding farther south for up to seven more miles. The trail ends by the ranger station at Anderson Lake County Park, site of Santa Clara County's largest reservoir.

Information and Contact

A $5 entrance fee is charged per vehicle. For more information, contact Santa Clara County Parks and Recreation Department, 298 Garden Hill Drive, Los Gatos, CA 95030, 408/355-2200, website: www.parkhere.org.

Directions

From San Jose, drive four miles south on U.S. 101 and take the Hellyer Avenue exit. Drive .25 mile to the Coyote Hellyer County Park entrance. Just beyond the entrance kiosk, bear left at the fork and park at the velodrome parking lot.

49 RUSSIAN RIDGE LOOP

Russian Ridge Open Space Preserve, off Highway 35
near Palo Alto

Total distance: 8.8 miles　　　　　**Biking time:** 2.0 hours

Type of trail: Dirt double-track

Type of bike: Mountain bike

Steepness: Rolling terrain　　　　　**Skill level:** Moderate

Russian Ridge is one of the few open-space preserves on Skyline Boulevard where beginning mountain bikers have a chance to ride without becoming discouraged by the technical nature of the trails. Conveniently, it's also more than 1,500 acres of windswept ridgetop paradise, which will charm you in every season of the year. In summer and fall, the hillsides turn gold and the grasses sway in unison to the ridgetop winds. In winter,

Russian Ridge Open Space Preserve offers easy to moderate trail riding through grasslands and spring wildflowers.

the trunks of the moss-covered oaks and laurels turn a bright verdant green. And in spring, the grasslands explode in a fireworks display of colorful mule's ears, poppies, lupines, goldfields, Johnny-jump-ups, and blue-eyed grass. This preserve is considered to be one of the best places to see wildflowers in the entire Bay Area.

As you admire the scenery, you ride on a smooth path through rolling hills. The route described here is a 4.2-mile loop plus an out-and-back of an additional 2.3 miles, making your total trip just shy of nine miles.

Begin riding at the trailhead parking area at the junction of Alpine Road and Skyline Boulevard/Highway 35. You start with a serious climb up Bay Area Ridge Trail to the top of Borel Hill, the highest named point in San Mateo County. (Stay to the right at two junctions.) At 2,572 feet, Borel Hill is just high enough to provide a 360-degree view of the South Bay, Skyline Ridge, and all the way west to the Pacific.

From there, you descend quickly for .5 mile (keep your speed down) to a major junction of trails near Skyline Boulevard. Take Bay Area Ridge Trail, continuing northwest (basically straight) for another .5 mile to a junction with Hawk Trail. Turn left on Hawk Trail, starting to loop back. You descend to the junction of Mindego Ridge Trail and Ancient Oaks Trail. If you're feeling energetic, turn right here and ride out and back on Mindego Ridge Trail, dropping 400 feet in elevation to the trail's end and then turning around and climbing back up.

Back at the junction of Mindego Ridge Trail and Ancient Oaks Trail, proceed southeast on Ancient Oaks Trail, riding through a remarkable forest of gnarled oak trees interspersed with equally gnarled Douglas fir trees, plus some madrones and ferns. Then cruise back out into the sunshine to join Bay Area Ridge Trail again. Close out your loop by riding on the connector trail back to the parking lot.

Options

If you want an easier ride, stick to the loop trail and skip the out-and-back on Mindego Ridge Trail, which has a sizable elevation gain on the return trip.

Information and Contact

There is no fee. The preserve is open from dawn until sunset. Free trail maps are available at the trailhead. For more information, contact Midpeninsula Regional Open Space District, 330 Distel Circle, Los Altos, CA 94022, 650/691-1200, website: www.openspace.org.

Directions

From I-280 in Palo Alto, take the Page Mill Road exit west. Drive 8.9 winding miles to Skyline Boulevard (Highway 35). Cross Skyline Boulevard to Alpine Road. Drive 200 feet on Alpine Road and turn right into the Russian Ridge entrance.

Or, from the junction of Highway 35 and Highway 9 at Saratoga Gap, drive seven miles north on Highway 35 (Skyline Boulevard). Turn left on Alpine Road, and then right into the preserve entrance.

50 OLD HAUL ROAD

Pescadero Creek County Park, off Highway 1 near Pescadero

Total distance: 10.0 miles   **Biking time:** 2.5 hours

Type of trail: Dirt road

Type of bike: Mountain bike

Steepness: Rolling terrain   **Skill level:** Moderate

Old Haul Road is an old logging route that runs for five miles between Pescadero Creek County Park and Portola Redwoods State Park. It tunnels through a dense forest of second-growth redwoods, providing a smooth dirt path that is ideally suited for beginning mountain bike riders. Built on an old railroad bed, the trail never gains more than 500 feet in elevation and has an easy grade in both directions.

Given these facts, you'd think it wouldn't matter which end of the trail you start from, but it does matter. Driving to the trailhead at Portola Redwoods State Park is a long, circuitous route from just about everywhere, and once you get there, you have to pay the state park day-use fee just to park your car. Then you're faced with a steep climb up the park road to access the bike trail. By the time you finally make it to Old Haul Road, you might easily be tired, hungry, and irritable.

Starting from the Wurr Road trailhead at Pescadero Creek County Park is a much better bet. It requires an easy, scenic drive from

Mountain bikers enjoy an easy out-and-back on the Old Haul Road at Pescadero Creek County Park.

Highway 1 on the San Mateo County Coast. There is no fee to park at the trailhead, and the trail begins about 50 feet from where you park your car. You drive in, you unload your bike, you ride. You retain your sense of humor.

Once on Old Haul Road, you'll enjoy a meandering cruise through the forest. The trail begins by a small picnic area near the rushing creek gorge at Pescadero Creek County Park, then heads east. From the start, this is a pleasant, rolling, up-and-down course, with only a few brief steep sections. The hard-packed dirt and gravel road rarely gets muddy except after the hardest rains. You'll see plenty of big stumps along the route, and, in the rainy season, multiple tiny streams run down the hillsides to empty into Pescadero Creek. The forest is somewhat drier on the western side of the trail, with California laurel mixed in among Douglas firs and second-growth redwoods.

Where Old Haul Road meets the Portola Redwoods State Park service road, turn your wheels around for a 10-mile round-trip. And remember that equestrians also enjoy Old Haul Road; keep your speed down, and yield the trail to horses if you see any on your trip.

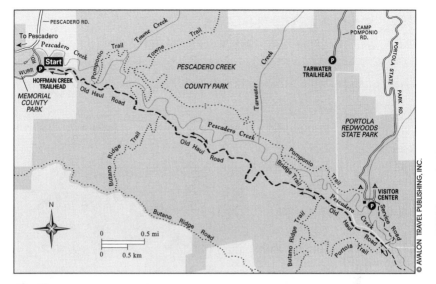

Options

Lock up your bike near where Old Haul Road meets the Portola Redwoods State Park service road. Walk about 150 feet up the paved road to where the Iverson Trail cuts off on your left. Follow Iverson Trail, crossing a bridge over Iverson Creek. In less than a mile, you come to tiny Tiptoe Falls, a pretty little waterfall in a canyon along Fall Creek. Even if the waterfall is running low, it's worth the trip just for this pretty walk through ferns and forest.

Information and Contact

There is no fee for parking at the Wurr Road trailhead for Old Haul Road. A Pescadero Creek County Park map is available at Memorial Park, .25 mile west on Pescadero Road. For more information, contact San Mateo County Parks and Recreation, 455 County Center, Fourth Floor, Redwood City, CA 94063, 650/363-4020, website: www.eparks.net. Or phone Memorial Park Visitor Center at 650/879-0212.

Directions

From Half Moon Bay, drive 15 miles south on Highway 1, then turn east on Pescadero Road and drive 9.8 miles. Turn right at the second entrance to Wurr Road, .25 mile past the entrance to Memorial Park. Drive .25 mile to the Hoffman Creek trailhead, where Old Haul Road begins.

Or, from I-280 at Woodside, take Highway 84 west for 13 miles to La Honda. Turn left on Pescadero Road and drive one mile, then bear right to stay on Pescadero Road. Continue 4.2 miles to Wurr Road on the left. Turn left and drive .25 mile to the trailhead.

51 SKYLINE-TO-THE-SEA TRAIL

Big Basin Redwoods State Park, off Highway 1 near Davenport

Total distance: 11.6 miles (plus 1.2-mile hike)   **Biking time:** 2.5 hours

Type of trail: Dirt double-track

Type of bike: Mountain bike

Steepness: Rolling terrain   **Skill level:** Easiest

Ah, bliss. Skyline-to-the-Sea Trail is the embodiment of a perfect easy bike trail. And even better, it's the easiest way to reach one of the Bay Area's premier outdoor destinations, 70-foot-high Berry Creek Falls. Sure, you can visit the waterfall the hard way, by hiking 5.5 hilly miles one-way from park headquarters at Big Basin Redwoods State Park. But why not go see Berry Creek Falls the easy way, by riding your bike 5.8 nearly level miles from the coast near Davenport, then walking in the last .6 mile? Riders of almost any ability can handle the wide dirt road, and the trip begins and ends at an easy-access trailhead right on Highway 1.

An easy ride through the redwoods leads to beautiful Berry Creek Falls.

While Berry Creek Falls is unquestionably the highlight of this ride, the entire trail is marked by beautiful scenery, including flowing Waddell Creek, ferns galore, alders, Douglas firs, and, of course, big redwoods. This trail is a winner every pedal crank of the way.

The trail, which is the western section of the 38-mile-long Skyline-to-the-Sea Trail, used to be even easier to ride, but heavy rains in the 1990s washed parts of it into Waddell Creek, forcing one stretch to be rerouted as narrow single-track with a few ludicrously tight turns. The vast majority of riders simply walk their bikes through this 100-yard stretch, which comes up at the three-mile mark. The rest of the trail is still very manageable, even for beginners.

The trail starts as pavement at the highway but turns to dirt after passing the small Rancho del Oso visitors center. It passes a few small farms, then quickly heads deeper into the canyon, becoming enveloped by the woods. You pass a few backpacking camps just off the route, used mostly by hikers following the entire length of Skyline-to-the-Sea Trail. At 3.4 miles is a crossing of Waddell Creek, where a sign directs trail users to the right to cross a long, narrow footbridge if the stream is too high to ford.

At 5.8 miles, you reach a bike rack and the end of the rideable section of Skyline-to-the-Sea Trail. Here, you must lock up your bike (don't forget your lock!) so you can take the 15-minute walk to the waterfall. With an impressive flow of water after winter rains, Berry Creek Falls creates a strong wind and a memorable sight. The waterfall never goes dry; this is one Bay Area cataract that is dependable even in the dry month of August, although its flow is greatly diminished. A bench on the viewing platform below Berry Creek Falls makes a perfect spot for lunch, if it isn't already in use by somebody else. Not surprisingly, this is a popular spot year-round. Plan a weekday trip if at all possible.

After getting an eyeful of the falls and its scenic canyon, your trip

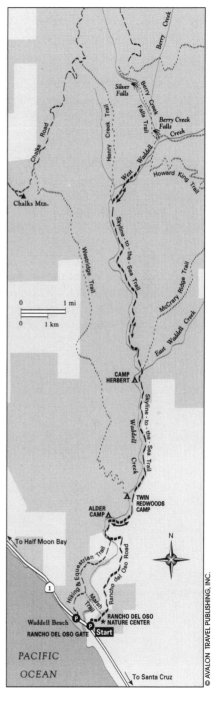

back is an easy downhill cruise. Beautiful Waddell Beach awaits when you return to your car at Highway 1.

Options
If you want to hike farther, you can see two more waterfalls—Silver Falls and Golden Falls, just upstream from Berry Creek Falls. Continue uphill on Berry Creek Falls Trail for 1.5 miles to the two falls, one shortly after the other.

Information and Contact
There is no fee. A map of Big Basin Redwoods State Park is available at the Rancho del Oso visitors center. For more information, contact Big Basin Redwoods State Park, 21600 Big Basin Way, Boulder Creek, CA 95006, 831/338-8860 or website: www.parks.ca.gov or www.bigbasin.org.

Directions
From Half Moon Bay at the junction of Highway 92 and Highway 1, drive south on Highway 1 for 30 miles to the Rancho del Oso area of Big Basin Redwoods State Park (across from Waddell Beach, 7.5 miles north of Davenport). Park on the east side of the highway by the Rancho del Oso gate.

Chapter 7

© ANN MARIE BROWN

Monterey and Big Sur

Monterey and Big Sur

It wouldn't be easy to choose the most spectacular stretch of California coastline, but if pressed, most beach connoisseurs would agree there is nothing quite as visually stunning as the 130 miles of cliffs, rocks, and waves that run from Davenport to San Simeon. Cyclists have been traveling this stretch of Highway 1 ever since the road was built in the 1930s. Along the way, they stop on top of 200-foot-high cliffs to admire the crashing surf, cross over concrete bridges spanning precipitous river gorges, and experience mile after mile of postcard-quality coastal scenery.

There is nothing to dislike here, from the mild climate to the wild landscape. Much of this area is isolated, undeveloped, and difficult to access, with high cliffs and few roads. Visiting this land means wandering along gravel beaches, watching sunsets over glimmering seas, and walking in the shadows of giant redwoods. South of Carmel, services are clustered in a few small towns: Big Sur, Lucia, Gorda, and San Simeon. In between are silence, solitude, and the sea.

In the midst of all this splendor, every winter and spring, like clockwork, a great natural spectacle occurs: Gray whales pass by on their long migrations. Traveling from their summer home in Alaska's Bering Sea to their winter breeding grounds in Baja, then back again a few months later, they leave hundreds of frothy spouts and occasional glimpses of fins or tails as their calling cards. Whale-watching is at its best December–May, on days when the sea is flat and deep blue, with no wind or whitecaps.

Besides watching whales, there's much more to keep a bicyclist occupied in the Monterey and Big Sur region. Mountain bikers cruise the trails of Wilder Ranch and Forest of Nisene Marks State Parks near Santa Cruz. Skinny-tire riders pedal the paved path at Henry Cowell Redwoods State Park or world-famous 17-Mile Drive, with its ocean lookouts, golf courses, and mansions. And riders of all styles and abilities can test out their wheels on the 14.5-mile Monterey Peninsular Recreation Trail, which runs from Marina to Pacific Grove, passing by highlights such as Monterey Bay Aquarium and Cannery Row.

Whatever kind of riding you enjoy, you'll find the right trail in the Monterey and Big Sur region. Here at "the greatest meeting of land and sea" lies a world of bicycling opportunities.

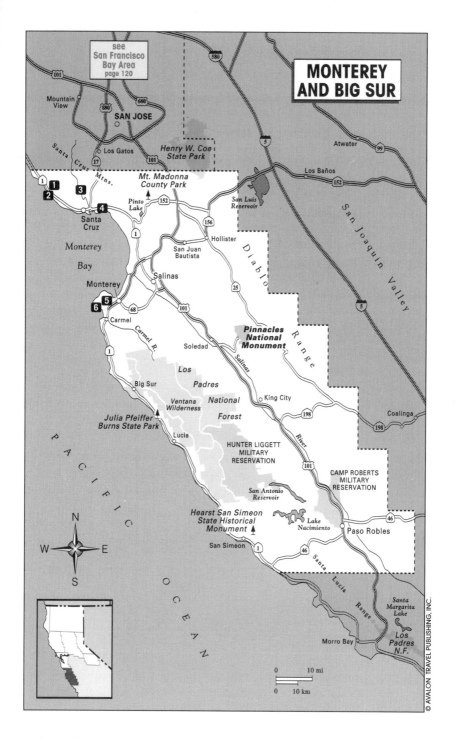

1 WILDER RIDGE & ZANE GRAY LOOP

Wilder Ranch State Park, off Highway 1 near Santa Cruz

Total distance: 6.0 miles   **Biking time:** 2.0 hours

Type of trail: Dirt double-track

Type of bike: Mountain bike

Steepness: Steep sections   **Skill level:** Moderate

Wilder Ranch State Park's 5,100-acre north side is almost completely the domain of mountain bikers. The experience here is a lot like visiting a mountain bike park at the ski areas around Tahoe or Mammoth. As you peer upward from the bottom of Wilder's coastal hills, dozens of bikers race toward you, each carving perfect S turns on the descent down the slope. The park's 30 miles of trails seem to have been built with mountain biking in mind: They roller-coaster, with plenty of twists, turns, and short-but-steep ups and downs.

Not surprisingly, it's a popular place, but there's no reason to be intimidated by the crowds, even on sunny, busy weekends. The park is large enough to accommodate everybody. Great views of Monterey Bay and the Pacific Ocean are a major plus, visible from several high points in these coastal hills. You just have to be willing to climb a bit.

Beginners need to choose their trails wisely, because many of Wilder's paths were built to take advantage of intermediate to advanced technical challenges, like stream crossings, rocks, and ruts. These would not be fun for the average easy rider. But if you are willing to crank up a 500-foot

wide views of coast and grasslands from the Wilder Ridge and Zane Gray Loop

ascent, Wilder Ridge Loop offers a good taste of the park's backcountry treats. Despite the hill, the trails are well signed and graded gently enough to be considered easy, with fantastic ocean views.

From the parking lot, ride your bike to the left (east), following the path past the restrooms, then taking the park road to the right. Turn left and walk your bike through the cultural preserve/ranch buildings, around the back and past the picnic tables and chicken coops, to a tunnel that leads underneath Highway 1.

Beyond the tunnel, ride past a horse-riding ring, then make a sharp left turn and head uphill. You are now on Wilder Ridge Loop Trail, and you have some serious climbing ahead. Pass a small pond on your left, then shortly a trail marker appears for Wilder Ridge Loop, which heads both left and right. Stay to the right on the double-track trail, saving the single-track fork for your return trip.

You can walk the steepest section of the hill, which lasts for only about 200 yards, and if you do, you probably won't be alone. The effort is well worthwhile, as you'll discover when you reach the top and take the left spur trail, which brings you to an incredible lookout over Monterey Bay in about 40 feet. Now pat yourself on the back, and maybe have an energy bar, too. Looking at the valley below, you'll be amazed at how far you've climbed.

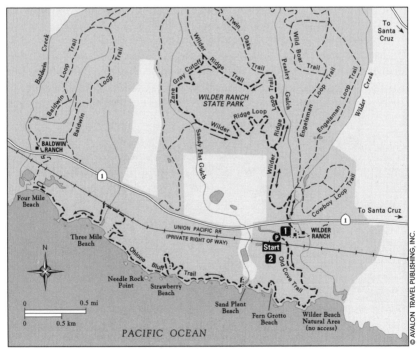

Get back on the loop when you're ready, continuing along the ridge for about .5 mile to Zane Gray Cutoff on the left, then ride down this single-track path until it meets up with Wilder Ridge Loop again—the single-track fork that you passed on the way in. Head left to close off the loop. While Zane Gray is a rather straight and practical trail, the single-track section of Wilder Ridge Loop has about a million curves and turns. Luckily, it's almost all downhill, but watch your speed or you can take a spill. When you finally meet the double-track section of Wilder Ridge Loop, turn right for an easy descent back to the cultural preserve and the parking lot.

Options

To make this trip easier, just ride up to the overlook, then turn around and ride back the way you came. Also, be sure to ride these trails after a period of dry weather, as rain and mud can make them far more difficult—especially the single-track sections.

Information and Contact

A $6 day-use fee is charged per vehicle. A park map is available from the entrance kiosk. For more information, contact Wilder Ranch State Park, 1401 Old Coast Road, Santa Cruz, CA 95060, 831/423-9703, website: www.parks.ca.gov.

Directions

From Santa Cruz, drive north on Highway 1 for four miles. Turn left into the entrance for Wilder Ranch State Park, then follow the park road to its end at the main parking area. You must walk your bike through the cultural preserve to access the tunnel under the freeway to the inland side of the park.

2 WILDER RANCH BLUFFS RIDE
Wilder Ranch State Park, off Highway 1 near Santa Cruz

Total distance: 7.6 miles   **Biking time:** 2.0 hours

Type of trail: Dirt double-track

Type of bike: Mountain bike

Steepness: Mostly level   **Skill level:** Easiest

Old Cove Landing and Ohlone Bluff Trails are exactly the opposite of all other trails at Wilder Ranch State Park. These trails are coastal; the park's other trails are inland. These trails are almost completely level; the park's other trails are roller-coastering climbs and descents.

dramatic oceanside bluffs at Wilder Ranch State Park

If the shoe fits, wear it. For easy riding, a cruise on Old Cove Landing and Ohlone Bluff Trails is a great way to spend an afternoon at Wilder Ranch State Park. The trails reveal many surprises, including dramatic cliffs and sea arches, a seal rookery, windswept beaches, and a hidden fern cave.

Old Cove Landing Trail begins from the main parking lot by the large signboard to the right of the restrooms. Begin riding on a level ranch road through the park's agricultural preserve—nearly 900 acres of brussels sprouts fields. The trail leads toward the coast, then turns right and parallels it. You're pedaling on top of sandstone and mudstone bluffs, the remains of an ancient marine terrace. In short order, you pass a wooden platform overlooking Wilder Beach, a critical habitat area for the endangered snowy plover, followed by the trail's namesake, the old landing cove—a remarkably narrow inlet where small schooners pulled in and anchored to load lumber in the late 1800s.

Continuing onward, cruise by a huge flat rock where harbor seals hang out, lying around in the sun to warm their flippers. At a wooden post marked as number 8, look down on Fern Grotto Beach, a small sandy cove. Tucked into its back wall is a shallow cave filled with sword and bracken ferns. A spur trail leads to it; carry your bike down and explore the cave if you please.

Beyond Fern Grotto Beach lie several more beaches. Accessing them, however, most often requires a little upper body strength. The bluffs above Sand Plant Beach are private farming property; during most of the year, bikers are not permitted to ride through, although you might get lucky and show up during a period when you are allowed. If the bluffs are closed off, you must follow the signs that direct you to carry your bike down to Sand Plant Beach and across the sand, then follow another trail back up to the bluffs on the beach's south side. Once you're back on the bluffs south of Sand Plant, the trail changes names to Ohlone Bluff Trail and travels 2.5 miles farther, past Strawberry Beach, Needle Rock, Three Mile Beach, and finally Four Mile Beach, a strip of sand well known for its clothing-optional tendencies. Beyond Four Mile Beach, the trail starts to head inland, so turn around and head back the way you came, enjoying the coastal scenery from the opposite perspective.

Options
You can cut this trip short anywhere you like. The views of the rugged coastline are excellent from all points on the trail.

Information and Contact
A $6 day-use fee is charged per vehicle. A park map is available for free from the entrance kiosk. For more information, contact Wilder Ranch State Park, 1401 Old Coast Road, Santa Cruz, CA 95060, 831/423-9703, website: www.parks.ca.gov.

Directions
From Santa Cruz, drive north on Highway 1 for four miles. Turn left into the entrance for Wilder Ranch State Park, then follow the park road to its end at the main parking area.

3 PIPELINE ROAD
Henry Cowell Redwoods State Park, off Highway 9 near Santa Cruz

Total distance: 6.0 miles   **Biking time:** 1.5 hours

Type of trail: Paved bike trail

Type of bike: Road bike or mountain bike

Steepness: Steep sections   **Skill level:** Easiest

Henry Cowell Redwoods State Park is celebrated for its ancient groves of coast redwoods. It's famous for its Roaring Camp Railroad steam trains, which roar over tracks carving through the center of the park. And it's well known for the San Lorenzo River, which provides good swimming for park visitors in summer and rushing waters for salmon and steelhead in winter.

Pipeline Road in Henry Cowell Redwoods meanders through dense forest.

But while bicyclists may enjoy all these aspects of Henry Cowell Redwoods State Park, what they'll really like is Pipeline Road, a paved service road that travels the park's length. It is closed to cars but open to bikers, hikers, and dogs on leash. The road has a few steep pitches, but much of it just rolls gently beside the San Lorenzo River or cruises along a ridgeline in a dense forest of redwoods, laurels, and Douglas firs. If you carry a bike lock on your Pipeline Road ride, you can visit another of the park's highlights—the observation platform on Ridge Fire Road, where a fine view encompasses Monterey Bay and some unusual flora.

The paved road begins behind the nature center, not far from the park's Redwood Trail Loop. (Make sure you walk this .25-mile trail through the redwoods before or after your bike ride.) Follow Pipeline Road on your bike, paralleling the San Lorenzo River and the hikers-only River Trail. You're in a forest of second- and third-growth redwoods; if you look carefully among them, you'll see giant stumps that belonged to the first growth of trees. In short order, you pass under a railroad trestle that crosses the San Lorenzo River, where a signboard displays a park map. Although the river is only a few inches deep in summer, it can be 20 or 30 feet deep during winter rains. Chances are good that as you ride along the river, you'll hear the wail of a train screeching around a curve in the canyon. The privately operated Roaring Camp Railroad runs through the park (the ticket office and station are near the parking lot where you left your car). When you hear one of its trains, you may think it sounds more like the "Wailing" Camp Railroad.

The first stretch of trail is pretty mellow, with many small ups and downs. The middle stretch is the harder, steeper part, with a .5-mile section that may force you to stop and walk your bike. Fortunately, the road is shaded by redwoods and Douglas firs, so at least you won't be overheated. The final stretch of road is easy again, featuring a nice level stint along the ridgeline. On this last stretch you reach an overlook point with a bench, from which you can see all the way down the San Lorenzo River canyon to Monterey Bay and the Pacific Ocean. A sea of conifers lies between you and the coast.

Keep riding beyond the overlook to a major junction of trails at three miles out, where Huckleberry Trail goes right, Pipeline Road continues straight ahead, and Powder Mill Fire Road and Graham Hill Trail head left. There's a picnic table at this junction, on the left side of Pipeline Road. The paved trail continues for another .5 mile, but it makes a serious descent and then ends abruptly at Graham Hill Road, at which point you would simply have to turn around and climb back up. Instead, make this junction your turnaround point, but before you make the fast and furious descent back to the trailhead, lock up your bike and take a walk to the park's observation platform. (Technically, you're allowed to ride there, but the road is ridiculously sandy. You might as well leave your bike and walk.)

Follow Powder Mill Fire Road gently uphill for .5 mile to the concrete observation deck, which offers a picnic table, hitching post, and water fountain, plus two surprising types of trees—knobcone pines and ponderosa pines. The latter, with its distinctive jigsaw-puzzle bark, usually is found at much higher elevations in places like the Sierra Nevada. Here, at 800 feet in elevation in the Santa Cruz Mountains, the ponderosa pine grows only in this strange "sand hill chaparral" community. This region's sandy soil is the remnant of an ancient ocean floor. Four million years ago, a shallow sea completely covered the area.

Walk up the observation platform's stairs for a somewhat obstructed view of Monterey Bay. (The forest has grown up around the observation platform since it was built.) Even if the view is only fair, the sunny platform is a fine place to lie down and take a nap.

When you return to your bike and Pipeline Road, remember that your downhill return is going to be fast. Be sure to keep your speed down and watch for hikers, bikers, and dogs coming uphill.

Options

After visiting the observation deck, return to your bike and backtrack on Pipeline Road to Ridge Fire Road. Turn left on Ridge Fire Road to connect to Rincon Fire Road and ride to Cathedral Redwoods, a peaceful grove of big trees.

Information and Contact

A $6 day-use fee is charged per vehicle. A park map is available from the visitors center. For more information, contact Henry Cowell Redwoods State Park, 101 North Big Trees Park Road, Felton, CA 95018, 831/335-4598 or, website: www.parks.ca.gov.

Directions

From Santa Cruz at the junction of Highway 1 and Highway 9, take Highway 9 north six miles to the right turnoff for Henry Cowell Redwoods State Park. Continue past the entrance kiosk to the visitors center and main parking lot. Follow the signs to the redwood grove and the nature center, then take the paved road that leads to the right of the nature center. Pipeline Road begins behind the nature center.

4 APTOS CREEK FIRE ROAD

Forest of Nisene Marks State Park, off Highway 1 near Aptos

Total distance: 5.2 miles   **Biking time:** 1.5 hours

Type of trail: Dirt double-track

Type of bike: Mountain bike

Steepness: Mostly level   **Skill level:** Easiest

Two major forces have shaped the land at Forest of Nisene Marks State Park: the railroad and unstable geology. Old-growth redwoods remained untouched in this steep and winding canyon for hundreds of years until the Loma Prieta Lumber Company came into ownership in 1881. Teaming up with Southern Pacific, they built a railroad along Aptos Creek and worked the land with trains, oxen, skid roads, inclines, horses, and as many men as they could hire, removing 140 million board feet of lumber over the course of 40 years. In 1922, when the loggers finally put their saws down, there were no trees left.

Luckily, Mother Nature has been busy in the last 80 years. Today, the canyon is filled with second-growth redwoods and Douglas firs, and the higher ridges are lined with oaks, eucalyptus, and madrones. Still, as you ride you occasionally pass a magnificent old stump, and it makes you hope that those lumber barons are sitting it out in purgatory.

Mother Nature was especially busy on October 17, 1989, when the park was the epicenter of the famous Loma Prieta earthquake, which forcefully shook the entire San Francisco Bay Area. You'll ride near the earthquake epicenter on this out-and-back tour, which follows Aptos Creek Fire Road for 2.6 miles.

The ride is densely shaded all the way and simple to follow, without a lot of technical challenges. The grade is so mellow on this stretch of Aptos Creek Fire Road that even children can ride it. From George's Picnic Area, the hard-packed dirt road parallels Aptos Creek, climbing almost imperceptibly. You pass two other picnic areas and several cut-offs for hikers-only trails. As you near the epicenter, you head briefly downhill and cross a steel bridge, then come to a large sign that reads: "Epicenter Area, 7.1 Earthquake, 5:04 P.M., October 17, 1989. You are in the vicinity of the earthquake's epicenter. Though there is little evidence here, slides and fissures occurred in more remote areas of the park." (This sign frequently gets stolen, and the park dutifully replaces it as often as it can afford. Don't be too surprised if it isn't there when you visit.)

A hiking trail leads to the exact epicenter from the left side of the earthquake sign. You must cross Aptos Creek and walk .5 mile. There is little to see at the epicenter, but it is pleasant to hike the path anyway, just to enjoy the dense second-growth forest. (Pack along a lock to use at the bike rack near the earthquake sign.)

Options

Aptos Creek Fire Road continues for 4.3 more miles to Sand Point Overlook at 1,500 feet in elevation, but it's a serious climb. Immediately beyond the earthquake sign, the trail enters a stretch known as Molino Incline, built for the loggers' narrow-gauge railroad, which makes several hairpin turns through which the road ascends 660 feet. If you can make it to the "Top of the Incline" in slightly more than a mile, the rest of the route seems easier.

Information and Contact

A $6 day-use fee is charged per vehicle. A map is available at the entrance kiosk. For more information, contact Sunset State Beach/Forest of Nisene Marks State Park, 201 Sunset Beach Road, Watsonville, CA 95076, 831/763-7063, website: www.parks.ca.gov.

Directions

From Santa Cruz, drive south on Highway 1 for six miles to the Aptos/State Park Drive exit. Turn left at the exit, drive .25 mile, then turn right on Soquel Drive and drive .5 mile. Turn left on Aptos Creek Road and drive 1.8 miles to George's Picnic Area.

5 MONTEREY PENINSULA RECREATION TRAIL

Monterey & Pacific Grove, off Highway 1 in Monterey

Total distance: 10.0 miles   **Biking time:** 2.0 hours

Type of trail: Paved bike trail

Type of bike: Road bike or mountain bike

Steepness: Mostly level   **Skill level:** Easiest

Good news happened at the close of the 20th century: After 25 years of red-tape wrangling, a final link in the Monterey Peninsula Recreation Trail was built through Sand City, making the trail a "nearly complete" 14.5 miles of car-free riding (29 miles round-trip). Nearly complete? Well, close enough: There's a short stretch where you must follow bike lanes through Seaside's shopping center, but otherwise, you're largely free of the dreaded gas-guzzler, except for street and parking lot crossings.

The truth is most people don't ride the entire trail, but it's nice to know it's an option. Easy riders would do well to stick to the most scenic, southern section, provided they can find a place to leave their car, which isn't always easy in tourist-laden Monterey. The easiest and cheapest parking is in the Monterey Harbor parking lot, at the corner of Del Monte Avenue and Washington Street. The bike trail leads in both directions from the lot, and the mileage above reflects riding both ways.

© ANN MARIE BROWN

a newly built stretch of the Monterey Recreation Trail

The stretch heading west to the town of Pacific Grove is unforgettable. All your senses are involved in the experience of this ride, but most of all your olfactory sense. Monterey smells wonderfully fishy, and the scent can be highly evocative—you may find yourself scheming to stow away on a freighter and live a life at sea.

Stick to your two wheels for now, though, and pedal toward Cannery Row and Monterey Bay Aquarium. Go very

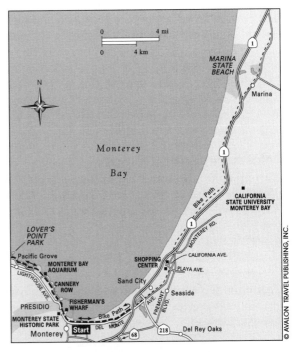

slowly and watch for pedestrians and especially kids, particularly near the aquarium. Also try to avoid the omnipresent four-wheeled, canopied rental bikes that take up more than half of the trail.

In between the bustling tourist areas are quiet stretches that belong only to you and the sea. We watched some scuba divers coming up out of the water and saw a pelican dive into the waves. We witnessed the sun turn bright orange and sink behind the harbor. South of Cannery Row, the trail leads into the wealthy neighborhood of Pacific Grove, with its bed-and-breakfast inns and restaurants. Views of the rugged, rocky coastline and the white-sand beaches get even better. This part of the trail is quintessential Monterey: Sea lions poke their heads out of the water, kayakers paddle by and wave, and sea otters float by on their backs, munching on abalone. The trail ends near Lover's Point, an enchanting seaside park near 17th Street. If you turn right and ride or walk down the road for about 100 yards, you can enter the park, explore its manicured lawns, and gaze out over the marine refuge below. Among a grove of windswept Monterey pines sit two interesting sculptures—one depicting a butterfly, and one of a child pointing to the sea.

When you return to your car, follow the bike trail in the opposite direction, toward Seaside. But don't expect the kind of scenery you just experienced.

The route to Seaside is far more pedestrian in nature, but it's a good way to roll out some miles and extend your trip for a 10-mile workout.

Options
Skip the ride to Seaside, and just ride out and back to Pacific Grove for a six-mile round-trip and the best scenery. Or try pedaling one of the more northern sections of trail. Another excellent starting point is "midtrail" at Laguna Grande Park in Seaside.

Information and Contact
There is no fee. For more information, contact Monterey Peninsula Regional Park District, 60 Garden Court, Suite 325, Monterey, CA 93940, 831/372-3196, website: www.mprpd.org.

Directions
From U.S. 101 in Salinas, take Highway 68 southwest to Highway 1. Take the Monterey Peninsula exit, which puts you on Camino Aguajito. Follow Camino Aguajito to Del Monte Avenue along the bay. Turn left on Del Monte and park in the Monterey Harbor parking lot, at the corner of Del Monte Avenue and Washington Street. The bike trail runs parallel to Del Monte Avenue.

---

6 17-MILE DRIVE
Off Highway 1 south of Pacific Grove

Total distance: 15.0 miles   **Biking time:** 2.0 hours

Type of trail: Paved road

Type of bike: Road bike or mountain bike

Steepness: Rolling terrain   **Skill level:** Moderate

One of the top reasons to ride your bike on world-famous 17-Mile Drive is because it costs eight bucks to drive your car on it, but biking is free. Another reason is because it's gorgeous. Before cars became the normal mode of transportation, 17-Mile Drive was navigated by horse-drawn carriages from Monterey's Hotel Del Monte. Tourists staying at the hotel in the late 1800s would be driven through Del Monte Forest and down to the same exquisite coastline that we see today, minus the sprawling golf courses (Pebble Beach Golf Links opened in 1919).

As you ride 17-Mile Drive, you may wish for those days of carriages instead of cars, because in the summer tourist season this road is extremely congested. Although nobody drives the scenic route fast (after all, drivers

The coastside leg of the 17-Mile-Drive offers close-up views of the crashing surf.

want to get their money's worth), I do not recommend riding it in summer, except perhaps in the early morning on weekdays. I would especially avoid weekends and holidays. Some of the route follows shoulderless roads, and the vast majority of drivers are gawking at the scenery, not watching for cyclists. This is not a ride for taking the kids on, but alert adult riders will thoroughly enjoy the trip, as long as they stick to riding in the off-season.

Three gates allow access to 17-Mile Drive. The Pacific Grove gate near Asilomar State Beach (see Directions, below) is probably the best place for bicyclists to start and end their trip, particularly if they want to follow my suggested route and not ride the entire 17-Mile Drive. Why not ride the whole thing? Only roughly half of the famous drive is actually along the coast; the rest weaves inland through hillsides covered with suburban-looking homes and cypress forests. Instead of riding the entire 17.4-mile loop, you can opt to go out and back from the Pacific Grove gate to Pebble Beach. This is a 15-mile round-trip, and you leave out the most strenuous hills while keeping in the best of the coastside scenery. After all, the coastal stretch is what everyone comes here for: ocean lookouts, impossibly green and fine-trimmed golf courses, showy mansions belonging to movie stars and the very wealthy, and the white sands and turquoise waters of Monterey Bay. There's no other drive (or bike ride) like it in the world.

The 17-Mile Drive is signed like crazy, so there is no chance of getting lost, despite numerous turns. To orient yourself, pick up a full-color map at the entrance gate when you sign your liability waiver to bicycle 17-Mile Drive.

Options

You can always add on a few more miles by completing the entire 17-Mile Drive instead of riding out and back on the coastal section. But be forewarned; about 1.5 miles beyond Pebble Beach you'll come to a doozy of a hill that continues up, up, and up for more than a mile. It's a workout.

Information and Contact

There is no fee. For more information, contact Pacific Grove Chamber of Commerce, P.O. Box 167, Pacific Grove, CA 93950, 831/373-3304 or 800/656-6650, website: www.pacificgrove.org.

Directions

From the junction of Highway 1 and Highway 68 north of Carmel, take Highway 68 northwest to Pacific Grove. Highway 68 ends at the Pacific Grove gate to 17-Mile Drive and the start of Sunset Drive. Parking is available on side streets off Sunset Drive or at Asilomar State Beach on Sunset Drive.

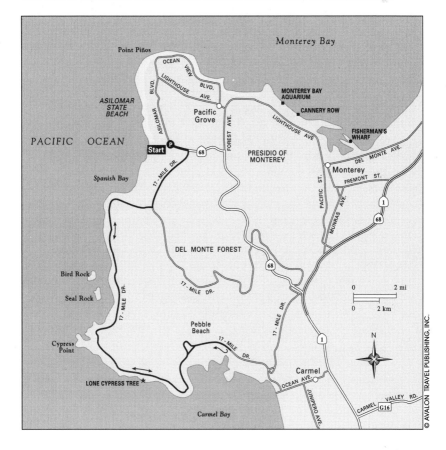

Chapter 8

© ANN MARIE BROWN

Yosemite and Mammoth Lakes

Yosemite and Mammoth Lakes

Plunging waterfalls, stark granite, alpine lakes, pristine meadows, giant sequoias, and raging rivers—you'll find them all in the Yosemite and Mammoth Lakes region, which encompasses not only world-famous Yosemite National Park, but also the popular recreation areas of Mammoth Lakes and the Eastern Sierra.

The centerpiece of this region, of course, is Yosemite National Park, a must-see on every traveler's itinerary. And what better way to see it than on two wheels, pedaling along the Yosemite Valley bike path? On a bicycle, you have wide-open views of Yosemite Valley's famous waterfalls, three of which are among the tallest in the world, plus the towering granite of El Capitan, Half Dome, and Sentinel Rock.

As scenic as the national park itself are the resort areas just to the east, particularly Mammoth Lakes on the U.S. 395 corridor. Best known for skiing and snowboarding in winter, the Mammoth area is also ideal for cycling in the warmer seasons. One of the greatest challenges for bike riders is dealing with the thin air at this altitude, which ranges 7,000–9,200 feet. Pavement and dirt-trail rides include easy loops near towns and more strenuous rides through alpine meadows, fir and pine forests, and sagebrush-covered plains.

The area east of U.S. 395 is dominated by Mono Lake, an ancient and majestic body of water covering 60 square miles. At more than 700,000 years old, Mono Lake is one of the oldest lakes in North America. Riding your bike near its lakeshore is a great way to experience one of the most unusual landscapes in California.

Key to enjoying your experience in Yosemite and Mammoth is planning your visit for the least crowded months of the year. Summer is the busiest time and best avoided. Springtime in Yosemite is ideal for viewing the valley's spectacular waterfalls. A visit before school lets out for the summer gives you a chance to see the famous valley without the masses.

Fall, too, is a fine time for cycling in and around Yosemite, and likewise, if there is a perfect time to visit the Eastern Sierra, it's in the transition between summer and winter. Autumn transforms the scenic canyons and pristine lakeshores into a wave of blazing color. The trees generally begin their color change early in September; peak viewing is usually in late September and early October. With an autumn show like this, why go to New England?

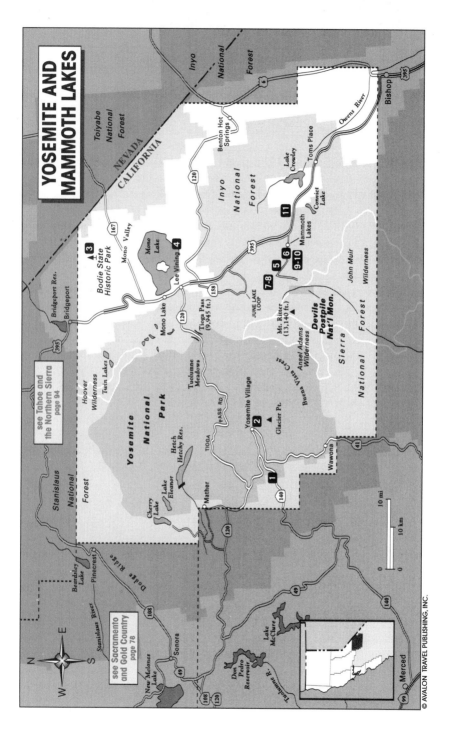

YOSEMITE AND MAMMOTH LAKES

© AVALON TRAVEL PUBLISHING, INC.

1 MERCED RIVER RAILROAD GRADE

BLM Folsom Resource Area, off Highway 140 near Mariposa

Total distance: 6.0 miles   **Biking time:** 2.0 hours

Type of trail: Dirt double-track

Type of bike: Mountain bike

Steepness: Mostly level   **Skill level:** Moderate

Merced River Railroad Grade is a mountain biker's dream trail. Pick a sunny April–June day, when the Merced River is running strong and the grassland wildflowers are blooming. Cruise along the wide, level path, enjoying nonstop river views and the entertainment of white-water rafters floating by. Feel the smooth gravel-and-dirt surface under your wheels and the wind in your hair.

The only way it could get any better than this would be if the trail continued farther than it does. Merced River Railroad Grade begins at the Bureau of Land Management's Railroad Flat Campground along the Merced River, only a few miles from the entrance to Yosemite National Park and Yosemite Valley. It takes a nearly five-mile drive on a dirt road to reach the camp and trailhead, but it's manageable in a passenger car. The first stretch of the railroad grade is rideable most of the year, although it can be quite hot in summer. After the first couple of miles, the trail can become impassable in winter and early spring, due to side streams that are not bridged. For scenery, the best season to ride here is late spring and early summer, when the foothill wildflowers are in bloom. To be assured of the longest possible ride, the best season to ride is autumn, when the trail will be dry.

Because it's an old railroad grade along the river, the trail is as flat as a pancake. You drive the first 4.8 miles of the grade to reach the trailhead, then leave your vehicle at Railroad Flat Campground. Walk your bike around the white metal gate signed "Do Not Block." One hundred yards beyond the white gate is a second, more formal gate. Shoulder your bike to heft it over the top, then enjoy the scene on the gate's far side, where Halls Gulch cascades down the hillside to join the Merced River. A bench sits here, at the official start of the trail.

Begin your ride. Everything should go smoothly in the first stretch. About .5 mile in, you pass the remains of an old diversion dam that was removed from the river. In the next mile, the canyon gets narrower and the river gets more ferocious as it builds up power for North Fork Falls. Between the second and third mile, the trail starts to get more rutted and rocky. Washouts sometimes occur during heavy rain years. (The quality of this part of the

Merced River Railroad Grade

trail varies greatly from season to season; before making a special trip, call the Bureau of Land Management for updated trail conditions.) At three miles out, you reach the point where the North Fork converges with the main fork of the Merced River. There is no bridge across the North Fork, and in spring you will be forced to turn back. (You may be joined by rafters on the trail here, who must portage at this stretch of river.) No matter; this makes an excellent turnaround spot. Just wheel your bike around, start pedaling, and watch the river roll by from the opposite perspective.

Options
If you ride this trail in late summer or autumn, you may be able to cross the North Fork of the Merced River and keep riding along the railroad grade. The trail continues beyond the North Fork for another six miles to Bagby.

Information and Contact
There is no fee. For more information, contact the Bureau of Land Management, Folsom Resource Area, 63 Natoma Street, Folsom, CA 95630, 916/985-4474, website: www.ca.blm.gov/folsom.

Directions
From Merced, drive 45 miles northeast on Highway 140 to Mariposa. Continue east on Highway 140 to the Briceburg Visitor Center on the left. Turn left at the visitors center and continue past it for 100 yards to the suspension bridge over the Merced River. Drive across the bridge and turn left, paralleling the river. Drive 4.8 miles to Railroad Flat Campground, where the road is gated off and the rail trail begins.

2 YOSEMITE VALLEY BIKE PATH

Yosemite National Park, off Highway 120 in Yosemite Valley

Total distance: 5.0 miles   **Biking time:** 1.5 hours

Type of trail: Paved bike trail

Type of bike: Road bike or mountain bike

Steepness: Mostly level   **Skill level:** Easiest

It's congested, it's crowded, and it can be a zoo on summer weekends, but hey, Yosemite Valley is still one of the greatest shows on earth. If you see it from your bicycle seat rather than your car window, you'll see it in the best possible way.

There is one critical tip for having the most enjoyable experience: Ride this trail as early in the morning as you possibly can, and get out of the valley before 10 A.M., when the day-users arrive en masse. If you can't bear to get up early, here's another option: Ride this trail pre-season (in April or May) or post-season (in October or November). Even then, try to do it on a weekday, not a weekend.

The best place to start your bike trip is at the Swinging Bridge picnic area along Southside Drive, just east of the trailhead for Four-Mile Trail. This gives you the chance to get out of your car and on your bike before you've driven all the way into the valley; you'll avoid the crowded parking lots at Yosemite Village. The paved bike trail starts just beyond the picnic area. Head straight for the wooden bridge across the Merced River, then ride through the big meadow that faces Yosemite Falls. The drama begins immediately with the sight of this stunning waterfall.

Ride over to the Lower Yosemite Falls trailhead, where you'll find a bike rack. Lock up your bike and take the .2-mile hike to the falls. When Yosemite Falls is running at its fullest (usually late March–early July), it's a sight to behold. In early spring, the waterfall flows with such force that onlookers get showered with spray, even while standing 50 yards away at the falls' overlook. Some people come prepared with their raingear.

Now steel yourself for the ride through Yosemite Village and past the visitors center, where the path can get extremely congested. Pay close attention to stop signs on the trail and the road intersections you must cross. Cars are plentiful on these cross-streets, and they don't always stop at crosswalks. Also, watch out for other trail users, who can be completely oblivious. Follow the trail, now paralleling Northside Drive, until you see the turnoff for Curry Village. Ignore this turnoff and head left instead. You move away from the road and things start to quiet down.

There's no need to drive your car in Yosemite Valley.

Now you can relax and cruise through the forest, crossing the Merced River again and going past the Pines campgrounds. At a signed junction, the trail turns to dirt; one fork heads to Mirror Lake in .6 mile, while the other curves right (still paved) to go to Happy Isles and Curry Village. Take the smooth dirt cutoff for about 30 yards until it joins with pavement again. This puts you on the paved two-lane road (with no cars) that leads to Mirror Lake. Be on the lookout for walkers, bikers, and in-line skaters, who share the trail.

On the road to Mirror Lake, you meet the only hill of your whole ride. If you've rented your bike in Yosemite Village, you aren't allowed to ride up the hill; there is a bike rack at the bottom where you must park your bike and walk (it's a liability issue with the rental bikes). If you're on your own bike, pedal away.

At the top of the hill, park your bike and walk around Mirror Lake. In spring, it is a lovely sight, but by late summer, the lake has mostly disappeared. Mirror Lake is not a true lake; it's a large, shallow pool in Tenaya Creek that varies in size from season to season. Over the years, the pool has undergone sedimentation—it has filled with sand and gravel from Tenaya Creek. Today, even in spring, the lake is quite shallow. Still, when Tenaya Creek is full of water, Mirror Lake is a sight to see. The view of Half Dome's 4,700-foot perpendicular face, seen from its base, is awe-inspiring. Directly in front of Half Dome is Ahwiyah Point; Mount Watkins is the prominent rounded peak on the left.

Most visitors mill around on the road side of the lake, swimming and sunning, but walking to the north side rewards you with a lovely hiking trail where you can find a little solitude.

When it's time to mount your wheels to make the return trip, don't go so fast that you miss the awesome view of Half Dome. About halfway down the hill is an incredible spot to look up and admire that huge piece of granite.

Options

If you drive farther into the valley and park near the Village Store, you can ride from there to Mirror Lake and back for a round-trip of three miles.

Information and Contact

There is a $20 fee per vehicle for entrance into Yosemite National Park. Keep your receipt, because the fee is good for seven days. Bike rentals are available in Yosemite Village. Park maps are available for free at the entrance stations. For more information, contact Yosemite National Park Public Information Office, P.O. Box 577, Yosemite National Park, CA 95389, 209/372-0200, website: www.nps.gov/yose.

Directions

From Merced, drive 70 miles northeast on Highway 140 to Yosemite National Park. Follow the signs toward Yosemite Valley, entering through the Arch Rock entrance station and continuing on El Portal Road, which becomes Southside Drive. Park alongside the road near the trailhead for Four-Mile Trail (on the right) or at the Swinging Bridge picnic area just past this trailhead (on the left). The bike trail begins at the picnic area. You can also pick up the bike trail from several other points in the valley, including the parking area near Curry Village or by the Village Store.

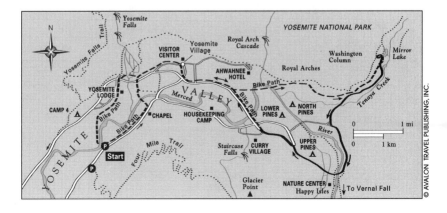

3 BODIE GHOST TOWN RIDE
Bodie State Historic Park, off U.S. 395 near Bridgeport

Total distance: 2.5 miles   **Biking time:** 1.5 hours

Type of trail: Dirt roads

Type of bike: Mountain bike

Steepness: Mostly level   **Skill level:** Easiest

"Are you sure we can ride in the ghost town?" We asked the park rangers on the phone before we made the long drive. "Absolutely," they said.

"Are you sure it's okay that we brought our bikes?" We asked at the kiosk as we paid our entrance fee. "Sure, just keep your speed down and be courteous," the ranger said.

Still, we felt like would-be criminals as we saddled up in the parking lot of Bodie State Historic Park, a fascinating and well-preserved Old West ghost town way out in the desert near Bridgeport. Bike riding in a state historic park is usually against the law. But sure enough, it's okay to ride here.

Bodie is just a little too large for families to walk the entire route through the ghost town, especially if the weather is hot. Cruising around Bodie on a bike, however, is perfect. You won't be riding for any long stretches, though; hence the mileage above is listed as only 2.5 miles, but the time required is 1.5 hours. At Bodie, there is so much to see and explore that you will constantly dismount your bike. If you have children

the well-preserved buildings of Bodie State Historic Park

© ANN MARIE BROWN

with you, you'll go even slower, because kids have a natural fascination with this type of living history.

Bodie, or what remains of it, is a California gold-mining ghost town that had its heyday in the 1870s, when it boasted more than 30 operating mines, 65 saloons, and a population of more than 10,000 people. It later suffered a steady and complete decline. The last inhabitants moved out in the early 1930s, and the town became a state historic park in 1962. Bodie is maintained in a state of "arrested decay," which means California State Parks employees don't fix it up, they just keep it from collapsing. Roofs are repaired, but floors are not, for example. This means that Bodie does not look like Disneyland's version of the Old West, it looks like the real Old West.

From the parking lot, ride straight down Green Street and start peering into the windows of homes that belonged to Bodie's townspeople. After the Gold Rush ended, many of them left Bodie in a hurry, often leaving their furniture in place and sometimes their dishes on the table. Pass the intersection with Main Street and ride up to Wheaton & Hollis Hotel on your left, which also housed the Bodie Store. The neighboring schoolhouse displays its still-hanging chalkboard and books open on the desks. Ride as far as you like up Green Street, then head back and explore Main Street in both directions, Make sure you peek in the windows of the saloon and general store. A highlight of the trip is a visit to Bodie Museum, right on Main Street, where you can view all kinds of paraphernalia left over from Bodie's lively past—old photographs, personal items left by local families, and even the town hearse.

Saving the best for last, ride out of town from the west end of Green Street and cross the park access road to Bodie Cemetery. It holds the gravestones of those who were deemed respectable in the community, while those who were not so respectable, like the town madam, are buried on the hill outside the cemetery's fence. The epitaphs on the gravestones give you a sense of the town's bawdy history.

Options

Bodie Road (Highway 270) and Cottonwood Canyon Road provide fun riding for mountain bikers who are prepared for occasional car traffic and extreme weather conditions. Carry water and food with you. Remember that if you start from the state park, you are heading downhill and will have to regain elevation on your return.

Information and Contact

A $3 per adult entrance fee is charged by Bodie State Historic Park. A map/brochure is available at the entrance kiosk. The park is open year-round, but it can be difficult to reach in winter. The best months to visit are June–October, depending on snow conditions. For more information, contact Bodie State Historic Park, P.O. Box 515, Bridgeport, CA 93517, 760/647-6445, website: www.parks.ca.gov.

Directions
From Lee Vining, drive north on U.S. 395 for 18 miles. Turn east on Highway 270 and drive 13 miles to Bodie State Historic Park. (The last three miles are very rough dirt road.)

◢ MONO LAKE SOUTH TUFA AREA TRAILS
Mono Lake Tufa State Reserve, off U.S. 395 at Mono Lake

Total distance: 4.0 miles   **Biking time:** 1.5 hours

Type of trail: Dirt roads

Type of bike: Mountain bike

Steepness: Rolling terrain   **Skill level:** Easiest

In an area rife with geologic oddities and fascinating natural phenomena, Mono Lake is hands-down the most unusual place to visit in the entire Eastern Sierra. With 60,000 surface acres of water and 16,000 acres of exposed shoreline, Mono Lake is bigger than you might expect—and being three times as salty as the ocean and 80 times more alkaline, it's weirder than you can imagine.

Surrounded by the snow-capped Sierra to the west and sagebrush desert to the east, Mono Lake is very beautiful. That's why you should bring your bike here and take a ride. Although the lake is ringed by dirt roads suitable for cycling, the best starting point is from the parking lot at the South Tufa Area of Mono Lake Tufa State Reserve. If you park there and ride on the four-wheel-drive road that leads northwest, past the overflow parking area, you get the best views of the lake, with little or no chance of cars kicking up dust in your face. When you return, lock up your bike and walk Mark Twain Scenic Tufa Trail (no bikes allowed), which leads from the South Tufa Area parking lot. This interpretive trail gives you an intimate look at the lake's strange coral-like structures, known as tufa.

Start by riding 100 yards from the South Tufa Area parking lot back up the access road, then turn right and pedal .9 mile (heading north) to a short cutoff on your right, a four-wheel-drive road. Follow it and ride down to a small parking area, where you are only about 50 yards from the lake and you can look back at the tufa spires to the south.

From this point, ride back past the South Tufa Area again, this time heading toward Navy Beach. The four-wheel-drive road you're on meets up

tufa spires and salty water at Mono Lake

with the improved dirt road to Navy Beach. Watch for car traffic here, as car-top boaters drive to this beach to launch their kayaks and canoes. Then return to the South Tufa Area parking for a four-mile round-trip.

You will likely see more gulls and seabirds on this ride than you can count. Mono Lake is the breeding ground for 85 percent of all California gulls. You'll also see desert wildflowers and sagebrush, which turns bright yellow in the late summer and fall. At any time of year, stellar views encompass snow-capped mountains to the west and wide open desert to the east.

Options
Take just the two-mile round-trip ride back and forth from the South Tufa Area parking lot to the four-wheel-drive parking area, skipping the ride to Navy Beach.

Information and Contact
There is no fee. Park maps are available at the South Tufa Area parking lot. For more information, contact Mono Lake Tufa State Reserve, P.O. Box 99 (Highway 395), Lee Vining, CA 93541, 760/647-6331, website: www.parks.ca.gov.

Directions
From U.S. 395 at Lee Vining, drive five miles south to the Mono Lake South Tufa exit, which is also Highway 120 east. Turn east and drive 4.6 miles to a dirt road on your left that is signed for South Tufa Area parking. Turn left and drive one mile to the parking area and trailhead.

5 INYO CRATERS LOOP

Inyo National Forest, off Highway 203 near Mammoth Lakes

Total distance: 10.0 miles   **Biking time:** 2.5 hours

Type of trail: Dirt and gravel roads

Type of bike: Mountain bike

Steepness: Steep sections   **Skill level:** Moderate

If you don't know what to expect when you first ride Inyo Craters Loop, you'll spend all 10 miles of the trip wondering where the heck the craters are. You don't find out until the end of the ride; you can't see the craters from the bike loop. The trail circumnavigates the craters but never goes close to them. To see the twin craters, you have to take a short hike from the trailhead parking lot before or after your ride.

With that understood, relax and enjoy the ride. Inyo Craters Loop is a classic Mammoth bike trip through cool pine forest and dusty desert flats. Although it is 10 miles long and will take a couple of hours to complete, the ride is relatively easy due to an elevation gain of less than 500 feet and smooth riding on firmly packed, pumice-lined logging roads. The key is to bring plenty of water and maybe a snack with you, especially if the day is hot. Also, make sure you know where you are going on this loop, since numerous logging roads crisscross the area. The trail is fairly well signed, but carry a map for extra security.

Start by riding .25 mile back down the parking lot access road, then turn left at the intersection of three dirt roads, which you passed as you drove in. Check for signs—you want to be heading west and then north on Forest Service Road 3S22. In .5 mile you reach and ride through Crater Flat, a wide-open meadow with an almost Arctic-looking panorama of the Sierra crest. The mountains seem to rise straight up from the dry desert floor.

Cross a small creek at about 3.5 miles in, then, .5 mile farther, cross the larger Deadman Creek. The first creek can be crossed by riding through the water or by dismounting and walking your bike to the right of the main trail, where the stream is shallower and you can rock-hop across. At Deadman Creek, walk to the left of the trail about 100 feet and find a small bridge over the water. Take a moment to notice all the flowers and greenery growing along Deadman Creek, a major contrast to the dry sagebrush country you've been riding through. Picnic tables here encourage a rest break, because you're almost halfway through the loop.

Continue right, paralleling the creek as it heads downstream, and turn right on Deadman Creek Road. What's that giant pile of rubble on your left? It's a glass flow, a heap of rocky leftovers formed from viscous lava. If you look closely, you may see shiny black rock in the pile; this is obsidian, a mineral coveted by rockhounds.

Ride east for two miles (the road gets wider and smoother as you go, and it becomes very level, easy riding), passing the signs for Deadman Campground and Obsidian Flats, until you reach Road 2S29, where you head southeast (a right turn). This leads all the way back to the paved Mammoth Scenic Loop in 2.5 miles, but you want to turn right onto 2S29D about a mile before the pavement, which becomes 3S22 and leads you back to the parking area. Save a little energy for the last two miles of the loop, as the trail can get a little soft and sandy and you may face a headwind.

Now that you've had a great ride and you're back at the parking area, it's time to see the craters. Put your bike back in your car and follow the hiking trail that starts from the middle of the parking lot. In a couple of minutes, you're there. Inyo Craters are evidence of the Mammoth area's fiery past, the remains of a volcanic explosion that occurred a mere 600 years ago. They are part of a chain of craters and other volcanic formations that reaches from Mammoth to Mono Lake. In early summer, one or both of the craters may have a tiny lake inside, left from winter snows. Read the interpretive signs, learn your geology lesson, then head back downhill.

Options

Don't ride the whole loop—just ride out and back through Crater Flat, turning around at the first stream crossing, for a seven-mile round-trip. Then walk the trail to the craters.

Information and Contact

There is no fee. For more information and a map, contact Inyo National Forest, Mammoth Ranger District, P.O. Box 148, Mammoth Lakes, CA 93546, 760/924-5500, website: www.fs.fed.us/r5/inyo.

Directions

From U.S. 395 in Lee Vining, drive 25 miles south to the Mammoth Lakes/Highway 203 cutoff. Take Highway 203 west for four miles, through the town of Mammoth Lakes, then turn right at Minaret Road and drive one mile to Mammoth Lakes Scenic Loop. Turn right on the scenic loop, then drive 2.7 miles to the turnoff for Inyo Craters. Turn left onto Inyo Craters Road and drive one mile to an intersection of three dirt roads. Bear right on the main, middle road and drive .25 mile to the Inyo Craters parking area. Ride your bike back out of the parking lot for .25 mile, returning to the intersection of three dirt roads. Make a hard left to begin on Inyo Craters Loop.

6 SHADY REST TRAIL

Shady Rest Town Park, off Highway 203 in Mammoth Lakes

Total distance: 5.0 miles   **Biking time:** 1.0 hour

Type of trail: Paved bike trail and dirt roads

Type of bike: Mountain bike

Steepness: Rolling terrain   **Skill level:** Easiest

Here's a trail perfect for families, in a town park that has all the great stuff that makes kids happy: soccer fields, a baseball diamond, a playground, and acres and acres of trees. Shady Rest Park is the place to go with your kids when they're tired of hiking, fishing, and having outdoor adventures in Mammoth, and they want something more like home. The park's bike trail has a one-mile paved section and a five-mile dirt-and-gravel section.

Most people start their ride at Shady Rest Campground and take the paved trail first, then connect to the dirt loop trail and ride around it. If you're on a mountain bike, I'd recommend the opposite: Drive and park all the way at the end of the paved trail, past the soccer fields, and ride the dirt loop trail first. More parking spots are available there, and the loop trail is more appealing to ride. It leads immediately into the pine forest and away from the developed areas of the park. You can always ride the paved trail at the end of your trip, out of the park and into the campground and back, just for fun.

The paved trail frequently has packs of six-year-olds flying by on their bikes, so keep your eyes open for them. The dirt trail, in comparison, usually has no one on it, although you may see riders on the adjacent Knolls Trail, which connects with Shady Rest for a short stretch.

The dirt stretch of Shady Rest Loop is fairly well signed, but when we rode it, some signs had been knocked over by errant riders. Watch carefully for the trail signs, since several dirt roads intersect with this loop. It helps to keep in mind that you should be following a clockwise loop. And remember to stop every once in a while to listen to the wind in the pines—one of the most pleasing sounds on earth.

Options

Knolls Trail is a more advanced mountain biking loop that connects with this loop. If you are up for a challenge, give this 10-mile loop a try.

Information and Contact

There is no fee. For more information and a map, contact Inyo National

Bikes are welcome, and actually encouraged, at Shady Rest Park.

Forest, Mammoth Ranger District, P.O. Box 148, Mammoth Lakes, CA
93546, 760/924-5500, website: www.fs.fed.us/r5/inyo.

Directions

From U.S. 395 in Lee Vining, drive 25 miles south to the Mammoth
Lakes/Highway 203 cutoff. Take Highway 203 west for 2.5 miles into the
town of Mammoth Lakes, then turn right into the access road for Shady
Rest Campground (just past the Forest Service Visitors Center sign).
Drive down this access road, past the campground, following the signs for
Shady Rest Town Park. Drive past the soccer fields and park at the end of
the road. Shady Rest Trail begins across from the paved bike trail. Look
for the Forest Service trail marker, which is a green circle on a post.

7 PAPER ROUTE & JUNIPER TRAILS

Mammoth Mountain Bike Park, off Highway 203
in Mammoth Lakes

Total distance: 6.5 miles **Biking time:** 1.5 hours

Type of trail: Dirt single-track

Type of bike: Mountain bike

Steepness: Rolling terrain **Skill level:** Moderate

The best thing about Mammoth Mountain Bike Park is that it gives mountain bike riders the opportunity to ride precious single-track trails that wind
through dense forests and break out into stunning ridgetop views. These

well-designed trails are a far cry from the usual two-lane dirt-and-gravel fire roads to which we are so often relegated. The price for admission is a bit steep, but bikers on a budget can purchase a discounted ticket that allows for limited gondola rides and shuttle services, plus all the trails you can reach under your own pedal power.

riding under the chairlift at Mammoth Mountain

One of the trails you can access with the discounted ticket is perfect for bikers looking for a casual ride. It's called Paper Route, and it leads from the east (left) side of the main lodge and bike-park entrance. Paper Route bears no resemblance to the suburban blocks many of us traveled as kids, tossing newspapers to supplement our meager allowances. Instead it is a narrow, winding stretch of single-track, with a few tree roots and rocks underfoot to keep things interesting. Several tight turns surprise you with big tree trunks appearing within inches of your handlebars. The trail is challenging, but not too much so. Even novice mountain bikers can have a good time, as long as they take it at their own pace. Paper Route's trickiest obstacles are moving targets—cute Belding ground squirrels that shuttle across the trail, always just ahead of your front tire. If you prefer larger obstacles, you'll also probably see deer on the trail, especially in its upper reaches.

Follow the right side of the Paper Route loop, heading uphill through Jeffrey pines until you cross an intersection with a trail called Follow Me. You end up right underneath the ski lift; suddenly the views open up and you're out of the woods. You can see all the way to Crowley Lake from several vantage points. Climb some more to Twin Lakes Lookout, where there is a convenient bench for resting and admiring the pretty double Twin Lakes. If you look closely, you can even make out the waterfall on their far side.

The Paper Route loop circles back down the mountain and then connects with Juniper Trail, a short but slightly more technical downhill that drops you off at the edge of the bike park at Lake Mary Road. From there, turn left on the road and ride .5 mile into town. (Turn left again at the stoplight.) Pick up the bike-park shuttle bus at Wilderness Outfitters, the outdoor store just past the stoplight. The bus runs every half hour, and it is a 10-minute ride back to Mammoth Mountain. Then off you go on your next ride.

Options

For a shorter route with less climbing, ride Paper Route to its intersection with Downtown, then ride Downtown all the way to—you guessed it—downtown, where you pick up the shuttle bus to return. This ride is almost all downhill, but it does not have the spectacular views of upper Paper Route.

Information and Contact

Mammoth Mountain Bike Park is open July–early October, weather permitting. Call for updates on season opening and closing dates. Ticket prices are $31 for trail use and unlimited gondola rides and shuttle van rides; $27 for trail use and limited gondola/van rides; and half price for children under 12. Bike-park maps are available for free. Helmets are required to ride at the park. Bike rentals are available. For more information, contact Mammoth Mountain Bike Park, P.O. Box 24, Mammoth Lakes, CA 93546, 760/934-0706 or 800/228-4947, website: www.mammothmountain.com.

Directions

From U.S. 395 in Lee Vining, drive 25 miles south to the Mammoth Lakes/Highway 203 cutoff. Take Highway 203 west for four miles, through the town of Mammoth Lakes, then turn right at Minaret Road and drive four miles to Mammoth Mountain Bike Park/Ski Area.

8 BEACH CRUISER TRAIL

Mammoth Mountain Bike Park, off Highway 203
in Mammoth Lakes

Total distance: 6.0 miles | **Biking time:** 1.5 hours

Type of trail: Dirt single-track

Type of bike: Mountain bike

Steepness: Steep sections | **Skill level:** Moderate

The big draw at all mountain bike parks, Mammoth Mountain included, is that you get to ride downhill to your heart's content without having to pay the price of grinding your way back uphill. You take the gondola or ski lift uphill, get off at the top, put on your helmet, and race downhill on exciting trails. You zip down the mountain, hardly ever having to pedal, then jump on a shuttle bus to be driven back to the gondola to start all over again.

Hey, call me old-fashioned, but I believe I should have to pedal once in a while. Taking a bus ride as part of my bike ride seems just a bit over the top. Riding in a gondola seems like heresy.

If you, too, believe that your bike pedals should not be used as foot pegs only, the Beach Cruiser Trail at Mammoth Mountain Bike Park gives you the opportunity to go up and down on a loop trail, returning to your starting point under your own power. There's something very simple and appealing about that, but it's not without a physical price. Beach Cruiser Trail requires an uphill climb lasting 30–40 minutes, working steadily and gradually with the help of lots of switchbacks. But the path is smooth, fine pumice, free of ruts, tree roots, rocks, and sand traps. It's a favorite trail of local riders at the bike park, because it offers a workout with many rewards.

Anyone can make the climb just by taking their time, gearing down, and spinning away. Don't be afraid to take a rest break at any point. The trail is almost completely forested, which keeps your body temperature down.

Get on your bike and start climbing on the trail just west (right) of the bike park/ski lodge building, underneath chairlift number 11. The trail goes up and up and up very gradually through a thick stand of Jeffrey pines. You may wonder if you will ever get out of these woods. But all at once, you reach an open ski run and a junction with a trail called Off The Top, and suddenly the trail levels out as you head around Red's Lake, elevation 9,300 feet. This is a perfect place to stop for a picnic or just lie around in the sun.

Shortly after Red's Lake, there is one more climb to make, and this one is a steeper grade than what you've faced so far. But immediately beyond it, you get your long-awaited downhill run all the way back to the bike-park entrance, a long bout of pure fun you have truly earned. Be sure to apply the brakes once in a while, though. The downhill side of the loop is more rutted and has some soft, sandy patches that can take you by surprise.

Options
Ride the bike park's gondola to mid-chalet (halfway up), then ride Trail Home and River Crossing, connecting to this Beach Cruiser loop and adding four more miles to your ride.

Information and Contact
Mammoth Mountain Bike Park is open July–early October, weather permitting. Call for updates on season opening and closing dates. Ticket prices are $31 for trail use and unlimited gondola rides and shuttle van rides; $27 for trail use and limited gondola/van rides; and half price for children

under 12. Bike park maps are available for free. Helmets are required to ride at the park. Bike rentals are available. For more information, contact Mammoth Mountain Bike Park, P.O. Box 24, Mammoth Lakes, CA 93546, 760/934-0706 or 800/228-4947, website: www.mammothmountain.com.

Directions
From U.S. 395 in Lee Vining, drive 25 miles south to the Mammoth Lakes/Highway 203 cutoff. Take Highway 203 west for four miles, through the town of Mammoth Lakes, then turn right at Minaret Road and drive four miles to Mammoth Mountain Bike Park/Ski Area.

9 HORSESHOE LAKE LOOP
Inyo National Forest, off Highway 203 in Mammoth Lakes

Total distance: 1.6 miles **Biking time:** 30 minutes

Type of trail: Dirt single-track

Type of bike: Mountain bike

Steepness: Mostly level **Skill level:** Moderate

The mileage rating for this trail should really be doubled, because there's a near-certain guarantee that you will ride this too-short single-track loop twice. Horseshoe Lake Loop is that good, although you might not guess it from the parking lot, where the scenery is quite eerie. Horseshoe Lake is surrounded by a barren-looking, partially dead Jeffrey pine forest.

It isn't fire or disease that caused all the dead trees, but rather carbon dioxide gas venting up through the soil, probably linked to some seismic action that occurred at Mammoth in 1989. The trees started to die in 1990, and since then, more than 30 acres have perished. The United States Geologic Survey and the Forest Service have been collecting air samples and say the area is perfectly safe for humans (although unsafe for tree roots), since the carbon dioxide dilutes quickly once it hits the air.

Still, the Forest Service closed the once-popular campground at Horseshoe Lake, and many visitors stay away. That's good news for bike riders who want to ride Horseshoe Lake Loop, also known as Waterwheel Trail. The reason for the waterwheel designation quickly becomes apparent when right from the start, you have four bridge crossings and four un-bridged stream crossings to negotiate. The first 150-yard section is often the trickiest part of the whole trail, and unless you have great technical riding skills, you should dismount and walk across the narrow bridges and streams. There's no reason to hurry—Horseshoe Lake, at elevation 8,950

Horseshoe Lake Loop

feet, is just plain gorgeous, dead trees and all. With its sandy shores and
backdrop of snow-crested, craggy mountains, it's a perfect example of
what makes Mammoth Lakes a prime summer destination.

After you've crossed creeks at the beginning of the loop, you can
start riding without interruption, but go slowly and enjoy your surroundings. Most of what you are pedaling through is classic Eastern
Sierra forest—Jeffrey pines growing in sand and pumice, with very little
undergrowth. But many small ravines flow into the lake, providing a
lush green contrast to the dry forest. One small stream in particular,
about halfway around the loop, is rich with wildflowers and greenery in
midsummer.

Shortly past this stream, you pass a couple of burned-down house foun-
dations. The lake views vanish as you ride through forest for the rest of the
trip. When you come out near Lake Mary Road, you have the choice of
riding back on the road or on the parallel gravel trail for the last .5 mile.

When you're done, well, the only logical thing to do is to ride the loop
again, or lock up your bike and walk it. This is definitely the kind of trip
you'll want to make twice.

Options
From this same trailhead, an easy road ride travels around Mammoth
Lakes Basin. If you don't mind sharing the road with cars, you can take
a nearly level 12-mile ride from Horseshoe Lake to Lakes Mamie, Mary,
and George.

Information and Contact

There is no fee. For more information and a map, contact Inyo National Forest, Mammoth Ranger District, P.O. Box 148, Mammoth Lakes, CA 93546, 760/924-5500, website: www.fs.fed.us/r5/inyo.

Directions

From U.S. 395 in Lee Vining, drive 25 miles south to the Mammoth Lakes/Highway 203 cutoff. Take Highway 203 west for four miles, through the town of Mammoth Lakes, to the intersection of Highway 203/Minaret Road and Lake Mary Road. Drive straight at this intersection, following Lake Mary Road five miles until it ends at Horseshoe Lake. Begin riding on the dirt road on the west side of the lake.

10 TWIN LAKES ROUTE

Inyo National Forest, off Highway 203 in Mammoth Lakes

Total distance: 3.0 miles   **Biking time:** 30 minutes

Type of trail: Paved road and bike trail

Type of bike: Road bike or mountain bike

Steepness: Mostly level   **Skill level:** Easiest

If you like sweeping views of granite crags, scenic glacial valleys, clear lakes, and plenty of wildlife and wildflowers, you've come to the right place. Might as well bring your bike, too.

Twin Lakes is the initial set of lakes you come to as you drive out Lake Mary Road, the first of more than 20 lakes in Mammoth Lakes Basin. Maybe that's why they've always had such a strong effect on me—I see Twin Lakes, and I know I've arrived in Mammoth. Good times always lie ahead.

The ride around Twin Lakes is a bit informal; there is a short paved bike trail, but mostly you ride on campground roads and the dead-end access road to Twin Lakes. You may have to deal with a car or two, but since the speed limit is only five miles per hour on the camp roads, this ride is safe even for families with small children.

Start by riding across the Twin Lakes bridge (which separates the lakes and the two campgrounds) heading into the upper campground. Cruise around, take your time—the views of the lakes and peaks from the bridge will seriously slow you down. When you reach campsites 36 and 37, look for the gravel road between them. Ride down it to a trail marked "Private Road, Public Trail." The private road to the right goes to some homes, so follow the single-track trail to the left. If you're on a mountain bike, you could ride, but there are obstacles and the trail is only a few hundred yards long, so you might as well walk your bike. The route tunnels through a very lush mixed forest, filled with dense undergrowth, including blooming columbine and corn lilies in midsummer. The trail takes you right to the base of Twin Falls, where the water streams down the mountain and pours into Upper Twin Lake. Late in the season, you can cross the stream at the base of the waterfall by rock-hopping, gaining a perfect view of the falls on one side and the lakes and their bridge on the other.

stopping along the Twin Lakes route

Return the way you came, riding back through the campground and over the Twin Lakes bridge, then pick up the short paved bike trail from where you parked your car. You'll see plenty of anglers fishing Twin Lakes, and ducks bobbing around on the water's surface, floating with the breeze. Continue alongside the lakes until the bike trail ends, then ride on Twin Lakes Road, still bordering the lakes, to its junction with Lake Mary Road. Turn around here if you wish, or follow the directions in Options, below, to extend your ride.

Options
Many other road rides are possible beginning from Twin Lakes, the most popular of which is riding out to Lake Mary Road, then turning south (right) and riding the loop around Lake Mary, or continuing on Lake Mary Road to its end at Horseshoe Lake. Watch for traffic on Lake Mary Road.

Information and Contact
There is no fee. For more information and a map, contact Inyo National Forest, Mammoth Ranger District, P.O. Box 148, Mammoth Lakes, CA 93546, 760/924-5500, website: www.fs.fed.us/r5/inyo.

Directions

From U.S. 395 in Lee Vining, drive 25 miles south to the Mammoth Lakes/Highway 203 cutoff. Take Highway 203 west for four miles, through the town of Mammoth Lakes, to the intersection of Highway 203/Minaret Road and Lake Mary Road. Drive straight at this intersection, following Lake Mary Road for 2.2 miles, then bear right on Twin Lakes Road and follow it for .5 mile, past the camp store. Park anywhere in the vicinity of the store or the lower Twin Lake.

11 HOT CREEK FISH HATCHERY & GEOTHERMAL AREA

Inyo National Forest, off U.S. 395 near Mammoth Lakes

Total distance: 4.0 miles   **Biking time:** 1.0 hour

Type of trail: Gravel and paved road

Type of bike: Mountain bike

Steepness: Rolling terrain   **Skill level:** Moderate

There aren't many places in California where you can end your bike ride with a dip in a hot spring, but at Hot Creek, you can. Not only that, but you start your ride at Hot Creek Fish Hatchery, where you are likely to see more trout swimming around than you've ever seen in your life. You can even bring your fly-fishing equipment with you on your bike trip—not for use at the hatchery, of course, but for casting into Hot Creek.

This route offers something for everyone. When I parked my car at the fish hatchery parking lot, some parents had brought their kids to look at the thousands of growing trout swimming in the holding troughs. When I rode the gravel road from the hatchery to Hot Creek, I saw dozens of anglers catch-and-release fly-fishing. Other mountain bikers happily rode past me, spinning their wheels in the warm sun. And farther downstream at the geothermal area were all these smiling hot spring–lovers, treading water in Hot Creek.

Start riding from the fish hatchery day-use parking lot, heading back out to Fish Hatchery Road. Ride east (left) toward the geothermal area on an alternately paved and gravel road. The paved sections will feel blissfully smooth in comparison to the bumpy gravel, which can be especially rough if the road was recently graded. If the bumps bother you, remember to stand up on your pedals as you ride and let your arms and legs take the jolting instead of your spine and brain.

The ride takes you through sagebrush country, past the rental cabins at Hot Creek Ranch and several stream-access parking areas. Mountain vistas are yours for the taking the whole way. The route is minimally up-hill on the way to the geothermal area, which means a nice easy cruise on the way back.

At two miles in, you reach the parking area for Hot Creek Geothermal Area. Peek over the parking lot's wall for a preview of your destination: a deep canyon with narrow Hot Creek winding through it, and bright turquoise, boiling hot pools right next to the stream. These pools are not where you will take a dip; their water is so hot that they could fatally burn you. Rather, the usable hot pool is right in the middle of Hot Creek's flow. Visitors simply wade into the stream, in which geothermally heated water rises up from underground and is cooled to manageable temperatures by the creek's flow. Exactly how hot the spring water is changes from season to season, and even day to day.

Lock up your bike at the parking lot, change into your bathing suit in the changing rooms, then walk down the short paved trail to the creek and hot springs. As you explore the stream canyon, be sure to stay away from the fenced and signed areas that the Forest Service has marked as "geolog-ically unstable." They're not kidding.

Options
After exploring around the hot pools and bathing in the river, you can add on to your trip by hiking the creekside trail that heads west, passing through the narrow and dramatic rocky canyon.

Information and Contact
There is no fee. For more information and a map, contact Inyo National Forest, Mammoth Ranger District, P.O. Box 148, Mammoth Lakes, CA 93546, 760/924-5500, website: www.fs.fed.us/r5/inyo.

Directions
From U.S. 395 in Lee Vining, drive 28 miles south, 2.8 miles beyond the Mammoth Lakes/Highway 203 cutoff, to the Hot Creek Fish Hatchery exit, where you turn left (northeast). Drive .9 mile on Hot Creek Hatchery Road to the hatchery parking area driveway, where you turn left and drive to the parking lot. Start your trip by riding from the parking area back to Hot Creek Hatchery Road. Turn left (east) to reach the geothermal area.

© JOHN KLEINFELTER

Northern California Mountain Bike Parks

The following downhill and cross-country ski resorts are transformed into mountain bike parks in summer. Mountain bikers pay a daily fee to ride all day on each park's trails. Most park fees include rides uphill on a chair-lift or gondola, so if you choose your trails carefully, all you have to do is coast downhill.

Mt. Shasta Bike, Board, and Ski Park, 104 Siskiyou Avenue, Mt. Shasta, CA 96067, 530/926-8610 or 530/926-8686, website: www.skipark.com.

Mammoth Mountain Bike Park, P.O. Box 24, Mammoth Lakes, CA 93546, 800/228-4947, 800-MAM-MOTH (626-6684), or 760/934-0706, website: www.mammothmountain.com.

Northstar-at-Tahoe, P.O. Box 129, Truckee, CA 96160, 530/562-1010 or 800/GO-NORTH (466-6784), website: www.northstarattahoe.com.

Squaw Valley USA, 1960 Squaw Valley Road, Olympic Village, CA 96146, 530/583-5585 or 800/545-4350, website: www.squaw.com.

Kirkwood Resort, P.O. Box 1, Kirkwood, CA 95646, 209/258-6000 or 209/358-3000, website: www.kirkwood.com.

Bear Valley, P.O. Box 5120, Bear Valley, CA 95233, 209/753-2834, website: www.bearvalleyxc.com.

Donner Ski Ranch, P.O. Box 66, 19320 Donner Pass Road, Norden, CA 95724, 530/426-3635, website: www.donnerskiranch.com.

Eagle Mountain, P.O. Box 1566, Nevada City, CA 95959, 800/391-2254, website: www.eaglemtnresort.com.

Northern California Bike Shops

Redwood Empire

Arcata
Life Cycle, 1593 G Street, Arcata, 707/822-7755
New Outdoor Store, 876 G Street, Arcata, 707/822-0321

Crescent City
Back Country Bicycles, 1331 Northcrest Drive, Crescent City, 707/465-3995

Eureka
Henderson Center Bicycles, 2811 F Street, Eureka, 707/443-9861
Pro Sport Center, 508 Myrtle Avenue, Eureka, 707/443-6328
Sport & Cycle, 1621 Broadway Street, Eureka, 707/444-9274

Shasta and Lassen

Chester
Bodfish Bicycles, 152 Main Street, Chester, 530/258-2338

Mount Shasta
The Fifth Season, 300 North Mount Shasta Boulevard, Mount Shasta,
    530/926-3606
House of Ski and Board, 316 Chestnut Street, Mount Shasta, 530/926-1303

Red Bluff
Fast Wheels Bike Shop, 233 Main Street, Red Bluff, 530/529-1388

Redding
Bikes Etc., 2400 Athens Avenue, Redding, 530/244-1954
The Bike Shop, 3331 Bechelli Lane, Redding, 530/223-1205, website:
    www.thebikeshop.cc
Chain Gang Bike Shop, 1180 Industrial Street, Redding, 530/223-3400,
    website: www.chaingangbikeshop.com
Redding Sports Limited, 950 Hilltop Drive, Redding, 530/221-7333
Sports Cottage, 2665 Park Marina Drive, Redding, 530/241-3115, website:
    www.sportscottage.com
Village Cycle, 3090 Bechelli Lane, Redding, 530/223-2320, website:
    www.villagecycle.net

Mendocino and Wine Country

Calistoga
Calistoga Bike Shop, 1318 Lincoln Avenue, Calistoga, 707/942-9687, website: www.calistogabikeshop.com

Cloverdale
Cloverdale Cyclery, 125 North Cloverdale Boulevard, Cloverdale, 707/894-2841

Fort Bragg
Fort Bragg Cyclery, 579 South Franklin Street, Fort Bragg, 707/964-3509

Healdsburg
Spoke Folk Cyclery, 201 Center Street, Healdsburg, 707/433-7171, website: www.spokefolk.com

Lakeport
The Bicycle Rack, 302 North Main Street, Lakeport, 707/263-1200

Mendocino
Catch-a-Canoe & Bicycles Too, 44850 Comptche-Ukiah Road, Mendocino, 707/937-0273, website: www.stanfordinn.com

Napa
Bicycle Madness, 2500 Jefferson, Napa, 707/253-2453
Bicycle Trax, 796 Soscol Avenue, Napa, 707/258-8729
Bicycle Works, 3335 Solano, Napa, 707/253-7000

Rohnert Park
Adventure Bike Company, 1451 Southwest Boulevard, Rohnert Park, 707/794-8594
Cambria Bicycle Emporium, 587 Rohnert Park Expressway, Rohnert Park, 707/206-9500, website: www.cambriabike.com

Saint Helena
St. Helena Cyclery, 1156 Main Street, Saint Helena, 707/963-7736, website: www.sthelenacyclery.com

Santa Rosa
The Bike Peddler, 605 College Avenue, Santa Rosa, 707/571-2428, website: www.norcalcycling.com
Dave's Bike Sport, 353 College Avenue, Santa Rosa, 707/573-0112, website: www.norcalcycling.com

Rincon Cyclery, 4927 Sonoma Highway, Santa Rosa, 707/538-0868, website: www.rinconcyclery.com

Sonoma
Goodtime Touring, 18503 Highway 12, Sonoma, 888/525-0453, website: www.goodtimetouring.com
Sonoma Valley Cyclery, 20093 Broadway, Sonoma, 707/935-3377, website: www.sonomavalleycyclery.com

Ukiah
Dave's Bike Shop, 846 South State Street, Ukiah, 707/462-3230
Ukiah Schwinn Center, 178 East Gobbi Street, Ukiah, 707/462-2686

Willits
The Bike Shop/Earthlab Energy Systems, 358 South Main Street, Willits, 707/459-3696
Suncycles, 151 North Main Street, Willits, 707/459-2453

Windsor
Windsor Bicycle Center, 9064 Brooks Road South, Windsor, 707/836-9111, website: www.windsorbicyclecenter.com

Sacramento and Gold Country
Angels Camp
Mountain Pedaler, 352 South Main Street, Angels Camp, 209/736-0771

Auburn
Auburn Bike Works, 350 Grass Valley Highway, Auburn, 530/885-3861, website: www.auburnbikeworks.com
The Bicycle Emporium, 483 Grass Valley Highway, Auburn, 530/823-2900, website: www.bicyleemporium.com

Carmichael
Carmichael Cycle, 5142 Arden Way, Carmichael, 916/488-5353, website: www.bicycleproducts.com

Chico
Campus Bicycles, 330 Main Street, Chico, 530/345-2081, website: www.campusbicycles.com
Chico Bike and Board, 845 Main Street, Chico, 530/343-5506
Cyclesport, 222 West Second Street, Chico, 530/345-1910

North Rim Adventure Sports, 178 East Second Street, Chico, 530/345-2453, website: www.northrimadventure.com

North Valley Cycles, 2590 Cohasset Road, Chico, 530/343-0636

Pullins Cyclery, 801 Main Street, Chico, 530/342-1055

Sports Ltd., 698 Mangrove Avenue, Chico, 530/894-1110, website: www.chicosportsltd.com

Citrus Heights

City Bicycle Works, 7885 Greenback Lane, Citrus Heights, 916/726-2453, website: www.citybicycleworks.com

Davis

ASUCD Bike Barn, University of California Davis, 1 Shields Avenue, Davis, 530/752-2575

B & L's Bike Shop, 610 Third Street, Davis, 530/756-3540, website: www.blbikeshop.com

Freewheeler Bicycle Center, 703 Second Street, Davis, 530/758-5460, website: www.freewheelerbikecenter.com

Ken's Bike & Ski, 650 G Street, Davis, 530/758-3223, website: www.kensbikeski.com

Davis Wheelworks, 247 F Street, Davis, 530/753-3118

Downieville

Downieville Outfitters, 310 Main Street, Downieville, 530/289-0155, website: www.downievilleoutfitters.com

Yuba Expeditions, P.O. Box 224, Downieville, 530/289-3010, website: www.yubaexpeditions.com

Elk Grove

Laguna Bike Shop, 7701 Laguna Boulevard, Suite 400, Elk Grove, 916/691-3251

Fair Oaks

The Bike Shop, 4719 San Juan Avenue, Fair Oaks, 916/961-9646

Bob's Cycle Center, 9920 Fair Oaks Boulevard, Fair Oaks, 916/961-6700, website: www.bobscyclecenter.com

Performance Bike, 5271 Sunrise Boulevard, Quail Point Shopping Center, Fair Oaks, 916/961-1488, website: www.performancebike.com

River Rat Inc., 9840 Fair Oaks Boulevard, Fair Oaks, 916/966-6777, website: www.river-rat.com

Folsom
Bicycles Plus, 705 Gold Lake Drive, Suite 320, Folsom, 916/355-8901, website: www.onlinecycling.com

Grass Valley
Mountain Recreation, 491 East Main Street, Grass Valley, 530/477-8006

Jackson
Jackson Family Sports, 225 East Highway 88, Jackson, 209/223-3890

Lincoln
Gold Country Bicycles, 150 Highway 65, Suite 104, Lincoln, 916/645-3753

Modesto
Valley Sporting Goods, 1700 McHenry Avenue, Suite D50, Modesto, 209/523-5681
World of Wheels, 1544 Standiford, Modesto, 209/522-0804

Nevada City
Tour of Nevada City Bicycle Shop, 457 Sacramento Street, Nevada City, 530/265-2187, website: www.tourofnevadacity.com

Paradise
The Bicycle Shop, 6133 Skyway, Paradise, 530/872-9363

Placerville
Golden Spoke Bike Shop, 679 Placerville Drive, Placerville, 530/626-8370
Placerville Bike Shop, 1307 Broadway, Placerville, 530/622-3015

Rancho Cordova
Bicycle Products of Rancho Cordova, 12401 Folsom Boulevard, Rancho Cordova, 916/351-9066, website: www.bicycleproducts.com

Rocklin
Sharp Bicycles, 6840 Five Star Boulevard, Rocklin, 916/630-8894, website: www.sharpbicycles.com

Roseville
Bob's Cycle Center, 378 North Sunrise Boulevard, Roseville, 916/784-2255, website: www.bobscyclecenter.com

Sacramento
American River Bicycle, 9203 Folsom Boulevard and 256 Florin Road, Sacramento, 916/427-6199, website: www.americanriverbikes.com
The Bicycle Business, 3077 Freeport Boulevard, Sacramento, 916/442-5246
City Bicycle Works, 2419 K Street, Sacramento, 916/447-7730, website: www.citybicycleworks.com
Natomas Bike Shop, 3291 Truxel Road, Sacramento, 916/641-8640, website: www.natomasbikeshop.com
Performance Bicycle Shop, 5271 Sunrise Boulevard, Sacramento, 916/961-1488, website: www.performancebike.com
Rest Stop Bike Accessories, 3230 Folsom Boulevard, Sacramento, 916/453-1870

Sonora
JT Cycles, 55 South Washington Street, Sonora, 209/536-9882
Sonora Cyclery, 13867 Mono Way, Sonora, 209/532-6800

Stockton
Performance Bicycle Shop, 6555 Pacific Avenue, Stockton, 209/951-5665, website: www.performancebike.com

Vacaville
Bicycle Products of Vacaville, 617 Elmira Road, Vacaville, 707/447-6399, website: www.bicycleproducts.com
Ray's Cycles, 400 Main Street, Vacaville, 707/448-1911

Woodland
Foy's Bike Shop, 352 West Main Street and 421 Pioneer Avenue, Woodland, 530/661-0900, website: www.blbikeshop.com
Main Street Cyclery, 1041 Main Street, Woodland, 530/661-6800, website: www.mainstreetcyclery.com

Yuba City
Twin Cities Bike and Repair, 980 Gray Avenue, Yuba City, 530/673-8409
Vans Bicycle Center, 622 Gray Avenue, Yuba City, 530/674-0179

Tahoe and the Northern Sierra
Bear Valley
Bear Valley Adventure Company, 1 Bear Valley Road, Bear Valley, 209/753-2834, website: www.bearvalleyxc.com

Homewood
Tahoe Gear, 5095 W. Lake Boulevard, Homewood, 530/525-5233

Hope Valley
Hope Valley Outdoor Center, 14655 Highway 88, Hope Valley, 530/694-2266

Kings Beach
Tahoe Bike and Ski, 8499 N. Lake Boulevard, Kings Beach, 530/546-7437

Kirkwood
Kirkwood Resort Adventure Center, 1377 Kirkwood Meadows Drive, Kirkwood, 209/258-7218, website: www.kirkwood.com

Northstar
Northsport at Northstar, Highway 267 at Northstar Drive, Northstar, 530/562-2268, website: www.skinorthstar.com

Olympic Valley
Squaw Valley Sport Shop, Squaw Valley Mall, Olympic Valley, 530/583-3356

Soda Springs
Java Summit Sports, 21501 Donner Pass Road, Suite 19, Soda Springs, 530/426-3567

South Lake Tahoe
Lakeview Sports, 3131 Harrison Avenue, South Lake Tahoe, 530/544-0183, website: www.tahoesports.com
Sierra Cycle Works, 3430 Lake Tahoe Boulevard, South Lake Tahoe, 530/541-7505
South Shore Bikes, 1132 Ski Run Boulevard, South Lake Tahoe, 530/541-1549
Tahoe Bike and Ski, 2277 Lake Tahoe Boulevard, South Lake Tahoe, 530/544-8060, website: www.tahoebikeandski.com

Tahoe City
Alpenglow Sports, 415 North Lake Boulevard, Tahoe City, 530/583-6917
The Back Country, 255 North Lake Boulevard, Tahoe City, 530/581-5861, website: www.thebackcountry.net
Cyclepaths, 1785 West Lake Boulevard, Tahoe City, 800/780-BIKE, website: www.cyclepaths.com
Olympic Bike Shop, 620 North Lake Boulevard, Tahoe City, 530/581-2500

Truckee

The Back Country, 11429 Donner Pass Road, Truckee, 530/582-0909

Paco's Truckee Bike & Ski, 11200 Donner Pass Road #6, Truckee, 530/587-5561, website: www.pacosbikeandski.com

San Francisco Bay Area

North Bay and San Francisco

Corte Madera

REI, 213 Corte Madera Town Center, Corte Madera, 415/927-1938, website: www.rei.com

Fairfax

Sunshine Bicycle Center, 737 Center Boulevard, Fairfax, 415/459-3334, website: www.sunshinebicycles.com

Larkspur

Village Peddler, 1161 Magnolia Avenue, Larkspur, 415/461-3091, website: www.villagepeddler.com

Mill Valley

Mill Valley Cycleworks, 369 Miller Avenue, Mill Valley, 415/388-6774, website: www.millvalleycycleworks.com

Novato

Bike Hut, 459 Entrada Drive, Novato, 415/883-2440

Classcycle, 1531-B South Novato Boulevard, Novato, 415/897-3288, website: www.classcycle.com

Pacific Bicycle, 132 Vintage Way, Suite F13, Novato, 415/892-9319

Petaluma

The Bicycle Factory, 110 Kentucky Street, Petaluma, 707/763-7515

Eastside Bicycles, 701 Sonoma Mountain Parkway, Suite B-6, Petaluma, 707/766-7501, website: www.eastsidecycles.com

Petaluma Cyclery, 1080 Petaluma Boulevard North, Petaluma, 707/762-1990

Sonoma Mountain Cyclery, 937 Lakeville Street, Petaluma, 707/773-3164

Point Reyes Station

Cycle Analysis, Highway 1, Point Reyes Station, 415/663-9164, website: www.cyclepointreyes.com

San Anselmo

Caesar Cyclery, 29 San Anselmo Avenue, San Anselmo, 415/721-0805

San Francisco

American Cyclery, 858 Stanyan Street, San Francisco, 415/876-4545, website: www.americancyclery.com

Avenue Cyclery, 756 Stanyan Street, San Francisco, 415/387-3155, website: www.avenuecyclery.com

Big Swingin' Cycles, 1122 Taraval Street, San Francisco, 415/661-2462, website: www.bigswingincycles.com

City Cycle of San Francisco, 3001 Steiner Street, San Francisco, 415/346-2242, website: www.citycycle.com

DD Cycles, 4049 Balboa Street, San Francisco, 415/752-7980, website: www.ddcycles.com

Free Wheel Bike Shop, 980 Valencia Street and 1920 Hayes Street, San Francisco, 415/643-9213, website: www.thefreewheel.com

Fresh Air Bicycles, 1943 Divisadero Street, San Francisco, 415/563-4824

Golden Gate Cyclery, 672 Stanyan Street, San Francisco, 415/379-3870

Lombardi's Sports, 1600 Jackson Street, San Francisco, 415/771-0600, website: www.lombardissports.com

Noe Valley Cyclery, 4193 24th Street, San Francisco, 415/647-0886

Nomad Cyclery, 2555 Irving Street, San Francisco, 415/564-3568, website: www.nomadcyclery.com

Ocean Cyclery, 1915 Ocean Avenue, San Francisco, 415/239-5004

Pacific Bicycle, 345 Fourth Street, San Francisco, 415/928-8466

Pedal Revolution, 3085 21st Street, San Francisco, 415/641-1264, website: www.pedalrevolution.com

Road Rage Bicycles, 1063 Folsom Street, San Francisco, 415/255-1351, website: www.roadragebicycles.com

Roaring Mouse Cycles, 1352 Irving Street, San Francisco, 415/753-6272, website: www.roaringmousecycles.com

Sports Basement, 1301 Sixth Street and Building 610 in the Presidio (Mason Street), San Francisco, 415/437-0100, website: www.sportsbasement.com

Valencia Cyclery, 1077 Valencia Street, San Francisco, 415/550-6600

Vision Cyclery S.F., 772 Stanyan Street, San Francisco, 415/221-9766, website: www.visionsf.com

San Rafael

Mike's Bicycle Center, 1601 Fourth Street, San Rafael, 415/454-3747, website: www.mikesbicyclecenter.com

Performance Bike, 369 Third Street, San Rafael, 415/454-9063, website: www.performancebike.com

Sausalito

A Bicycle Odyssey, 1417 Bridgeway, Sausalito, 415/332-3050, website: www.bicycleodyssey.com

Sausalito Cyclery, 1 Gate Six Road, Sausalito, 415/332-3200, website: www.mikesbicyclecenter.com

East Bay

Alameda

Alameda Bicycle, 1522 Park Street, Alameda, 510/522-0070, website: www.alamedabicycle.com

Cycle City, 1433 High Street, Alameda, 510/521-2872, website: www.cyclecityusa.com

Stone's, 2320 Santa Clara Avenue, Alameda, 510/523-3264

Albany

Solano Avenue Cyclery, 1554 Solano Avenue, Albany, 510/524-1094, website: www.solanoavenuecyclery.com

Antioch

Bikes for Life, 1344 Sunset Drive, Antioch, 925/754-8025

Schwinn City, 814 A Street, Antioch, 925/757-0664, website: www.schwinncity.com

Berkeley

Bent Spoke, 1615 University Avenue and 6124 Telegraph Avenue, Berkeley, 510/540-0583 or 510/652-3089, website: www.thebentspoke.com

Left Coast Cyclery, 2928 Domingo Avenue, Berkeley, 510/204-8550, website: www.leftcoastcyclery.com

Mike's Bikes, 2133 University Avenue, Berkeley, 510/549-8350, website: www.mikesbicyclecenter.com

Missing Link Bicycle Shop, 1988 Shattuck Avenue, Berkeley, 510/843-7471, website: www.missinglink.org

REI, 1338 San Pablo Avenue, Berkeley, 510/527-4140, website: www.rei.com

Velo Sport, 1650 Martin Luther King Way, Berkeley, 510/849-0437, website: www.velosportbicycles.com

Castro Valley

Castro Valley Cyclery, 20515 Stanton Avenue, Castro Valley, 510/538-1878, website: www.cvcyclery.com

Eden Bicycles, 3313 Village Drive, Castro Valley, 510/881-5000, website: www.edenbicycles.com

Clayton
Clayton Bicycle Center, 5411 Clayton Road, Clayton, 925/672-2522

Concord
REI, 1975 Diamond Boulevard, Concord, 925/825-9400, website: www.rei.com

Danville
California Pedaler, 495 Hartz Avenue, Danville, 925/820-0345, website: www.californiapedaler.com
Danville Bikes, 115 Hartz Avenue, Danville, 925/837-0966
Pegasus Bicycle Works, 439 Rail Road Avenue, Danville, 925/362-2220, website: www.pegasusbicycleworks.com
Alamo Bikes, 1469 Danville Boulevard, Danville, 925/837-8444

Dublin
Dublin Cyclery, 7001 Dublin Boulevard, Dublin, 925/828-8676, website: www.dublincyclery.com

El Sobrante
El Sobrante Schwinn Cyclery, 5057 El Portal Drive, El Sobrante, 510/223-3440
The Pedaler, 3826 San Pablo Dam Road, El Sobrante, 510/222-3420, website: www.theped.com

Fremont
The Bicycle Garage, 4673 Thornton Avenue, Suite A, Fremont, 510/795-9622, website: www.bicyclegarage.com
Performance Bike, 39121 Fremont Boulevard, Fremont, 510/494-1466, website: www.performancebike.com
REI, 43962 Fremont Boulevard, Fremont, 510/651-0305, website: www.rei.com
Tri City Sporting Goods, 40900 Grimmer Boulevard, Fremont, 510/651-9600, website: www.tricitysportinggoods.com

Hayward
Cyclepath, 22510 Foothill Boulevard, Hayward, 510/881-5177, website: www.cyclepathhayward.com
Witt's Bicycle Shop, 22125 Mission Boulevard, Hayward, 510/538-8771

Lafayette
Hank and Frank Bicycles, 3377 Mt. Diablo Boulevard, Lafayette, 925/376-2453
Sharp Bicycle, 969 Moraga Road, Lafayette, 925/284-9616

Livermore

Livermore Cyclery, 2752 First Street, Livermore, 925/455-8090, website: www.livermorecyclery.com

Cal Bicycles, 2053 First Street, Livermore, 925/447-6666, website: www.calbicycles.com

Martinez

Martinez Cyclery, 4990 Pacheco Boulevard, Martinez, 925/228-9050, website: www.martinezcyclery.com

Oakland

Cycle Sports, 3241 Grand Avenue, Oakland, 510/444-7900, website: www.cyclesportsonline.com

Hank and Frank Bicycles, 6030 College Avenue, Oakland, 510/658-1177

Wheels of Justice, 2024 Mountain Boulevard, Oakland, 510/339-6091, website: www.wojcyclery.com

Pioneer Bike Shop, 11 Rio Vista Avenue, Oakland, 510/658-8981

Pleasant Hill

Mike's Bikes, 1741 Contra Costa Boulevard, Pleasant Hill, 925/671-9127, website: www.mikesbicycles.com

Pleasant Hill Cyclery, 1494 Contra Costa Boulevard, Pleasant Hill, 925/676-2667, website: www.pleasanthillcyclery.com

Pleasanton

Bicycles Pleasanton, 525 Main Street, Pleasanton, 925/461-0905, website: www.bicyclespleasanton.com

San Leandro

Robinson Wheel Works, 1235 MacArthur Boulevard, San Leandro, 510/352-4663, website: www.robinsonwheelworks.com

Walnut Creek

Encina Bicycle, 2901 Ygnacio Valley Road, Walnut Creek, 925/944-9200, website: www.encinacycles.com

Performance Bike, 1401 North Broadway, Walnut Creek, 925/937-7723, website: www.performancebike.com

Rivendell Bicycle Works, 2040 North Main Street, Walnut Creek, 925/933-7304, website: www.rivendellbicycles.com

Peninsula and South Bay

Belmont

California Sports & Cyclery, 1464 El Camino Real, Belmont, 650/593-8806

Burlingame

Summit Bicycles, 1111 Burlingame Avenue, Burlingame, 650/343-8483, website: www.summitbicycles.com

Campbell

Performance Bike, 1646 South Bascom Avenue, Campbell, 408/559-0495, website: www.performancebike.com

Wheel Away Cycle Center, 402 East Hamilton Avenue, Campbell, 408/378-4636

Cupertino

Cupertino Bike Shop, 10493 South De Anza Boulevard, Cupertino, 408/255-2217, website: www.cupertinobike.com

Daly City

Broadmoor Bicycles, 150 San Pedro Road, Daly City, 650/756-1120, website: www.broadmoorbicycles.com

Half Moon Bay

The Bike Works, 20 Stone Pine Center, Half Moon Bay, 650/726-6708

Los Altos

The Bicycle Outfitter, 963 Fremont Avenue, Los Altos, 650/948-8092, website: www.bicycleoutfitter.com

Chain Reaction Bicycles, 2310 Homestead Road, Los Altos, 408/735-8735, website: www.chainreaction.com

Los Gatos

Crossroads Bicycles, 217 North Santa Cruz Avenue, Los Gatos, 408/354-0555

Los Gatos Cyclery, 652 North Santa Cruz Avenue, Los Gatos, 408/399-5099, website: www.losgatoscyclery.com

Summit Bicycles, 111 East Main Street, Los Gatos, 408/399-9142, website: www.summitbicycles.com

Menlo Park

Menlo Velo, 433 El Camino Real, Menlo Park, 650/327-5137

The Bike Connection, 622 Santa Cruz Avenue, Menlo Park, 650/327-3318

Milpitas
Sun Bike Shop, 1549 Landess Avenue, Milpitas, 408/262-4360

Mountain View
Off Ramp, 2320 El Camino Real, Mountain View, 650/968-2974, website: www.offramp.com

Palo Alto
Bike Connection, 2011 El Camino Real, Palo Alto, 650/424-8034, website: www.bikeconnection.net

Mike's Bikes, 2180 El Camino Real, Palo Alto, 650/493-8776, website: www.mikesbicyclecenter.com

Palo Alto Bicycles, 171 University Avenue, Palo Alto, 650/328-7411, website: www.paloaltobicycles.com

Redwood City
Chain Reaction Bicycles, 1451 El Camino Real, Redwood City, 650/366-7130, website: www.chainreaction.com

Go Ride Bicycles, 2755 El Camino Real, Redwood City, 650/366-2453, website: www.goridebicycles.com

Performance Bike, 2535 El Camino Real, Redwood City, 650/365-9094, website: www.performancebike.com

San Bruno
Bike Route, 568 San Mateo Avenue, San Bruno, 650/873-9555

San Carlos
Broken Spoke, 782 Laurel Street, San Carlos, 650/594-9210

REI, 1119 Industrial Boulevard, San Carlos, 650/508-2330, website: www.rei.com

Velo Bicycle Shop, 1316 El Camino Real, San Carlos, 650/591-2210

San Jose
Calabazas Cyclery, 6140 Bollinger Road, San Jose, 408/366-2453, website: www.calabazas.com

Fast Bicycle, 2274 Alum Rock Avenue, San Jose, 408/251-9110

The Hyland Family's Bicycles, 1515 Meridian Avenue, San Jose, 408/269-2300, website: www.hylandbikes.com

Pacific Bicycle, 1008 Blossom Hill Road, San Jose, 408/264-3570

Reed's Sport Shop, 3020 Alum Rock Avenue, San Jose, 408/926-1600, website: www.reedssportshop.com

REI, 400 El Paseo de Saratoga Shopping Center, San Jose, 408/871-8765, website: www.rei.com

Santa Teresa Bikes, 503 West Capitol Expressway, San Jose, 408/264-2453, website: www.fifthwave.com/stbikes

Trail Head Cyclery, 14450 Union Avenue, San Jose, 408/369-9666, website: www.trailheadcyclery.com

Willow Glen Bicycles, 1110 Willow Street, San Jose, 408/293-2606, website: www.willowglenbicycles.com

San Mateo

Cyclepath, 1212 South El Camino Real, San Mateo, 650/341-0922, website: www.cyclepath.com

Talbots Cyclery, 445 South B Street, San Mateo, 650/342-0184

Santa Clara

Calmar Cycles, 2236 El Camino Real, Santa Clara, 408/249-6907, website: www.calmarcycles.com

The Off Ramp, 2369 El Camino Real, Santa Clara, 408/249-2848, website: www.offrampbicycles.com

Shaws' Lightweight Cycles, 45 Washington Street, Santa Clara, 408/246-7881, website: www.shawscycles.com

Sunnyvale

Walt's Cycles, 116 Carroll Street, Sunnyvale, 408/736-2630, website: www.waltscycles.com

Monterey and Big Sur

Capitola

Cycle Works, 1203 41st Avenue, Capitola, 831/476-7092

Carmel Valley

Bay Bikes at the Village, 10 East Carmel Valley Road, Carmel Valley, 831/659-2453

Gilroy

Sunshine Bicycle Shop, 311 First Street, Gilroy, 408/842-4889, website: http//:sunshinebicycles.com

Hollister
Off the Chain Bikes, 341 Tres Pinos Road Suite 106, Hollister, 831/636-0802, website: offthechainbikes.com

Monterey
Adventures by the Sea, 299 Cannery Row and 201 Alvarado Street, Monterey, 831/372-1807, website: www.adventuresbythesea.com
Aquarian Bicycles, 486 Washington Street, Monterey, 831/375-2144
Bay Bikes, 585 Cannnery Row and 99 Pacific Street, Monterey, 831/655-2453, website: www.baybikes.com
Joselyn's Bike Shop, 398 East Franklin Street, Monterey, 831/649-8520, website: www.joselynsbicycles.com

Pacific Grove
Winning Wheels, 318 Grand Avenue, Pacific Grove, 831/375-4322

Salinas
Bobcat Bicycles, 141 Monterey Street, Salinas, 831/753-7433, website: www.bobcatbicycles.com

Santa Cruz
Another Bike Shop, 2361 Mission Street, Santa Cruz, 831/427-2232, website: www.anotherbikeshop.com
Bicycle Trip, 1127 Soquel Avenue, Santa Cruz, 831/427-2580, website: www.bicycletrip.com
The Bike Shop, 1325 Mission Street, Santa Cruz, 831/454-0909
Family Cycling Center, 914 41st Avenue, Santa Cruz, 831/475-3883, website: www.familycycling.com
The Spokesman Bicycles, 231 Cathcart Street, Santa Cruz, 831/423-5683, website: www.spokesmanbicycles.com
Sprockets, 1420 Mission Street, Santa Cruz, 831/426-7623, website: www.sprocketsbikes.com

Scotts Valley
Scotts Valley Cycle Sport, 245 Mt. Hermon Road, Scotts Valley, 831/440-9070, website: www.svcyclesport.com

Seaside
Sports Center Bicycle, 1576 Del Monte Boulevard, Seaside, 831/899-1300

Watsonville
Trey's True Wheel, 1431 Main Street, Watsonville, 831/786-0200

Yosemite and Mammoth Lakes

Fresno
Cyclopath Fresno, 6459 N. Blackstone, Fresno, 559/432-2990
Tri Sport, 132 W. Nees Avenue, Suite 111, Fresno, 559/432-0800

Madera
Sierra Cycle Works, 1501 Howard Road, Madera, 559/674-3315
Mammoth Lakes
Footloose Sports, 3043 Main Street, Mammoth Lakes, 760/934-2400, website: www.footloosesports.com
Mammoth Mountain Bike Shop, 1 Minaret Road, Mammoth Lakes, 800/228-4947, website: www.mammothmtn.com
Mammoth Sporting Goods, 1 Sierra Center Mall, Old Mammoth Road, Mammoth Lakes, 760/934-3239, website: www.mammothsporting-goods.com
Sandy's Ski and Sport, 3499 Main Street, Mammoth Lakes, 760/934-7518

Merced
Kevin's Bikes, 60 W. Olive Avenue, Merced, 209/722-2228

Index

F

Fall Creek: 223

Fallen Leaf Lake Road: **108**, 108–110

Fallen Leaf Lake Trails: 110–111

Falls Loop Trail: 57–58, **58**

family trails: Angora Lakes Trail 112–113; Aptos Creek Fire Road 238–239; author's top five 7; Bear Valley Trail 131–133; Bizz Johnson National Recreation Trail 49–50; Bodie Ghost Town Ride 254–256; Contra Costa Regional Trails 178–179; Corte Madera Trail 206–208; General Creek Loop 104–106; Half Moon Bay Bike Path 205–206; Howarth Park Trail 65–67; Iron Horse Regional Trail 176–177; Lafayette-Moraga Regional Trail 173–175; Lafayette Reservoir 171–173; Lake Almanor Recreation Trail 45–47; Lake Chabot West & East Shore Trails 184–186; Las Gallinas Wildlife Ponds 146–148; Los Gatos Creek Trail 215–217; Lost Man Creek Trail 25–27; Quarry Road Trail 84–87; Ranch Trail 203–204; Sawyer Camp Recreation Trail 199–201; Shady Rest Trail 260–261; Spring Lake Park Trail 65–67; Stump Beach Cove Trail 62–64; Tennessee Valley Trail 161–163; Tiburon Bike Path 150–152; tricycles/training wheels 8–9; Twin Lakes Route 267–269; Union Valley Bike Path 114–115

Fern Canyon Trailhead: 24

Fern Canyon Trail (Russian Gulch State Park): 57–58, **58**

Fern Canyon Trail (Van Damme State Park): 59–60, **60**

Fern Grotto Beach: 234

Fibreboard Freeway Loop: 97–99

Filoli Estate: 202

first aid: 3–4

Fish Loop Trails: 36–38, **37**

Five Brooks Trailhead: 133, **138**

Five Mile Recreation Area: 80

Follow Me Trail: 262

Folsom Lake & Dam: 87–88

Folsom Lake State Recreation Area: 87–89

food: 2

Forest of Nisene Marks State Park: 238–239

forest trails: Angora Lakes Trail 112–113; Aptos Creek Fire Road 238–239; Beach Cruiser Trail 263–265; Bear Valley Recreation Area 115–116; Bear Valley Trail 131–133; Blackwood Canyon 102–103; Clikapudi Creek Trail 39–41; Coastal Trail 21–23; Cross Marin Trail/Sir Francis Drake Bikeway 137–139; Eagle Lake Trail 47–48; Fallen Leaf Lake Trails 110–111; Fern Canyon Trail (Russian Gulch State Park) 57–58; Fern Canyon Trail (Van Damme State Park) 59–60; General Creek Loop 104–106; Hammond Trail 27–28; Horseshoe Lake Loop 265–267; Howland Hill Road 19–20; Inyo Craters Loop 258–259; Juniper Trail 261–263; Lake Almanor Recreation Trail 45–47; Lake Ilsanjo Trail Loop 67–69; Laurel Dell Fire Road 155–157; Lost Man Creek Trail 25–27; Mills Peak Lookout 95–96; Old Haul Road 221–223; Olema Valley Trail 133–134; Paper Route Trail 261–263; Pipeline Road 235–238; Pygmy Forest Trail Loop 61–62; Shady Rest Trail 260–261; Shoreline Trail 148–150; Siskiyou Lake North Shore 35–36; Skyline-To-The-Sea Trail 224–226; Sugar Pine Railway 89–90; Twin Lakes Route 267–269; Union Valley Bike Path 114–115; Waters Gulch & Fish Loop Trails 36–38; Wildcat Creek Trail 168–169; Yosemite Valley Bike Path 251–253

Four Mile Beach: 235

Fox Tail Trail: 181, **181**

Notes

Notes

Notes

Notes

Notes

Notes

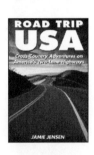